Planning Labour

International Studies in Social History

General Editor: Marcel van der Linden,
International Institute of Social History, Amsterdam

Published under the auspices of the International Institute of Social History, Amsterdam, this series offers transnational perspectives on labour and working-class history. For a long time, labour historians have been working within national interpretive frameworks. But interest in studies contrasting different national and regional experiences and studying cross-border interactions has been increasing in recent years. This series is designed to act as a forum for these new approaches.

Recent volumes:

Volume 32
Planning Labour: Time and the Foundations of Industrial Socialism in Romania
Alina-Sandra Cucu

Volume 31
Categories in Context: Gender and Work in France and Germany, 1900–Present
Edited by Isabelle Berrebi-Hoffmann, Olivier Giraud, Léa Renard and Theresa Wobbe

Volume 30
What Is Work? Gender at the Crossroads of Home, Family, and Business from the Early Modern Era to the Present
Edited by Raffaella Sarti, Anna Bellavitis and Manuela Martini

Volume 29
Laborers and Enslaved Workers: Experiences in Common in the Making of Rio de Janeiro's Working Class, 1850–1920
Marcelo Badaró Mattos

Volume 28
Labour, Unions and Politics under the North Star: The Nordic Countries, 1700–2000
Edited by Mary Hilson, Silke Neunsinger and Iben Vyff

Volume 27
Rescuing the Vulnerable: Poverty, Welfare and Social Ties in Modern Europe
Edited by Beate Althammer, Lutz Raphael and Tamara Stazic-Wendt

Volume 26
The History of Labour Intermediation: Institutions and Finding Employment in the Nineteenth and Early Twentieth Centuries
Edited by Sigrid Wadauer, Thomas Buchner and Alexander Mejstrik

Volume 25
Bread from the Lion's Mouth: Artisans Struggling for a Livelihood in Ottoman Cities
Edited by Suraiya Faroqhi

Volume 24
Bondage: Labor and Rights in Eurasia from the Sixteenth to the Early Twentieth Centuries
Alessandro Stanziani

Volume 23
Migration, Settlement and Belonging in Europe, 1500–1930s
Edited by Steven King and Anne Winter

For a full volume listing, please see the series page on our website:
http://www.berghahnbooks.com/series/international-studies-in-social-history

PLANNING LABOUR

Time and the Foundations of Industrial Socialism in Romania

Alina-Sandra Cucu

berghahn
NEW YORK • OXFORD
www.berghahnbooks.com

First published in 2019 by
Berghahn Books
www.berghahnbooks.com

© 2019, 2025 Alina-Sandra Cucu
First paperback edition published in 2025

All rights reserved. Except for the quotation of short passages
for the purposes of criticism and review, no part of this book
may be reproduced in any form or by any means, electronic or
mechanical, including photocopying, recording, or any information
storage and retrieval system now known or to be invented,
without written permission of the publisher.

Library of Congress Cataloging-in-Publication Data
Names: Cucu, Alina-Sandra, author.
Title: Planning labour : time and the foundations of industrial socialism in
 Romania / Alina-Sandra Cucu.
Other titles: Planning labor
Description: New York : Berghahn Books, 2019. | Series: International studies
 in social history ; volume 32 | Includes bibliographical references and
 index. |
Identifiers: LCCN 2019002248 (print) | LCCN 2019007092 (ebook) | ISBN
 9781789201864 (ebook) | ISBN 9781789201857 (hardback : alk. paper)
Subjects: LCSH: Socialism--Romania--Cluj-Napoca--History--20th century. |
 Government ownership--Romania--Cluj-Napoca--History--20th century. |
 Central planning--Romania--History--20th century. | Romania--Economic
 policy--1945-1989. | Working class--Romania--Cluj-Napoca--History--20th
 century. | Cluj-Napoca (Romania)--Economic conditions--20th century. |
 Cluj-Napoca (Romania)--Social conditions--20th century.
Classification: LCC HX375.C58 (ebook) | LCC HX375.C58 C83 2019 (print) |
 DDC 331.109498/4--dc23
LC record available at https://lccn.loc.gov/2019002248

British Library Cataloguing in Publication Data
A catalogue record for this book is available from the British Library
EU GPSR Authorized Representative
LOGOS EUROPE, 9 rue Nicolas Poussin, 17000, LA ROCHELLE, France
Email: Contact@logoseurope.eu

ISBN 978-1-78920-185-7 hardback
ISBN 978-1-83695-325-8 paperback
ISBN 978-1-83695-326-5 epub
ISBN 978-1-78920-186-4 web pdf

https://doi.org/10.3167/9781789201857

Contents

List of Tables	vi
Foreword. What *Was* the Plan? And What Was It Meant to Do?	vii
Don Kalb	
Acknowledgements	xii
Introduction	1

I. PRIMITIVE SOCIALIST ACCUMULATION IN CLUJ

1	Productive State Apparatuses: Taking Over the Factories, 1944–1948	37
2	'More Precious Than Gold': Labour Instability and the 'Stickiness' of Everyday Life	75
3	'Workers', 'Proletarians' and the Struggle for Cheap Labour	109

II. TIME AND ACCUMULATION ON THE SHOP FLOOR

4	'Hidden Reserves of Productivity' and the Quest for Knowledge	147
5	Productive Flows and Factory Discipline	178
6	Planned Heroism and Nonsynchronicity on the Shop Floor	204
Epilogue. Really Existing Socialism as Nonsynchronicity		228
Bibliography		235
Index		243

Tables

2.1 1938 wages in Cluj. Industrial skilled vs. unskilled workers.   81
2.2 Hours worked per week for the industrial workers in Cluj in 1938.   81
3.1 Migration destinations in 1966.   115
3.2 Average monthly income (Romanian Lei).   121
3.3 Gender structure of industrial workforce in Cluj in 1938.   135
3.4 Income structure for the families of the Tobacco Factory women.   136

FOREWORD
What *Was* the Plan? And What Was It Meant to Do?

Don Kalb

As 'really existing socialism' was dying and the new capitalism was not yet born, Katherine Verdery posed the urgent question with characteristic clarity: 'What *was* socialism, and what comes next?' (my emphasis). She ventured that 'next' might be a new feudalism rather than the capitalism most Western and Eastern commentators were hoping for. But in retrospect she seems to have been wrong-footed by the old historical schemas. She could easily be forgiven. What came next was a dependent semi-peripheral capitalism with oligarchic tendencies, a fuzzy hierarchical configuration that in the early 1990s could easily have been mistaken for a new feudalism, but which in the following decades became incorporated in transnational capitalist logics, lending it a more dynamic twist than Verdery could have perceived in the rubble of the socialist collapse.

Alina Cucu has written an important, rich and subtle book, *Planning Labour*. It has been written at a time in which questions about postsocialist futures cannot possibly be answered on a local level anymore – and of course they could not either in 1990, which was Verdery's methodological mistake. In general, it has been hard to think beyond capitalism of late. Alina Cucu has decided it is therefore time to go back to the old questions about socialism. And she answers them in perfectly cerebral, post-Cold War mode. She goes back to 1950s Romania, to Cluj-Napoca, looks closely at what was happening with labour regimes in two factories, and wonders about what is probably the most central question that can be posed in this context: what was the Central Plan?

The postwar literature on which Verdery based her idea of socialism (associated with János Kornai and others) has seen central planning as a bureaucratic system for allocating quantifiable factors in which the prices, given the presumed absence of capitalist value and therefore accounting, were soft and fuzzy. They were objects of political negotiation rather than economic calculation and fact. Cucu does not reject this approach in its entirety but shifts the perspective decidedly towards a reading that is rooted not in economics but in a historical anthropology of labour and class. The picture that emerges is thrilling. The plan, for her, was a collective performative exercise in what might be called 'synchronization' amid deep and tense non-simultaneity. It tried to call into being a working class that was, as such, as yet absent. At the same time, it was trying to empirically manage and coordinate the concrete productive practices of that projected working class in the here and now. But it was also seeking to cast that working class into the dream model of the future idealized socialist worker, perfectly assimilated to the behavioural and ideological requirements of socialism as a mode of production.

What emerges from this shift of vision is not the classic picture of failure. Rather, we get a visceral and dynamic sense of the Promethean effort that East European socialists were willy-nilly engaged in as they were trying to create a new society. The plan was the key tool for doing so. It did not just produce a centrally planned economy but rather a whole new type of society with a new man and new woman, a new childhood, new temporal rhythms, spatial structures, and new social relationships of solidarity, inequality and hierarchy. Moreover, the plan had to simultaneously secure socialist accumulation. Socialist growth was essential for its survival. Socialism in that sense could never be fundamentally different from capitalism, Cucu proposes as she revisits the debates of the 1920s and 1970s–80s. Both systems had to produce working classes via dispossession of the peasantry, and had to extract and secure a surplus from those classes for reinvestment, growth, and maintaining their elites and cadres.

Cucu is careful, then, to distinguish her approach from the classical historical revisionism of the totalitarianism thesis associated with the work of Sheila Fitzpatrick, Lewis Siegelbaum and Ronald Suny, and others. Her point is not that life in really existing socialism was different from the ideological blueprint, nor more richly differentiated than both Stalinism and Liberalism were willing to allow, even though that was obviously the case. Rather than bringing in 'the social', she brings in 'class'. By looking at the plan from the vantage point of her two factories in Cluj-Napoca, she is trying less to bring in endless local specificities or social differentiations – though she does that too, and enjoyably so – than seeking to return to the key universal contradictions that emerged in all socialist societies. Here then, is a local historical ethnography of labour, exemplarily executed, with stark universalizing ambitions. What was 'The Plan' and what *was* it meant to do? Her answer: managing those contradictions.

Cucu grasps back, convincingly, to the older relational conception of class, which was so important for Marx and for his basic idea of modes of production. Class here is not equated with hierarchy, status or distinction, nor necessarily seen as a bounded group that recognizes itself as such, let alone a discourse – all things that class has been seen to be during the neo-liberal decades and generally within positivist sociology (with apologies to Bourdieu). Rather, class is conceived as a set of ineluctable relationships of exploitation and extraction, indeed of power, domination and rule, including potential forms of counter-power; relationships that are essential to be maintained if wider social accumulation must be secured. Class, for Cucu then, is not about difference, nor even just inequality, but about immanent relational contradictions as they develop over time and space.

As if this theoretical bravery is not enough, she then goes back to Trotsky and Preobrazhensky in order to pinpoint the classic problems of socialist accumulation after the 1917 revolution. It is here also that she introduces her key notions of nonsynchronicity, taken from Ernst Bloch, and combined and uneven development, derived from Trotsky. Both notions are witnessing a marked revival these days in anthropology, development studies, and international relations. Cucu moulds them together into an original anthropological and historical tool that allows her to understand the fundamental mission of the Central Plan in new ways, and to start a micro historical-ethnographic investigation on labour in a Transylvanian city that is driven by big theoretical and historical questions.

What were those basic contradictions that the plan was meant to manage? Uneven development was the key one. Socialism emerged in spaces that were still very largely rural, and most of these rural economies were underdeveloped, hardly specialized, penetrated by capital and the city in the form of debts, poverty, putting out networks, seasonal and circular migration, and large-scale commuting, apart from the marketing of agricultural produce. Cucu rightly says that Romania in 1950 was not fundamentally different from Russia in 1920 in that respect. Temporary urban work was taken on to subsidize rural reproduction. But under socialism, rural reproduction was also targeted to produce various subsidies to urban industrialization. This was the key contradiction that the plan had to manage. Preobrazhensky, in the early 1920s, had theorized primitive socialist accumulation: someone had to be taxed on behalf of reinvestment in industry. The peasantry was the main source of those transfers. In Russia, enforced collectivization of the countryside made that possible. In Romania and Central Europe, it was precisely the time lag between the initial socialist industrialization and the later collectivization that facilitated such transfers, a time lag that was organized and coordinated within the plan. An essential part of those transfers sprang from the continued availability of pools of cheap unskilled labour in the wider surroundings of the urban industrial sites. Such labour hardly resembled the ideal type of the socialist worker, let alone the Stakhanovite. It was oriented towards time schedules and lifeworlds other than the plan, rooted in the rhythms of the countryside. Massive labour turnover remained therefore a basic characteristic of the factory regimes studied by Cucu. But primitive socialist accumulation targeted the full-time industrial labourer too. As a category they were supposed to harbour 'hidden reserves of productivity' that had to be discovered and tapped to the full by the plan and the party state. And while the Stakhanovite cult was meant to instil socialist competition among workers, the investments into working-class everyday life and social reproduction were never meant to equal the surplus extracted from their labour. High prices, insufficient supply and low quality of food and shelter remained characteristic for the early years of the plan that Cucu studies, and for many years after. This produced its own systematic antagonisms and divisions among working classes in which different ethnic backgrounds could always be manipulated to play into further social divisions. Gender too remained a fundamental axis of difference, whereby female labour was never rewarded as much as male labour was, lest socialist accumulation would stutter. As the labour transfers from the surrounding countryside would decline in the 1960s, the gender axis of socialist accumulation would gain in importance, as would systematic population transfers from the underdeveloped provinces further away, and new consequent urbanizations.

The plan managed these uneven histories and asynchronicities on behalf of the making of a shining socialist future until the last pools of exploitable labour in socialism had been exhausted, and pressures for more investments in social reproduction, more and better supplies, more and better jobs, had begun to mount and could hardly be resisted by force or contingent concession any longer. It was only then that the plan began to fail in a substantial and historical sense beyond soft and fuzzy prices. It was at that precise moment that socialist accumulation began to stutter. It was not different in the capitalist welfare states in the West. The competing social and ideological models of the European twentieth century began to collapse at the exact same time that their populations had finally begun to resemble their ideal type of literate trained urban industrial worker-citizen – sometime between 1970 and 1990. Also, in that respect, there was no contrast between the really existing socialist and really existing capitalist worlds. Further accumulation now required new dispossessions and new and wider spatial integrations and reorderings. This of course lies outside the purview of this fascinating book, but is certainly suggested by the rich historical ethnographic reading of the first five-year plan in Cluj and the close observation of the János Herbák and Armătura factories in the late 1940s and early 1950s. Alina Cucu has written a book that is not only a great joy to read; pregnant with deep insights, it will stimulate socialist labour historians and global labour historians to rethink their visions, methods and questions.

Don Kalb is Professor of Social Anthropology at the University of Bergen. He is also a Senior Researcher at Utrecht University and a Visiting Professor at the Max Planck Institute for Social Anthropology, Halle/Saale. He is the Founding Editor of *Focaal – Journal of Global and Historical Anthropology* and of *Focaalblog*.

Acknowledgements

These pages come with a fragile hope that the future will honour labour's toil and recognize it as foundational for our history. I dedicate them to the workers in Cluj.

Marcel van der Linden believed in this book before I even knew what it was going to look like. He strongly encouraged me to work through the most difficult questions and to always strive to be a better historian, despite not having been trained as one.

The book has its roots in the PhD dissertation I defended at the Department of Sociology and Social Anthropology at Central European University in Budapest, where I learned the craft of research from my professors and my colleagues. It is easier when struggles to understand power are shared. My research would not have been possible without Don Kalb's unabated belief in its potential, and without his ability to create broad spaces in which I could grow and learn. Prem Kumar Rajaram put his endless patience to good use, and opened up for me a more nuanced conceptual vocabulary that will stay with me for a long time. My heartfelt gratitude goes to Tom Rooney, my academic-writing instructor at CEU, who taught me not only how to write better but also how to think better. If I am truly lucky, all the paragraphs I will ever write will be marked by Tom's tireless pursuit of clarity.

My research benefited immensely from dialogues with scholars of East Central Europe. During these years, Mark Pittaway, a most wonderful historian, died at an unfairly young age. Had it developed in a face-to-face dialogue with him, this book would have been better. Martha Lampland's fresh thinking about labour in the region was a continuous source of inspiration. My work bears the intellectual influence of one of the most generous and knowledgeable people I have met. As labour history in Romania is in its infancy, one can feel lost between the huge amount of archival material and the almost total lack of systematic scholarship on the topic. I cannot imagine this journey without the aid of two excellent

Romanian historians, Mara Mărginean and Adrian Grama, who offered me their selfless help and friendship.

I am grateful to friends who read and commented on chapter drafts: Emily Brownell, Barbara Hahn and Victoria Fomina. I also thank those people who shared data with me at different stages: Alexandra Ghiț, Camelia Badea, Oana Pop and Elena Chiorean. I warmly acknowledge the help of all those whose wit, dedication and passion placed important bricks at the foundation of my intellectual growth. During my stay at Max Planck for the History of Science in Berlin, my colleagues furthered my interest in knowledge and its relationship to productive reasoning. My colleagues from the 'Moving Crops' working group keep expanding my horizons to new worlds of marvels.

I was lucky enough to spend the academic year 2017/18 at re:work in Berlin, where I was surrounded by the best intellectual collective I could have imagined. One could hardly dream of a more stimulating or supportive environment for writing a book. My friends at re:work rekindled the hope that there are academic places out there where people take their work and political commitments more seriously than they take themselves.

The writing of this book has been an important part of my life, one that I shared with people I deeply care about. My friends, some new, some old, found unexpected ways to encourage me from Cluj, Budapest, Vienna, Bucharest, Leipzig and Berlin. I have been lucky to be surrounded by people whose intellectual curiosity, passion for life, resilience, sense of humour and kindness challenge me to be a better scholar and, hopefully, a better person. Thank you Victoria Fomina, Natalia Buier, Celia Revilla, Thorsten Storck, Veronica Lazăr, Magda Crăciun, Mihai Olaru, Simion Pop, Irina Culic, Cristina Raț, Cosmin Colios, Raul Cârstocea, Aron Szele, Görkem Akgöz, Hannah Ahlheim, On Barak, Bridget Kenny, BuYun Chen, Emily Brownell, Luisa Steur and Michael Stanley-Baker.

Jakob literally helped me to stay sane during this process, while at the same time ensuring that the good crazy that makes us pour our souls onto white pages stayed with me until the end. The road ahead is long and winding.

And finally, this book is my family's as much as it is mine. My mother and my grandmother made sure there was love and care behind every written word. Mimi made sure there was laughter. And without Ada, nothing would ever have been possible.

Introduction

> How can you take as a whole a thing whose essence consists in a split?
> —Leon Trotsky, The History of the Russian Revolution

Tensions and Contradictions of Industrial Socialism

In June 1949, only a few months after the implementation of the first central economic plan, an article from the programmatic journal of the Romanian Workers' Party – *Class Struggle* – opened with a special quote from Stalin's *Problems of Leninism*.

> It would be foolish to believe that the production plan can be reduced to a mere sequence of figures and tasks. In fact, the production plan is the *living and practical activity* of millions of people. The reality of our production plan lies in the millions of working people, who are building a new life. The reality of our program is constituted by living people, it is us together with you, it is our will to work, our readiness to work in a new way, our determination to accomplish the plan. Do we have that determination? Yes, we do. Well then, our production program can and must be fulfilled.[1]

Originally, the quote was part of a speech addressed to the Soviet's new economic executives at the end of the first Soviet Five-Year Plan. At the end of the 1940s, Stalin's words were acquiring a new life in the context of the East Central European transition to central planning. For the next few years, the quote circulated widely among the Romanian party activists and factory managers through countless articles, lectures and reports.[2] It was going to accompany their efforts to establish control over the factories, the cities and the countryside, as well as the struggles of millions with the new realities of work and everyday life.

In the broadest sense, the 'living and practical activity' that sustained the Romanian planned economy in its formative years is the subject of this book, which illuminates how the plan's 'mere sequence of figures and tasks' came to embody the contradictions of primitive socialist accumulation deriving from the multivocal nature of labour: as creator of value, as living labour and as bearer of emancipatory politics. I explore the limits and possibilities of a political imaginary that fetishized planning as instrumental in resolving these contradictions through elaborated mechanisms of knowledge production and disciplining practices. More concretely, I examine how the postwar expansion of a cheap and flexible workforce set the constraints for the emergence of a historically specific shop floor regime, predicated on an uneasy synthesis between Taylorist politics of productivity and heroic mobilization. I read these transformations in a temporal key, as an encounter between the different horizons of a civilizing process, of capital accumulation and of everyday life, as they materialized in the plan figures and in the shop floor practices that sustained them.

In order to understand how the contradictory nature of labour – as labour power, as living labour and as political subjecthood – was reflected in the ordinary operations of planning, the book attempts to answer several interrelated questions. Who were the workers of early socialist factories? How did the socialist state keep the cost of labour low? How did the relationship between the city and the countryside play out in labour's reproduction, expansion and control? How were the new labour regulations translated into local realities? How did the workers respond to these societal changes with their own classed, ethnicized and gendered strategies of reproduction? And finally, how were the daily struggles to (re)produce a cheap labour force reflected in the possibility of controlling workers, mobilizing them and unearthing their practical knowledge on the shop floor?

To answer these questions, the book explores the day-to-day practicalities of introducing Soviet-style economic planning and its functioning as an essential instrument of capital accumulation in the factories of Cluj (Kolozsvár in Hungarian), between 1944 and 1955.[3] Functioning for centuries as the administrative, symbolic and cultural capital of the region, Cluj was an ethnically mixed city with a complicated history of belonging in between Hungary and Romania, and with a central role in the negotiation of the 'Transylvanian question'.[4] Both the interwar economic policy of investment and the first decades of socialist industrialization left the city mostly bereft of large-scale manufacturing, making it into a good case for analysing socialist accumulation at the margins, where its contradictions were harder to tame, and where ethnic lines of fracture between the Hungarian and the Romanian population magnified the class ones.

The investigation starts from the struggles for control over the factories at the end of the Second World War, it continues through the implementation of the One-Year Plan in 1949, and it concludes with the successes and failures of the First Five-Year Plan in 1955. During the postwar reconstruction years, the negotiation of industrial peace involved a constant struggle to contain labour unrest against the background of ever-intensifying inflation, the fall of workers' real wages and the precariousness of everyday life. In 1949, the implementation of planning marked a turn to a logic of productivity and rationalization of the production process that mirrored, with variations and with different ideological justifications, the Western social contract of the 1950s.[5] On a larger historical scale, this period represented a foundational moment in the Romanian transition to industrialism – a transition that had already started in the interwar period but condensed much of its depth in the first decade after the Second World War, when it became strong enough to radically transform social life.

In the short term, the 1945–1955 decade articulated the generalized effort for the normalization of life in the aftermath of the Second World War. In the longer run, it laid down the foundations of industrial socialism by grounding the economic mechanisms and the social arrangements that constituted its spine for more than forty years. The achievements and failures of these years represented an Eastern European reinterpretation of the Stalinist answer to long-term backwardness and economic isolation. The Soviet response was itself a peripheral variation of an essentially Western modern project, which equated progress with industrialization. Socialist industrialization was not politically neutral. It prompted the emergence of an industry that simultaneously reflected the logic of capital accumulation and a logic of historical advancement with progressive aims. Planning was the ultimate expression of this contradictory simultaneity and its critical solution.

During this decade, 'really existing socialism' was articulated as a bureaucratically managed accumulation regime, which depended on a particular combination of surplus extraction mechanisms. As primitive socialist accumulation, it relied on the direct dispossession of the capitalist class and of a part of the peasantry through the nationalization of the means of production and through the collectivization of land; on the exploitation of the countryside as a pool of cheap raw materials, food and manpower; and on the externalization of costs for the reproduction of a cheap and flexible labour force. As expanded reproduction proper, it directly hinged on a restrictive wage policy and centrally planned politics of productivity of a Taylorist inspiration.

Based on the investigation of the formative years of industrial socialism in Romania, I advance a three-step argument about the historical stakes played out in the apparently banal act of planning labour. First, the plan functioned as the direct unifier of the sphere of production, reproduction and exchange, and as such, it was constitutive for the ways in which social relationships became objectified in state socialism. Second, the implementation of central planning generated a tension between the worker as the creator of capital accumulation and the worker as the ideal subject/object of an emancipatory political project. Deeply rooted in the local practices and relations that made surplus extraction possible, this tension went beyond the daily struggles around legitimacy on the shop floor.[6] It was a class tension that further effected the Romanian 'workers' state' as a fragile state, caught between a historically progressive mission and the practical task of creating and managing social production processes. Third, amidst these tensions, state socialism emerged as a conflicting temporal regime marked by the state's efforts of keeping together the temporal horizons of accumulation on the shop floor, of workers' everyday life, and of the Bolshevik civilizing mission. Controlling, instrumentalizing and working through multiple temporalities became essential aspects of governance, and found their expression in the very act of planning.

The book embraces a materialist bottom-up epistemological perspective on planning, which makes the specificity of labour as resource transparent. It shows how plan figures and tasks embodied the polyphonic nature of socialist labour as value producing, as living labour and as political undertaking. Unlike in market societies, in centrally planned economies, living labour acquired its character of commodity, and thus of social labour, within exchange relations that were not only anticipated but also secured.[7] Far from simply imposing the plan as a bureaucratic instrument upon an amorphous population and territory, the economic executives of the 1950s had to articulate an entire field of politics in which the calculation of wages or the anticipation of investments were never taken for granted as simple technicalities. Most importantly, the efforts of the socialist planners revolved around the difficulties of generalizing industrial employment as a source of livelihood, the practical universe of the reproduction and expansion of labour, as well as the incorporation or workers' nonsynchronous horizon of expectations into life on the shop floor.

Hence, the book analyses how the tasks of the plan had to be juggled against the multiple temporalities of primitive socialist accumulation: the historical 'leap forward' of early socialist industrialization as a solution to backwardness and economic isolation; the chronology of investment, which privileged heavy industry over consumer goods and agriculture, previously industrialized areas over the underdeveloped ones, and the city over the village; the different rhythms set by the new economic executives for the nationalization of the factories and for the collectivization of land; the pace at which the workforce was released from the countryside; the tempo at which people's bare necessities were met; and the pulse of workers' attempts to reproduce their experience of being in the world in terms of class, ethnicity and gender.

On the shop floor, these temporalities of primitive socialist accumulation produced the regime's own version of 'nonsynchronicity'[8] – an amalgam of archaic, contemporary, and future-oriented forms of living and working – that constrained the possibility to discipline and mobilize labour. These conflicting temporal horizons would haunt planners and factory managers when trying to articulate the mixture between Taylorism and labour heroism, which marked the politics of productivity of early socialism.

The book draws on Martha Lampland's analysis of the commodification of labour in Eastern and Central Europe. Following a Postonian line of critique, Lampland argues that 'the process of commodifying labor has been fully realized under socialism in conditions thought to be inimical to capitalist development generally, and to commodification in particular'.[9] Focusing on village life in Hungary, she reveals how 'the final blossoming of commodity fetishism' was carried forward by state policies and local managers' practices, which further produced a social fabric dominated by individualist and utilitarianist values. She moves the focus from the centrality of markets in the commodification of labour to the expanding field of possibilities to sell one's labour power that emerged with the socialist industrialization. While in *The Object of Labor* she convincingly shows how commodification could be 'bred and fostered' in a planned economy, Martha Lampland's subsequent work is essential for understanding how calculating the value of labour stood under the sign of modernist rationalization that traversed the interwar period, the Second World War and early socialism. This was the period when the concerted efforts of scientists and bureaucrats materialized the 'substantial infrastructure' that made the functioning of markets and planning possible.[10]

My analysis goes one step further to show how a Soviet-inspired form of primitive accumulation and the operations of central planning came about not only through the conjugated efforts and negotiations of socialist planners, managers and scientists, but also through the rearticulation of the production/life nexus. I read plan figures as being simultaneously an expression of objectified labour-power, whose price could be calculated and included in the production cost of any manufactured good, and as the end result of the complex dynamics in which labour and the state came to be entangled in the first decade after the Second World War. Understanding how labour appeared in the plan figures cannot be separated from the 'definite historical conditions' under which it became a commodity or from workers' living selves. The plan, too, should 'bear the stamp of history'.[11]

The remainder of the Introduction takes a closer look at the central notions of the book: socialist accumulation and planning. The second and third sections place the mechanisms of surplus extraction and the class relations they produced on the ground into a broader conversation regarding primitive socialist accumulation in the region. The fourth section lays down the foundation for an epistemological rethinking of central planning. It makes the point that the top-down, idealist perspectives prevailing in the scholarly literature have missed out the granular realities of socialist economies when taking labour for granted, as simply another 'resource' to be planned and calculated. The last section explores the analytical opportunities opened by industrial Cluj as a case, and by the factory as a site of accumulation and governmentality.

Primitive Socialist Accumulation in the Romanian Context

Forcefully imposed in the aftermath of the Second World War as a prize for the crucial role played by the Soviet Union in the Allied victory, the 'really existing socialism' of Eastern and Central Europe represented the embodiment of a political project of fighting against long-established forms of backwardness and uneven development through a vast programme of industrialization. In its initial stage, it unfolded as a class war against privately owned capital, better-off categories of the peasantry, clergy, and conservative intellectuals. The top-down 'class struggle' was the stepping stone for a governing minority, who came to rule the countries in the region for almost half a century, and whose modernizing ethos went hand in hand with the privatization of power.

Scholars of Eastern and Central Europe have long debated the essence of 'really existing socialism' in the countries of the region. In the attempt to classify these historical configurations as state capitalist, transitional or socialist, researchers used diverse criteria such as the nature of property relations; the absence of markets; the endemic shortages, bargaining, and hoarding along the production chains; the (im)possibility of economic calculation without freely fluctuating prices; the emergence of the state bureaucracy as a 'new class'; and the continuing alienation and exploitation of industrial workers on the shop floor.[12] As Michael Burawoy points out, what these perspectives had in common was the fact that socialism became in the scholarly imagination everything capitalism was not.[13] Naturally, the concrete functioning of state socialism did not accommodate too well the assumptions of this comparison, especially when articulated in an ahistorical critique that unproblematically opposed dictatorship to freedom, illegitimacy to democracy, violence to consent, ideology to facts, planning to market, or waste to efficiency.

Since the very beginning, the Marxist tradition itself was split by heated arguments around the nature of the Soviet regime and its European satellites, with scholars debating if the historical embodiment of socialist ideas should be labelled as 'state capitalism', 'state monopoly capitalism', 'bureaucratic state capitalism', or 'degenerated workers' state'.[14] For Trotskyists in the revolutionary heat of the 1920s, and for Western Marxists like Ernest Mandel and Paul Sweezy, who were still holding hopes of a world revolution in the mid twentieth century, the Bolshevik trajectory was simply a transitional regime.[15] They brought into the conversation the lack of spontaneous exchange, the central setting of prices, the more equal forms of redistribution, and the reinvestment of surplus 'for the good of all' to argue that Soviet and Soviet-inspired socialism represented a historical bridge between capitalism and communism, necessarily containing elements of both. This historical passage was unavoidably violent, but it would lead to a better, fundamentally different world.

For other leftist thinkers, any similarity of really existing socialism with the capitalist system came to be considered as a sign of malfunctioning and as a historical failure of the initial revolutionary project.[16] They argued that socialist modernization in the Soviet Union and its satellites epitomized a combination of exploitative practices and scientific ethos that stood under the same sign as the capitalist one. The developmental projects in the region might have had equalitarian aims but they were inherently harmful to workers, since the resources for sustaining these projects came from wage labour and from the appropriation of surplus. In a devastating critique, Moishe Postone went on to claim that these regimes were simply new forms of 'political administration and economic distribution of the *same* mode of production' like the capitalist ones.[17]

In relation to these debates, my analysis starts from some basic assumptions. As this book will show, if we refocus our inquiry on production rather than redistribution, exchange, or political arrangements, the postwar East Central European regimes appear as contradictory social formations, subjected to regionally specific alignments of constraints, but set out to transcend these constraints through productive arrangements very similar to the Western ones. For the period analysed here, these productive arrangements were articulated around the logic and mechanisms of primitive accumulation.

To support the reading of early socialism as a historical configuration primarily centred on a logic of accumulation, one only needs to notice that the aim of economic activity was always *over*fulfilling the plan, and that the rise in production thus obtained was used to further increase future targets. 'Socialist accumulation' also occupied a central place in the political imaginary of the 1950s, when socialist planners and other economic executives were heavily debating terms like 'value', 'surplus', 'productivity', 'return rate', and 'profitability of investments' in their endeavour of establishing the new categories of political economy.

As an 'ideal type', early socialist accumulation combined two elements: the squeezing of the private sector (primarily agricultural) in relation to the state sector (largely industrial) on the one hand, and workers' 'self-exploitation' on the other. 'Primitive socialist accumulation' was defined by Yevgeni Preobrazhensky as 'the accumulation in the hands of the state of material resources obtained chiefly from sources lying outside the state economic system',[18] and it came to be postulated as the central axis of development in the Soviet Union in the 1930s. It was a response to the fundamental problems posed by the transition to socialism in a backward, primarily agrarian society, and in the absence of the much-expected socialist revolutions elsewhere: the need of an absolute and constant increase of capital, and the more rapid expansion of the state sector compared to the private one.[19]

For Preobrazhensky – as well as for Marx – primitive accumulation referred both to expropriation in its material sense, and to a fundamental change in social relations, expressed chiefly as class displacement.[20] And it was constitutive of capitalism and socialism alike. Preobrazhensky used the concept of primitive accumulation not in the classical liberal sense of 'previous accumulation' – as Adam Smith called it – but as an answer to two entangled questions. First, where should resources for growth come from during the transition period to socialism? Second, how should the relations of production transform, in order to allow socialism to become self-sustainable? The answer to these questions was that the 'process of extending and consolidating the state economy' was meant to proceed 'both at the expense of its own forces and resources – that is, the surplus product of the workers in state industry – and at the expense of private, including peasant ... economy'.[21]

Therefore, primitive socialist accumulation relied on small agricultural production for provisioning the rapidly developing industrial centres and for ensuring an important part of the Soviet international grain trade. It revolved around the idea of replacing forced deliveries – which had proved catastrophic for the Soviet space – with financial techniques of squeezing the peasants. Generally, these techniques involved introducing unequal terms of exchange between industry and agriculture – price scissors – in favour of the former.[22] Preobrazhensky's unequal exchange solution was completely rejected in the beginnings of the Soviet industrialization debate and labelled as a form of exploitation of the peasantry by the working class, only to be later adopted and transposed in a violent key by Stalin during the collectivization.[23] It was in this later version that the unequal reliance of the city on the countryside was transferred as a developmental option in East Central Europe.[24]

Drawing the lines of the British particular experience onto the canvas of a country 'privileged by its backwardness' profoundly affected the making of the Soviet working class in the first decades of the twentieth century. In England, this process started with the enclosure movement as a precondition for the progressive transformation of agriculture according to the laws of capitalist production. In the classical account of the transition from feudalism to capitalism, the role of the state was to hasten the process by supporting the landlords against the rural population, by expanding territorially and economically in colonies, and by creating the modern system of taxation. In the transition to socialism, the state relied on differential taxation, manipulation of prices, and land appropriation proper. Although the Soviet state had the resources of monopoly capital at its disposal, it was not this 'extraordinary power' of the state but rather an acute sense of its fragility that convinced Preobrazhensky of the historical necessity and urgency of his solution.[25] The vulnerability of the Bolshevik state came not only from the social and economic devastation of the interwar period or from the class war raged against the peasantry and formerly better-offs, but also from its direct involvement in industrial production. Revisionist historians of Soviet industrialization have convincingly shown how, as 'the surplus product of the workers in state industry' became the second pillar of primitive socialist accumulation, it brought forward an exploitative wage policy, the prevalence of shock work, impossible production targets and appalling living conditions. These developments combined with the intense politicization of the shop floor to produce a factory regime dominated by absenteeism, fluctuations and shortages, and permanently threatened by riots and strikes.[26]

These unfoldings also proved crucial for Eastern and Central Europe in the first decade after the Second World War. As the book will show, the early Romanian socialist accumulation was articulated around the double mechanism highlighted by Preobrazhensky for the Soviet case. First, it rested on the possibility of surplus extraction through politics of productivity that combined a Taylorist system of targets and incentives with workers' heroic mobilization on the shop floor. Second, it relied on preserving a non-socialist exterior that would function as a source of goods and raw materials, and as a reservoir of cheap labour for the expanding factories.

In a labour-intensive regime, which had little to count on except for making people work more, faster and better, the socialist planners imagined the factory as the depository of 'hidden reserves' of productivity that had to be revealed in the act of work through learning, discipline and technologies of the self. The combination of planned heroism – manifested through practices like shock brigades, socialist competitions and the Stakhanovite movement – and a hyper-rationalization drive were characteristic for the First Five-Year Plan. As a result, the shop floor became the space of encounter between the efforts to ensure the 'scientific organization of the production process' and the hope to achieve workers' enthusiastic consent to managerial (thus state) authority.

The rationalization impulse and the search for the 'hidden reserves' of the shop floor in workers' mobilization and practical knowledge was not simply a faithful imitation of the Soviet blueprint. It was also dictated by the severe lack of capital and by the destabilizing war reparations Romania had to pay to the Soviet Union in the aftermath of the Second World War. The first wave of socialist investment privileged pre-existing industrial agglomerations and was directed towards industries producing export commodities like oil, cement and lumber, which took priority even over heavy industry branches like metallurgy or industrial equipment building.[27] In the early phase of planning, after the countries in the Eastern bloc refused the extension of the Marshall Plan in the region, limited access to credit for buying the necessary industrial equipment came only from the Soviet Union and from Czechoslovakia. The chronic lack of capital drew the main lines of the early socialist industrialization: high intensity of labour and associated politics of austerity, which translated into an oversized accumulation fund in comparison to the consumption fund, and touched every aspect of workers' lives: rationing of food and other consumer goods; lack of housing, heating or sanitation; and wages that did not allow workers' survival on industrial employment alone. All these were played out against the dynamics of the two central acts of primitive socialist accumulation: the nationalization of industry and the collectivization of land.

The nationalization of the means of production and of the financial sector took place as early as June 1948, less than one year after the communists were officially installed as the sole government party. After the nationalization had been announced in the communist press as being 'the first act of socialist accumulation', the most important industrial, commercial and financial units became state owned in only one day, while the remainder of local industry and services would not be incorporated in the state sector until 1952. Nevertheless, things went differently for agriculture, with collectivization proceeding at a considerably slower pace.

Following the Soviet historical path, the collectivization of land in East Central Europe was supposed to constitute a solid starting point for the socialist project. While Western capital instituted the colonies and invented the Third World as a reservoir for continuous primitive accumulation, the not-yet-socialist village represented the state economy's Other for the communist governments of the 1950s. Whether through price scissors, coerced deliveries, appropriation of liquidities, or forced collectivization, the peasant's surplus was extracted and redirected towards industrialization and towards the growing needs of the urban population. The expropriation of the agricultural population had to ensure the needed increase in the agricultural output, the release of the labour force for the rapidly growing industry, and the internal market for industrial products. The brute force of the state was the instrument of this accumulation form, in itself an economic power – 'the midwife of every old society which is pregnant with a new one', as Marx would have put it.[28] A significant part of the peasantry witnessed the dissolution of the old society as a history of expropriation. It was going to be 'written in the annals of mankind in letters of blood and fire',[29] while the rural population was to be progressively reduced to a number that matched the requirements of the labour force in the countryside. Ideally, at the end of collectivization, it was not land anymore but employment that was going to decide the possibility to survive, both in the city and in the village.

Agricultural policy was crucial in the context of the struggles for taking over the political power immediately after the war. In 1945, hoping that it could count on the votes of the poor and middle peasantry, the Romanian Communist Party initiated an agrarian reform to redistribute land confiscated from Nazi sympathizers and German citizens. But the fragmentation of land that followed in its trail was soon to become a problem, especially since Romania was an important exporter of agricultural products and raw materials. The issue was compounded by the severe drought following the end of the Second World War, which also produced a massive wave of internal migration.

Between 1948 and 1952, the agricultural policy of the communist government revolved around promoting the establishment of voluntary cooperatives and investing in their gradual mechanization. Ana Pauker – the Romanian Workers' Party's secretary for agriculture – and Vasile Luca – the head of the finance ministry – endorsed a policy of equitable exchanges between the city and the countryside, as well as a balanced development of heavy and light industry.[30] Nevertheless, Stalin's pressures for forced collectivization in the socialist bloc, the impossibility of controlling the deliveries of the mid-size peasant households, the impact of agricultural prices and the effects of peasants' cash reserves on the growing state economy pushed the Romanian state towards a new stance regarding the dynamics between economic sectors. Thus, the initial strategy of primitive socialist accumulation shifted towards rapid industrialization, price scissors favouring the urban over the countryside, and a new push towards the expropriation of land.[31] The offensive of 1952 was followed by concessions in 1953, under the threat of protests like elsewhere in Eastern Europe. In 1955, at the end of the First Five-Year Plan, the socialist sector in agriculture covered only one-quarter of the total cultivable land.[32] The last (and most violent) wave of collectivization started in the late 1950s and ended in 1962, when the state declared that the formation of cooperatives had been concluded and most of the agricultural land was now part of the socialist economy.

Nationalization and collectivization were indeed powerful processes meant to solve a fundamental contradiction of capitalism: the one between private appropriation of surplus and the social character of production. Not far from Preobrazhensky's initial vision, their unfolding created a new social fabric, which was fundamentally classed, gendered and ethnicized. In this book, I explore these forms taken by primitive socialist accumulation from a processual angle, and I show how their different progressions in time mattered no less than the change in property relations they brought forward. More concretely, I argue that the slower rhythm of collectivization compared to the nationalization of industry proved essential for the socialist labour regime. Especially in the first decades of socialism, maintaining a (mainly rural) non-socialist exterior, which could be used as a resource for food, raw materials and manpower, was a crucial condition for rapid industrialization. The different rhythms of the nationalization of the means of production and of the collectivization of land represented integral parts of how dispossession and displacement shaped the structure of possibility for the reproduction, expansion and control of labour.

Postponed Proletarianization and the Workings of Class

In the logic of early socialist accumulation, postponed proletarianization was the direct consequence of the slower rhythm of the collectivization of agriculture. It was coupled with a systematic effort to keep workers' real wages down,[33] and to ensure that the population, especially the rural one, would partly bear the social reproduction costs of the labour force. In this sense, time functioned as a top-down, purposeful instrument of class formation that impacted people's lives for several generations. On the ground, the tension between bringing manpower into the factories and preventing people from flooding the cities was going to encounter workers' and peasants' own strategies for reproducing the lives they once knew, or for making industrial wages into an opportunity to escape those lives.

Early socialist Romania was an emerging industrial regime where workers were difficult to find and then to keep in the factory. In an agrarian country with a low level of urbanization, the growth of industry had to rely on categories of labourers who were anything but the ideal revolutionary proletarians. Factories functioned and expanded not only with the help of their core urban labourers but with the help of a largely unskilled workforce made up of soldiers, prison mates, women, temporary labourers and young professional trainees. For these factories, the peasant worker (not the proletarian) was the central figure of early Romanian industrialization. The antagonisms of socialist construction in conditions of backwardness were inscribed onto his body. As a commuter or as a young migrant living in the factory barracks, he (mainly 'he' for the first working generation after the war) brought 'barbaric' rhythms and routines into the city, sanctioned by old urbanites with contempt. Making Stakhanovites out of these peasants became the ultimate transformative victory of the state over a reluctant population.

By exploring the reproduction of a heterogeneous labour force in Cluj factories, the first part of this book reveals the emptiness of the central category of the socialist project – 'the worker' – and unpacks the employment regime that emerged in the late 1940s and the early 1950s in cities that were peripheral to socialist accumulation. The first three chapters show that the early socialist labour regime was non-homogeneous and volatile, and was shaped not only by the instrumental logic of the new economic executives but also by local configurations of livelihood. In order to capture the entanglement between production and life as the crux of socialist accumulation, a deeper understanding of the workings of class in socialism is needed.

By 'class', I understand the field of forces that embeds people in historically specific mechanisms of surplus extraction, appropriation and distribution, and in the power relations that enforce them, (re)produce them and legitimize them. These fields of forces structure people's possibilities of survival, and affect their moral economies and political imaginaries. My understanding of class is meant to capture not only mechanisms of exploitation and domination, but also people's positioning in relation to these mechanisms, to their corresponding institutional arrangements, and to each other.

Although from a Marxist perspective the extraction of surplus is always at the root of class as an analytical category, the processes that make this extraction possible are never purely economic. Processes of economic valuation resort to people's experience as a whole, as constituted by technological advancement and corresponding transformations in the production process. They are mediated through various forms of oppression, and are reproduced through complex narratives, which are fed no less by the experience of work than they are by structures of feelings in which love, friendship, religious ardour and ethnic belonging are central.[34] From this angle, far from being merely empty nominal categories, 'classes' appear to be imbued with life. They are seen here as experiential realities, continuously shaped by the changing power relations they are part of, and in return permanently transforming these relations through people's specific knowledges and practices. For me, class becomes a modest instrument of discovery,[35] a project for local-national-global explorations, a tool for understanding how people in their daily struggles 'make history in the factories, in the barracks, in the villages and on the streets'.[36]

In recent decades, the emergence of a scholarship focused on localized practices and relations, as they were lived in factories, in agricultural fields in people's homes, has illuminated the contested terrain of state socialism. This growing literature embodied the hope that the stereotypical way of seeing state socialist regimes as homogenous, grey and lifeless entanglements of populations and territories that were fully subjected to the Soviet rule would be dismantled forever. The scholarship was going to be salutary, and the stereotypical views would be replaced with in-depth explorations of shop floor politics,[37] emerging urban identities,[38] radically transforming generational experiences,[39] counterintuitive conceptions of work and personhood,[40] specific notions of 'solidarity' and 'efficiency',[41] complex forms of controlling time and bodies,[42] material and emotional forms of dispossession,[43] patterns of consumption,[44] or participation in extensive transnational networks of economic knowledge.[45]

This literature has accomplished many of the hopes it was initially invested with, and has undoubtedly enriched our understanding of forty-five years of European history. Nevertheless, it has also revealed that, on the ground, the experience of socialism was indeed remarkably structured. In Hungary, Poland and Romania, workers used the same tactics to escape the control of their foremen; managers negotiated plan figures and resources in the same way; and during the collectivization, peasants everywhere cried more when the party activists took their animals than when they confiscated their inanimate tools. Even jokes and moralizing stories circulated in the same form in various countries. But if these similarities are not simply to be explained through the ordinary appeals to 'the Soviet model', top-down decisional flows, or sheer violence, how can they be accounted for? In this book, I emphasize the need for a return to class as a compelling strategy to think through the striking similarities between the postwar East and Central European regimes, without falling back into the trap of homogenizing their histories.

The programme for class analysis in socialism that underlies my research can be summarized in three points. First, there is a wider recognition of the contingency of class relationships and a strong argument against the teleological understanding of class formation processes. Second, I move from the traditional understanding of 'class structure' towards an exploration of the mutually constitutive relationship between the state and the workers, which connects 'the local' with broader historical processes and political power to social production. Third, the image of a monolithic state needs to be replaced by an exploration of socialist governmentality, which allows a rethinking of the exercise of power as part and parcel of ordinary productive practices.

Together with the previously unthinkable historical possibility of socialism in a backward country, the new party leaders in East Central Europe inherited from the Bolsheviks an 'economistic view of production and a voluntaristic view of politics'[46] that produced a rather impoverished notion of class. This view of politics was a continuation of the belief in the fracture between base and superstructure, as well as in the primacy of the productive forces as the engine of history, which pervaded leftist debates after the Second International. These debates established a chronology of societal transformation that started with (capitalist) industrial modernization, which was then subjected to the whip of planning and state rationality. Technological progress and ever-higher productivity came first, followed by improvements in workers' living standards and a heightened sense of being on the good side of history.

Relegating the political to matters of the state and reducing production to technological advancement according to ineluctable laws of progress were two sides of the attempt to drive class struggle out of the factory, into a purely discursive realm. The shop floor was imagined as a pre-political space, which the party could mould into the desired shape. But because of its productive core, power in socialism could never be separated from the workings of class, on whose lines of tension the boundary between state, society and economy were negotiated. Although the socialist project was supposed to linearly produce a working class to match a specific vision of historical advancement, on the ground it encountered real people with their own life strategies, dreams and desires. The dominant narrative on East Central European regimes assumes that these strategies, dreams and desires were simply smashed by the socialist states in their drive to encompass life and to mute struggles. However, the book shows that far from disappearing, people's everyday strategies for reproducing their lives imposed themselves on the new regime, leaving the state with no choice but to use them as a problematic – though often fertile – ground for socialist accumulation and politics.

As a result, the socialist state was a fragile one, fractured between opposite roles: a workers' state guiding an emancipatory project for an emergent class, and a manager state creating and running social production processes. In other words, the fragility of the socialist state resided in the contradiction between its functioning as a manager of an accumulation regime and its needs to imagine an emancipatory project, not only *for* the workers but also *together with* them. This tension was the result of a specific articulation of class in history, and the consequence of its placement under incongruous temporal horizons.

This fragility has been partially captured in the revisionist historians' accounts of how the Soviet workers were dealt with after the October Revolution.[47] But their focus on 'the social' – so welcome at the time – almost closed the theoretical possibility of rethinking the notions of 'class' and 'state' in socialism. This discussion was also basically absent from the literature on workers' states focusing on the East Central European regimes, even when rich histories of social change, production politics and shop floor negotiations were produced.

When the nature of the socialist states in Eastern and Central Europe was explicitly addressed, the analysis focused on the shifting nature of the social contract between labour and the party state, and on 'the limits of dictatorship.' Going beyond the usual notions of shortages and bargaining as identifiable limits of state power, Mark Pittaway returns to the idea that the relationship between the workers and the state was definitory for the socialist configuration.[48] He shows how the Stalinist-type forced industrialization of Hungary had in fact many limitations, since informal wage bargaining, labour indiscipline and managers' lack of authority over the workers were common occurrences. One of the end results of Mark Pittaway's comparative analysis of factory regimes in postwar Hungary is the reconceptualization of the exercise of state socialist power as always constrained and limited in its daily encounters with the working class.

Pittaway's work is essential for understanding how the day-to-day practicalities of state functioning in the factory impacted its struggle for legitimacy. He proposes 'a historically contingent definition' of legitimacy, which in Hungary was established and eroded several times between 1944 and 1958, and it remained partial and uneven, fluid and contested for decades after. Instead of the total power presupposed by a 'dictatorship', in the daily operations of the Hungarian factories Pittaway observes a modest project of state functioning, 'a state of affairs in which a given regime's claim to rule met with a sufficient degree of acceptance to ensure that it was able to acquire the necessary degree of 'infrastructural' power to rule on a day-to-day basis, and thus appear as a coherent, unified actor ruling above the rest of society'.[49] From this perspective, repression itself appears as an epiphenomenon, which was rooted in the fight against the growing perception of the socialist state's political illegitimacy.

While my book can definitely be read as an argument about the fragility of the socialist state, this argument is related neither to its political legitimacy, nor to the unexpected effects of its ideology. My view on the fragility of the socialist state is rooted in the Marxist tradition of conceptualizing the state itself as a relation of production, this time both as institutionalized capital and as the single guardian of capital formation.[50] Scholars of socialism often read the historical configurations in the region as status hierarchies due to the absence of private property over the means of production. Nevertheless, this reading leaves out the ways in which the state acted *as capital*, with accumulation as its explicit goal. Here, I take the position that postwar countries were class societies simply because they were structured around mechanisms of capital accumulation, articulated directly by the state. From this it follows that in its capacity of creator and manager of social production processes, the socialist state became highly sensitive not only to workers' capacity to mobilize politically but also to the everyday workings of class on the shop floor, and beyond.

The fragility of the state was compounded by the problems of safeguarding capital accumulation in a mainly agrarian country, where the 'proletarians' were still in project, and 'socialist workers' were problematic both as a category of rule and as a much-needed economic resource. This understanding of the state is related to planning and to the regimes of knowledge, discipline and temporality it entailed, and it leads us to the factory as the space where the 'everyday forms of state formation'[51] in socialism unfolded.

Understanding the state itself as a relation of production also suggests that the boundaries between 'the state', 'economy' and 'society' might not be so different from the ones between 'production' and 'life'. Although the aim of planning was the making of socialist economy as a whole, it also required the weaving of a specific social fabric made of structured and structuring relations, practices and subjectivities. Unsurprisingly, an identifiable tendency towards what I could call 'programmatic embeddedness' was manifest in the early years of planning in the practical drive towards a societal project founded on the explicit recognition of the production's characteristic of being immediately social. In this project, economy, society and the state were constituting each other in a dialectical relationship that embraced the plan as its ultimate expression. Nevertheless, as modern states, socialist states needed to appear as 'ideological projects of cohesion and unity'.[52] As such, they were continuous exercises in institutionalizing political and economic power as 'at once integrated and isolated' narrative structures that gave 'an account of political institutions in terms of cohesion, purpose, independence, common interest and morality'.[53] The crux of this account was the intersection between production and life.

Thus, the investigation of socialist accumulation and planning proceeds through an effort to understand the stakes of real workers trying to live their lives and make sense of them in the tumultuous and uncertain historical present of the 1950s. Following the trajectory of the relationship between labour and the state during the period when central economic planning was implemented, I examine the material roots of the worker's transformation into the subject/object of a particular mission that came with a promise of freedom, equality and emancipation for all. Recounting the stories of the women and men who became both the targets of the socialist construction project and its bearers allows glimpses into how the fundamental stickiness of everyday life combined the modernizing ethos of planning with a set of modest local negotiations around the lines of labour control, maintenance and expansion. Following Alf Lüdtke's understanding of *Alltagsgeschichte*, the book reveals the fundamental category of rule in socialism – the 'worker' – as a problematic category. Its content uncomfortably glided between contradictory political signifiers, which emerged as locally mediated expressions of the instrumental logics of the state. The next section turns to the ways in which the plan itself captured these logics, and to the social fabric they sought to reproduce.

Planning Labour on and beyond the Shop Floor

Scholarship on centrally planned economies has been organized around several tenets regarding the nature of the plan as a bureaucratic instrument of coordination: the plan replaced the market as a mechanism for synchronizing supply and demand; it functioned in a top-down manner, although the power of the socialist managers depended on their ability to attract resources from the government; labour was just another economic resource to be planned; and economic activity followed a temporal organization according to the party directives.[54] As the main pillars on which the analysis of socialist regimes rested, these ideas had important analytical consequences for how we understand the political economy of East Central Europe in the second half of the twentieth century and beyond. I discuss them one by one in what follows.

First, the academic obsession with state socialism as a system articulated around coordinated redistribution has obscured the role of planning in securing the conditions for the accumulation of capital – that is, the creation and realization of value.⁵⁵ Socialist economies came to be conceptualized as allocative mechanisms without the possibility of exchange through the markets, whose absence or limited role has been taken for granted.⁵⁶ Especially for the early socialist decades, the plan has been understood as taking over the allocation function of the capitalist market, and came to be unambiguously conceptualized as its opposite.

The exploration into the struggles to reproduce labour and the managerial efforts required to make the shop floor function is taken here as an investigation of the issues faced by the socialist economic executives to ensure the creation and extraction of surplus, once its capitalization had already been secured at the moment of planning. While there is no question about the fact that the nationalized factories of the Eastern bloc aimed at creating surplus product, no consensus related to the possibility of equating this surplus product with value has been reached. While some authors considered that valorization continued to be a reality for the socialist regimes, others assumed the suspension of the law of value after the nationalization of the means of production, in the absence of free markets, and in the context of a generalized impossibility to use the rate of profit as a meaningful economic category.⁵⁷ This lack of consensus was not only a feature of Western Marxism but also a painful spot for the economists of Eastern Europe, whose debates about the continuing operation of the law of value in socialism had concrete consequences for the activity of planning.⁵⁸

I start from the observation that East Central European communists in the 1950s explicitly saw planning as a condition of possibility for safeguarding socialist accumulation.⁵⁹ The plan itself functioned as a matrix which made both the operation of the law of value *and* its violations possible. These violations were not more definitory for socialism than they have been for capitalism – they were just more transparent, and assumed integral dimensions of a societal project.

More concretely, the plan represented an attempt to (chrono)logically collapse the creation of value and its realization, as well as the spheres of production and exchange. At the moment of planning, a certain good was assigned a price, which was based on the production cost and acquired a monetary expression. Planning the production cost started from the calculation of the necessary expenditure of labour time, and it concluded through a financialized synthesis of productive and unproductive wages, raw materials, the required intermediate goods, fuels and electricity, the transportation costs, the amortization rate of investment in fixed capital, and the benefit of every industrial unit at each stage of the production chain.⁶⁰ From here, manufactured goods had two possible routes. On the one hand, consumer goods were sold to the population, and their prices were centrally set by the government, based on a combination of their actual production cost and the reaction of the population (taken as proxy for the market) to their usefulness and quality. The means of production, on the other hand, were incorporated in the pool of fixed capital owned by the state. As scholars of socialism have argued, the accumulation of fixed capital represented the central mechanism of creating an internal market for the production chains functioning at national and regional level.[61] The models of growth through the development of heavy industry and constructions produced a logic of investment that operated as a powerful maker of the territory/population nexus, and according to which places and regions competed against each other for the resources allocated by the socialist state.

In the last instance, socialist planners aimed towards an economy where the realization of value was not only possible but also secured in advance, not left to the whims of the market. They calculated production costs based on the expenditure of abstract labour, harmonized prices between goods, and ensured that surplus was further capitalized through safeguarding exchanges and investments that could further expand the economy. The new economic executives of the 1950s might not have reached a consensus around the categories of political economy and their specificity in socialism, but they certainly acted *as if* the law of value had to operate in the newly emerging world as a foundation for socialist accumulation.

Second, literature on state socialism tended to hypostatize the political as an autonomous sphere, having a unidirectional, top-down impact on the 'economy'. This meant an assessment of the 'successes' and 'failures' in terms of the collision between the plan as an idea and what happened when things were actually getting done in production. However, academic idealism goes against the logic of the socialist planners.

The political economy of planned economies was intentionally performative, in the crudest sense of being a discourse acting upon and producing its object.[62] In the historical configuration of really existing socialism, economic categories were explicitly employed with the aim of changing reality on the ground. I claim that fetishizing 'the plan' as a bureaucratic instrument obscures the set of activities, practices and relations that actually accounted for much of its performative power. The book considers planning as the daily weaving of material webs of practices and relations within which the socialist factory emerged as an object of governmentality, with its own conflicting regimes of knowledge, discipline and time. It re-establishes a materialist perspective on socialist planning, deeply embedded in the local context of the 1950s factories in Cluj, to show that the plan was actively produced not only in the offices of the new economic executives but also on the shop floor.

Consequently, the starting point of my investigation was to unpack the very notion of a 'centrally planned economy'. Instead of starting from a top-down image of a 'planned' and 'centralized' socialist economy and assessing its functioning parameters in terms of success and failure, I realized an in-depth exploration of planning and centralization as scaled processes and relations, focusing on the way the plan was transformed into economic, political and everyday practices within productive spaces, and on how, in return, these practices were both enabling and constraining for the exercise of state power. Thus, the book is not set to explore how the plan was envisioned and implemented by the state, but how 'the economy' and 'the state' – understood here in its double determination as 'state-system' and 'state-idea' – were produced in the factory, within a bundle of practices and evermore structured interactions.[63]

Third, and most importantly, scholars of socialism have been inclined to equate labour with any other economic resource that could be calculated, allocated or hoarded. Most of the time, previous analyses painted state socialism as a historical configuration dominated by the bureaucratic fetish of the plan, which laid down the foundation of exclusive managerial prerogatives. Bureaucratic coordination of redistribution was thus considered the central function of the plan, which translated into an obvious lack of interest in its role in the transformation of the production/life nexus.

Academic conversations on central planning have been grounded in the 1970s–1980s economic debates, when the winds of economic restructuring, the opening towards Western markets and a strong technocratic reformist ethos were infusing the question of the specificity of socialist systems with a new life. János Kornai's neo-institutionalist analyses continue to stand out in the dialogues about the functioning principles of centrally planned economies. The core of Kornai's work opposed the 'soft budget constraints' of socialist units facing no possibility of bankruptcy to the 'hard budget constraints' of the capitalist companies.[64] The Hungarian economist convincingly showed that since the allocation of investments, raw materials and labour was decided through arbitrary political decisions, the control over resources was unstable. This generalized uncertainty pushed the factory managers to counteract the central planners by employing a widespread strategy of hoarding. Since the activity of the economic units was interconnected, the misallocation of resources and the resultant forms of hoarding made the production chains of socialist economies be plagued by shortages, including by a pervasive shortage of labour.

For scholars who have followed Kornai's lead, the 'endemic shortage economies' of socialism appear as redistributive systems functioning in a property vacuum, where the utility maximization logic of the socialist managers competing for state investments stood in stark contrast with the rationality of the capitalist ones, who needed to compete for demand on the free market. From this angle, power in socialism was simply a function of the actors' allocative capacity, while the aggregate effect of local actors trying to get by within the institutional frame of 'deficient' property relations and diffuse responsibility was a gradual paralysis of the socialist economy as a whole. This made socialism function in a perpetual – if hidden – crisis, in which resources were limited and the requests for investments were always inflated. Consequently, scholarship on state socialism and postsocialism focused on the chronic shortages that plagued socialist economies and on their immediate consequences: the hoarding of raw materials and labour; the practice of fake reporting, which made an accurate estimation of the economic situation difficult; the relentless competition for investments and allocation of resources, which gave rise to intricated economies of favours; the identity between consumer/provider and surveiller/surveilled types of relationship; and the pervasive personalization of relations between factory managers and state executives at different levels of hierarchy, which sometimes came to be equated with the feudalization of the socialist systems.[65]

This book will show that planning labour meant dealing with a very different type of 'resource', not only for the obvious reason that workers had their own voice and rationality, but also (and crucially) because the mechanisms of surplus extraction that made socialist accumulation possible depended on *if* and *how* labour was reproduced, expanded and controlled. In other words, it depended on localized class relations and experiential realities, which meant not only consuming living labour in the production process but also creating it.

Harnessing labour power meant unearthing workers' resilience to hardship, their willingness to commit to shop floor hierarchies and their practical knowledge. As this book will show, socialist planners and factory managers led a continuous fight for reorganizing the process of production in the direction of increased efficiency and managerial control, as well as for materializing Taylorist-oriented politics of productivity on the shop floor. In effect, although hailing the workers as political subjects, the mechanisms of socialist accumulation bore an uncanny resemblance to the ones emerging on the peripheries of the capitalist system.[66]

And finally, I will show that the unfolding of economic activity according to the plan was not the only way in which time mattered. At the most basic level, like in other Taylorist-inspired and labour-intensive industrial regimes, time discipline was supposed to constitute the foundation of an early socialist system of efficiency, which was predicated on the necessity of eliminating waste and on a historically specific form of expanded rationality. A continuous tendency towards what we can call time–time compression was essential to the materialization of socialist accumulation in a historical moment dominated by hunger for capital, scarce resources, and technological backwardness.

As politics of anticipation and calculation, plan indices stood at the core of the socialist modernization project and functioned as the bearers of a concrete historical possibility to catch up, whose objectives were ideally measurable. Planning as working ahead time functioned as a measure of the radical nonsynchronicity the socialist project met on the ground, understood here as the uneasy coexistence on the shop floor of ideas and practices belonging to different historical epochs. Labour heroes and slackers stood at the ends of a quantifiable continuum that opposed the hope for a bright future to the fear that past ways-of-doing would penetrate the factory walls. People themselves were placed not only on a quantifiable spectrum of successes and failures in fulfilling the plan indices, but also in relation with the horizon of communism as an ethical ideal. Plan figures could then become concrete and immediate expressions of workers' historical consciousness, and the party could entertain the old belief that workers' political subjectivity could be rooted directly in production.

The socialist plan can be understood as the expression of a never resolved synthesis of conflicting temporalities: the time of production colliding with the time of politics. 'Time of production' refers to the state's managerial strategies for compressing as much work in as little time as possible, and to their practical requirements and consequences for the factory life. 'Time of politics' was the other side of the temporal logic of socialism, which related individual workers to a civilizing project meant to transform them from 'simple-minded peasants' to proletarians. Since productivity came to be expressed in a temporal language and the plan figures ultimately connected it to the performance of the individual worker, it was not long before time itself became essential for deciding upon who could become a comrade and who was meant to remain 'just workforce'.

The relationship between time and planning stood both as the foundation of socialist accumulation and as the neuralgic point of socialist politics of development that vitally effected people's lives and work. In order to control the planning process, the state had to learn how to master different and often conflicting temporal horizons. The bright future of socialism required not only a sacrificial and rhythmic present, but also a segmentation of all futures in manageable pieces, in fragments of history yet to be foreseen, and which were then adjusted according to the real unfolding of the plan. Juggling time is a crucial dimension of any act of governance. But the totalizing capacity of this exercise made socialist central planning unique, and placed its contradictions at the very heart of Romanian industrial modernization.

Industrial Cluj as a Case

To follow these lines of inquiry, I carried an exploration from below of production politics in Cluj/Kolozsvár, a city in Transylvania that was culturally and economically contested along ethnicized class lines. At the end of the Second World War, Cluj was not what we would call an industrial city. The few factories that had developed in the interwar period employed a core of skilled urban workers, both men and women, who worked especially in leather, textiles, and metallurgical manufacturing. The largest factories in the city had paternalist features and carried their social infrastructure into the 1950s. There were many artisans and craftsmen in the city, but in most cases their production was small-scale and family based, maybe with one or two apprentices around the workshop, while their distribution networks were restricted to their own neighbourhoods. The imposing cultural and religious centre was surrounded by neighbourhoods in which people combined small-scale industry with agriculture, while the suburbs preserved their rural aspect and supported the provisioning of the city.

If Cluj was not an interwar industrial hub like Reșița, Łódź or Petrograd, it was even less a classical 'socialist' city emerging from nothingness like Magnitogorsk or Nowa Huta. In the period explored in this book, Cluj did not feature modernist architecture or huge industrial plants and it did not foster long-distance migration to produce young autonomous workers like those descending from the Soviet-inspired posters in other European regions. The city hardly featured as an industrial hub on the economic map of early socialism. And although its industry did grow in the postwar years, Cluj did not benefit from the first two waves of investment that changed the landscape of other Romanian regions in the 1950s and 1960s. Consequently, Cluj becomes a case for understanding socialist planning at the margins of postwar economic life. It is precisely its relatively marginal position that reveals the contradictory nature of labour in Romania, a space where 'proletarians' were generally absent and where socialist industry often needed to rely on a non-socialist, non-industrial and non-urban exterior.

While industrial Cluj went almost unnoticed by scholars of labour, it featured prominently in the social sciences as a terrain for ethnic struggles and as an important cultural and educational heart, central both for the Romanian and the Hungarian nation-building projects.[67] Located in the centre of Transylvania, the city shared the history of contested belonging of the whole region and it had its own special place in modernization processes and in the national imaginary of two different states. But as the book will show, the battle for Cluj was also a battle for its productive resources, which makes class crucial for the understanding of local relations. Although systematically hidden under ethnicized processes of identification, class actually featured as importantly in the history of Cluj as ethnicity and regional belonging. There is a different story to be told about the profound transformations of the city, one that cannot be grasped without accounting for people's mundane concerns in the factories and beyond.

Because of the way political and economic rights have been historically fragmented in Transylvania, assuming an ethnic identity or a class identity have never been separated processes in Cluj. Like the rest of East Central Europe, Transylvania lived through centuries of economic and political dependency. As a region, it shared most of its history with the Hungarian Kingdom and with the Habsburg Imperial space. At the turn of the twentieth century it was incorporated in Romania, one of the poorest agrarian countries in Europe at the time. The complex history of the region also shaped the city's occupational structure and its ethnically segregated nature was a salient characteristic until recently. Integrated for centuries into the economic circuits of the Austro-Hungarian Empire, Cluj became one of the relatively industrialized cities of Greater Romania after 1918.

Before the Second World War, a quarter of the city's population were workers, and most of them lived in the northern part, combining their time in the factory with independent work for others and with gardening. For centuries, most labourers, craftsmen and tradesmen in the city were Hungarian and Jewish. The same goes for the industrial workforce, which was also predominantly Hungarian, especially its core of highly skilled male workers. Romanians, although a majority in Transylvania, lived mostly in the countryside and so constituted a minority in urban areas. Nevertheless, the interwar period saw the rudiments of a collaboration between Hungarian capital and a thin layer of the Romanian bourgeoisie in the upper echelons of factory administration and management.

The two neighbourhoods of the city where industry was concentrated had started to develop in the nineteenth century as part of the commercial circuit of the former Habsburg Empire. A railway connected the north-western neighbourhood, where the Railways Workshops' labourers worked and lived, with the north-eastern one, well known for its Hungarian and Jewish craftsmen, artisans and vendors. At the beginning of the twentieth century, some of the best artisans in the north-eastern part of the city had been employed at Renner Brothers, a leather and footwear manufacturer owned by a Jewish Hungarian family. In the following years, the male workers brought their wives and daughters along, making the footwear factory one of the most feminized workforces in the city. The small family business constituted the core of the Dermata industrial complex, a factory I focus on in-depth in this book. For a short period after the nationalization, the factory was going to be named after the communist illegalist János Herbák.

In 1930, over six thousand enterprises had been registered by the *Industrial Record* in Cluj, most of them functioning in these districts. Of these enterprises, 116 had been categorized as 'medium' or 'large', but only two of them actually employed more than a thousand workers: Dermata and the Railways Workshops. Several other factories were employing 250 to 500 workers in various branches: metallurgy, electricity, textiles, leather, paper, printing, and chemical production. The leather and textile industries employed most skilled workers in the city, many of them Hungarian and Jewish. Many of these enterprises had disappeared by 1938 as a direct consequence of the economic crisis, which slowed down the industrial development of the city. In the late 1930s, unemployment and poverty accompanied the high number of bankruptcies and affected more than one-fifth of the working-class families in Cluj. It proved catastrophic for the Jewish population, which heavily relied on industrial employment and trade.

Between the wars, life was bustling in the working-class neighbourhoods. Four permanent markets and two fairs took place in this part of the town. They were 'at least as good as the ones in the city centre, if not better', as the former workers are still fondly remembering them today. Around the neighbourhood's churches, people built networks of support for old people and orphans, and helped the opening of several confessional schools. Around the most important factories in the city, Dermata and the Railways Workshops, the unions supported mutual aid societies, choirs, orchestras, and sporting teams. In the cosmopolitan sporting scene of the city, Hungarian workers' clubs and associations were the oldest in the city. The railroad workers, the butchers, and the commercial employees had their own clubs. Another workers' club was founded to accommodate all those who wanted to manifest their love for sport but could not find a place in the factory or guild teams. They often played against the other teams in the city, teams built around notions of belonging that had as much to do with class as with ethnic divisions: the City Athletic Club – the team of the Hungarian middle class; Universitatea – the club of the Romanian students; Haggibor – the Jewish merchants' team.[68]

Small but relatively strong communist cells had also been organized in the Dermata factory and the Railways Workshops – and acted illegally during the two successive fascisized regimes – the Romanian one in the late 1930s and the Hungarian one during the Second World War. A small but active cell had also been organized by the women at the textile factory, which was soon to be renamed Varga Katalin, after the leader of the Transylvanian miners' movement in the 1840s. The Tobacco Factory – the only factory that employed mainly unskilled Romanian women – had the weakest union and no known connection to any leftist movement in Transylvania.

The 1920s and 1930s strikes by the Dermata labourers were also decided in the north-eastern side of the city. Probably the male workers discussed their claims at the tables of the small pubs scattered around the workshops and warehouses. And maybe the vines in the neighbourhood's gardens stood witness when the women from the footwear factory had convinced each other to join the protests under the lead of their social democrat unions. From these neighbourhoods, in 1933, the workers from Dermata started their solidarity march with the Railways Workshops employees, only to face prison and death together. Anger and despair must have haunted the streets when tens of workers were fired, beaten and arrested during the events.

The city's economy between the wars had also been part of an ethnic theatre where belonging and possession could not be separated. The interwar politics of 'nostrification' of the Romanian state had been strongly felt in the city's financial sector, which had become dominated by the largest Romanian banks. Romanian capital had penetrated industry to a lesser extent, focusing on those sectors that could sustain infrastructural development. For instance, the Brick Factory, founded by a group of Jewish owners, had been transformed into 'an economic unit with exclusively Romanian interests' in 1923, when the city of Cluj, the Transylvanian Bank and the Agricultural Bank – all Romanian – had become its shareholders. The share of the Romanian capital in the city's industry was going to increase in the late 1920s, when the Romanian Central Bank for Industry and Trade became the main shareholder at Dermata.

The interests of Romanian capital often collided with the manifestations of Hungarian and Jewish economic nationalism in banking, trade and industry. These local forms of economic nationalism weaved together the reproduction of the labour force with the reproduction of Hungarianness and Jewishness. Many Hungarian and Jewish banks and factories organized or financially supported orphanages, schools and apprenticeship centres, all of them constituting an important infrastructure for professional and religious education, which became central in the identification processes within the city.

The start of the Second World War reversed the effect of these politics. A process of re-Hungarianization of the economic life started in the autumn of 1940, when the Second Vienna Arbitration decided that Northern Transylvania was going to return to Hungary, while the southern part of the region was to remain part of Romania. Who owned what became more important than ever, not only as a means of economic domination but also as a way to demonstrate better managerial competences and to assert the superiority of Hungarianness in terms of industriousness. Nevertheless, some Romanian banks kept their branches in the biggest Transylvanian cities by reorienting their loans towards Hungarian enterprises.

Jewish economic activity was restricted, and most of the time controlled by the Hungarian authorities through appointed managers and endless inspections. Although the Hungarian government adopted a gradual approach towards the dispossession of the Jews in order not to destabilize trade and industry, the expropriations of Jewish property became a daily occurrence towards the end of the war. All Jewish property came to be considered *de jure* Hungarian in 1944, when the Final Solution was applied to the Northern Transylvanian territories.

The local elites, however, sought to sustain a political vision that would have preserved the Transylvanian specificity in relation to the Hungarian motherland: more populist, with a more favourable ear to the labour question, and more inclined to a social contract between labour, the state and capital, which was also supposed to make workers less vulnerable to the Bolshevik wind of change. Communist allegiances remained stronger in Transylvania when compared to Hungary, where the Communist Party had been outlawed immediately after Bela Kun's revolution in 1919. However, during the war, the hunting down of the communist leaders extended to the Transylvanian territories, which soon came under the spell of the populist discourse of the Arrow Cross – the extreme right party in Hungary.

As the issue of Transylvania as a contested territory became central for the negotiations of the German military alliances with both Romania and Hungary, ethnic conflict became more and more expressed in racialized terms, with politicians and researchers on both sides arguing for the existence of biological differences between the Hungarians and the Romanians, and for the superiority of their nation.[69] Notions of 'civilization' and 'progress' became intertwined with the concept of 'cleanliness', with roots in an ethnicized class structure and in the rural/urban division between Romanians, Hungarians and Jews.

Since the Second Vienna Arbitration had allowed individuals to opt for the state where they were ethnically majoritarian, thousands of refugees fled from and to the city. As Holly Case shows, the refugees' situation was complicated. Many of them came to Kolozsvár without having a support network in the city. Between 1940 and 1943, Hungary spent around 36 million pengő on aid for more than two hundred thousand refugees. They received a daily allowance of two pengő forty fillér from the Hungarian government, and were sheltered in refugee camps, which were soon to be dismantled only to give way to the expansion of the city's slums due to the severe housing shortage and to the swelling of the local population.

As Kolozsvár became the second most important city in Hungary, its industry got absorbed into the German war effort. From the nearly five thousand refugees who were seeking jobs in September 1940, almost fifteen hundred were still unemployed one year later. Due to the material shortages caused by the war, the presence of the refugees was contributing to the narrowing down of employment in the largest factories of the city. The ethnic structure of the labour force changed, not only because many Hungarian workers arrived in the city but also because the unskilled Romanian workers preferred to leave the factories soon after the Vienna Arbitration. At Dermata, almost all of the seven hundred Romanian workers either opted for Romania or were dismissed by the Hungarian management of the factory.

At the end of the war, Cluj once again became the symbolic and administrative capital of a Romanian region. The historically conflictual relations between the Romanians and the Hungarians represented a significant source of fragmentation of workers' moral economies in Transylvania. The Romanian workers could hardly identify with the prewar labour struggle, and perceived it as alien and belonging to the Hungarians. The postwar waves of rural–urban migration further created a fragmented understanding of what it meant to be a 'Romanian', a 'Hungarian' or a 'Clujean'. The association between 'newcomer', 'peasant' and 'worker', and the distinction between this clusters of markers and the one comprising 'real' Clujean, 'intellectual' and 'Hungarian' were permanently enforced within the political negotiation for what the place should stand for. The fact that the working class in a Romanian workers' state was Hungarian opened a broad space for the hopes that the Hungarians would continue to dominate the urban space. In this symbolic field, the celebration of manual work came to be translated as a celebration of Hungarianness. Because in Transylvania class interests and class consciousness could not be separated from the lived definitions of citizenship, the articulation of ethnic belonging became more and more salient in the first years after the war, complicating working-class identities and narratives, muddling labour's interests, and making the political project of building a society for all workers difficult.

Although it started as a peripheral site in the emerging postwar Romanian economy, during the next twenty years Cluj was going to develop a flourishing industry and attract enough people from rural areas to change the ethnic balance in the city. From a Hungarian city of learning and culture in which the Romanian intellectuals played their own card in articulating the right to the city, in the mid-1960s Cluj became a Romanian-dominated city concentrating more than two-thirds of its population in the industrial areas. The face of the city changed forever due to an intensive wave of industrialization – the third one in the territorial logic of socialist construction – which brought Romanian peasants into the newly built working-class neighbourhoods. Rural/urban and unskilled/skilled cleavages continued to reproduce hierarchies historically constituted along class and ethnic lines after centuries of domination and marginality. For Clujeni, the complex play with nationalism of the socialist governments has always represented more than just 'discourse'. It appealed to long-lasting resentments and bitterness, partially responsible both for the fragmentation of working-class identity and for the creation of a powerful ideological interplay between the 'Party-state' and the 'nation',[70] with the complex relationship between class and ethnicity as one of the fundamental mediators through which political subjectivities were produced.

The factory becomes the ultimate site where the core contradictions of socialist accumulation were enacted and mediated, not only because heavy industrialization was a central feature of the socialist developmental project, but also because in a socialist regime production management was imagined as a fundamental part of the 'problematics of government'.[71] What was spectacular about the socialist factories was the double permeability of their boundaries: on the one hand, the factories' care and control of their workers extended outside their walls; on the other hand, workers' lives and worries penetrated the factory space, transforming it in unexpected ways. This intersection made the factory a crucial object of governance and governmentality, a contested space for the encounter of specific 'political rationalities' and 'governmental technologies', between concepts of government, their moral justifications, and the totality of techniques and procedures that supported the exercise of power.

Grounded in a relational, processual, and critical realist epistemological stance, my exploration made use of a diversity of sources, which reflect the rarely heard voices of ordinary labourers and local managers. These voices can shed plausible light on what was hidden in the plain in the early years of the Romanian socialist accumulation: its contradictory unfolding and the problematic nature of the plan as its key solution. In order to illuminate industrial planning from below, my investigation led me to the archives in Cluj, Bucharest and Budapest where I studied production minutes, economic reports, proceedings of the county and city committees of the Romanian Workers' Party meetings, instructions from the ministries to the factories, along with local newspapers and legislation. Life histories of the workers from Cluj, memoirs, newspaper interviews, and countless informal conversations with old inhabitants of the city rounded the picture of the formative years of the Romanian socialism. Although my findings are based on archival sources or oral testimonies about the past, my treatment of the case was ethnographic. My hope was to capture the vivid, complex, and contradictory substance of 'everyday life in its extra local and historical context'[72] through a 'virtual participation' in the 1950s factories in Cluj.

While industrial Cluj as a whole constitutes the object of inquiry, a bottom-up perspective on planning required an understanding of the variations in the labour process and in the positioning of different factories in the developmental logic of the state. Thus, in addition to the paper trails of the city and county party committees, governmental documents and local newspapers, I focused more in-depth on the archives of two factories: János Herbák, a leather and footwear factory, founded at the beginning of the twentieth century, and Armătura, a producer of domestic and industrial faucets and fittings, which emerged in 1949 through the nationalization and the unification of three formerly private workshops. The twelve hundred people working at Armătura in 1949 were mainly former craftsmen in the nationalized workshops. János Herbák was one of the largest factories in the city, employing over four thousand workers in 1948, a largely feminized workforce around a core of skilled male workers. Due to the nature of the labour process in leather manufacturing and to its rapid growth, János Herbák was more vulnerable to labour turnover, and more dependent upon a semi-proletarian workforce living in the countryside and commuting to town for work. Like most industrial units in the country in the first years of planning, both factories had to contend with absenteeism, stealing and other disciplinary problems. Factory managers had very limited possibilities to fire workers, since they were faced with endemic labour shortages, permissive legislation regarding workers' behaviour, constraining employment regulations, and fierce unofficial competition for labour. Following the hard postwar years, both factories enjoyed a peak of commercial success during the socialist period. Until 1960, Armătura enjoyed a monopoly position, being the only factory of its kind in Romania. János Herbák would eventually become the city's export jewel. In the 1970s, under the name of Clujana, its products were going to carry the rediscovered Romanian nationalist ethos of the late socialist regime into the world, and were going to be equally cherished at home, where being in possession of a Clujana pair of shoes became a sign of distinction among the city dwellers.

Notes

1. Stalin, 'New Conditions – New Tasks', 559. Speech delivered at a Conference of Economic Executives, 23 June 1931 (originally published in *Pravda*, No. 183, 5 July 1931). Author's translation from Romanian.
2. 'The party' always refers to the Romanian Workers' Party (later the Romanian Communist Party). Full names will be used for all the other political parties in existence in Romania until 1947.
3. I will switch between the two names according to the rapidly shifting political situation of the city in the twentieth century.
4. Case, *Between States*.
5. Maier, 'The Postwar Social Contract'.
6. Pittaway, *The Workers' State*.
7. Baronian, *Marx and Living Labour*.
8. Bloch and Ritter, 'Nonsynchronism'.
9. Lampland, *The Object of Labor*, 1.
10. Lampland, *The Value of Labor*.
11. Marx, *Capital*.
12. Djilas, *The New Class*; Konrád and Szelenyi, *The Intellectuals*; Kornai, *The Socialist System*; Kornai, 'Resource-Constrained; Kornai, 'The Soft Budget Constraint'.
13. Burawoy, *Politics of Production*.
14. The idea that socialism would degenerate into a dictatorial regime that would oppress workers rather than genuinely attempt to emancipate them is as old as the struggles between various factions of the Left. Its roots are to be found in Bakunin's anarchist critique against Marx's theory of the state, and in his prediction that 'the true despotic and brutal nature of all states, regardless of their form of government', would prevail in a dictatorship of proletariat (see Bakunin, 'The International and Karl Marx', 319). Bakunin's prophecy was that new elites would 'corrupt' socialism by monopolizing scientific knowledge and expertise, and by dominating workers in their own interest. Fears of excessive centralization and concerns with the transformation of the party and its relationship with the masses in a proletarian state were expressed by people coming from very different leftist traditions, from social democrats like Karl Kautsky, to anarcho-communists like Emma Goldman, or revolutionary socialists like Rosa Luxemburg. For a synthesis of these critiques, see Howard and King, 'State Capitalism'.
15. Mandel, 'Theory of State Capitalism'; Sweezy, *Post-Revolutionary Society*.
16. See Cliff, *State Capitalism in Russia*. The tendency to consider both really existing capitalism and really existing socialism as (equally) exploitative and unjust regimes was advanced more and more after the Fourth International, when the Trotskyst tradition split into several groups like Johnson-Forest Tendency and *Socialisme ou Barbarie*. See van der Linden, 'Socialisme ou Barbarie'.
17. Postone, 'Necessity, Labor, and Time', 741; Postone, *Time, Labor and Social Domination*.
18. Preobrazhensky, *The New Economics*.
19. Ibid. See also Millar, 'A Note'; and Day, 'On "Primitive" and Other Forms'.

20. Glassman, 'Primitive Accumulation, Accumulation by Dispossession'.
21. Preobrazhensky, *The New Economics*, 226.
22. Price scissors were not a Soviet phenomenon. In interwar Romania, they were supported, opposed and implemented in various forms. See Madgearu, *Agrarianism, Capitalism, and Imperialism*.
23. Erlich, 'Preobrazhensky'; Nove, *Economic History of the USSR*.
24. The adoption of collectivization was a response to the 1920s fierce struggles encountered by the unfolding of the Bolshevik politics on the ground. Although predicated upon the alliance between peasants and workers (*smychka*), Soviet industrialization was cornered by peasants' resistance at every step. 'Secure the Harvest!' was the mid-1920s motto that reflected a practical need and the seed of a vision in which the 'countryside' was conceived as a homogeneous supporting bloc *against* the needs of the towns; see Corrigan, Ramsey and Sayer, *Socialist Construction*; Cliff, *State Capitalism in Russia*; and Binns, 'State Capitalism'. According to this version of the narrative, as trade rapidly declined, radical solutions were adopted to support the rapid tempo of industrialization in the Soviet Union: the peasants were expropriated and forced onto large farms to increase agricultural production and make people in the countryside available for industry. For a well-taken point against this version of the Soviet industrialization, the reader might refer to Millar, 'Soviet Rapid Development'; Millar, 'Mass Collectivization'; and Ellman, 'Did the Agricultural Surplus Provide the Resources'.
25. Preobrazhensky, *The New Economics*.
26. Kotkin, *Magnetic Mountain*; Fitzpatrick, *Everyday Stalinism*; Filtzer, *Soviet Workers and Stalinist Industrialization*; Siegelbaum and Suny, *Making Workers Soviet*.
27. Montias, *Economic Development*.
28. Marx, *Capital*, 916.
29. Marx, *Capital*, 875.
30. Levy, *Ana Pauker*; Verdery and Kligman, *Peasants under Siege*; Iordachi and Dobrincu, *Transforming Peasants*.
31. Levy, *Ana Pauker*.
32. Montias, *Economic Development*, 88–91.
33. Through what Adrian Grama calls 'politics of austerity'; see Grama, 'Laboring Along'.
34. Steinberg, 'The Great End of All Government'.
35. Kalb, 'Bare Legs Like Ice'.
36. Trotsky, *History of the Russian Revolution*, xvi.
37. Haraszti, *A Worker in a Worker's State*; Burawoy and Lukács, *Radiant Past*; Pittaway, *From the Vanguard*; Kenney, *Rebuilding Poland*.
38. Lebow, *Unfinished Utopia*; Pobłocki, 'The Cunning of Class'.
39. Yurchak, *Everything Was Forever*.
40. Lampland, *The Object of Labor*.
41. Dunn, *Privatizing Poland*.
42. Verdery, *What Was Socialism*.
43. Verdery and Kligman, *Peasants Under Siege*.
44. Fulbrook, *Power and Society*.
45. Bockman, *Markets in the Name of Socialism*; Bockman and Eyal, 'Eastern Europe'.
46. Corrigan, Ramsey and Sayer, *Socialist Construction*, 43.
47. Filtzer, *Soviet Workers*; Fitzpatrick, *Everyday Stalinism*.
48. Pittaway, *The Workers' State*; Pittaway, *From the Vanguard*.
49. Pittaway, *The Workers' State*, 5.
50. Corrigan, Ramsey and Sayer, *Socialist Construction*.
51. Painter, 'Prosaic Geographies'.
52. Abrams, 'Notes', 122.
53. Abrams, 'Notes', 117.

54. Ellman, *Socialist Planning*. For a critique of how the definition of socialism as 'shortage economies', with corresponding behavioural patterns and rationality, has been unproblematically employed in the anthropology of postsocialism; see Thelen, 'Shortage, Fuzzy Property'.
55. The problem of equating capitalism itself with the functioning of markets, and the markets with an abstract space of free exchanges, would deserve a special discussion, but it goes beyond the scope of this Introduction.
56. In Kornai's words, '[t]he overwhelming role of the market is replaced by the predominance of central management. The usual name given to this form of coordination is "central planning". A more appropriate characterization is one of bureaucratic coordination, central control, a system of enforced instructions. This is a "command economy"'. Kornai, 'Socialism and the Market'.
57. For the position that the law of value was still operating in state socialism, and for a review of the debates in Romania, see Petrovici, *Zona urbană*. For the opposite claim, that the law of value was actually suspended in socialism, see Clarke, 'The Contradictions'.
58. Petrovici, *Zona urbană*.
59. For the idea of primitive socialist accumulation in the Soviet Union, see Preobrazhensky, *The New Economics*; Erlich, 'Preobrazhensky'; and Millar, 'A Note'. The core discussion of uneven and combined development appears in the same context. See Trotsky, *History of the Russian Revolution*. For recent reinterpretations of the concept of uneven development, see Harvey, *Spaces of Global Capitalism*; Allinson and Anievas, 'Uses and Misuses'; Anievas and Matin, *Historical Sociology*; Dunn and Radice, *100 Years*.
60. During the first years of planning, the state produced an impressive number of publications to help the planners, the factory managers and the accountants with the calculative technologies involved in the production cost.
61. Petrovici, *Zona urbană*.
62. MacKenzie, Muniesa and Siu, *Do Economists Make Markets?*
63. Abrams, 'Notes'.
64. Kornai, *The Socialist System*.
65. Verdery, *What Was Socialism?* The negotiation power of the industrial labourers was also seen as an important consequence of the labour shortage; see Burawoy, *Politics of Production*.
66. There are scholars who, at least in principle, have tried to move beyond the socialist/capitalist divide and have highlighted the similarities of industrial production in socialist and capitalist countries. See Creed, *Domesticating Revolution*.
67. Case, *Between States*; Brubaker et al., *Nationalist Politics*.
68. Faje, 'Playing to Win'.
69. Case, *Between States*.
70. For the most comprehensive analysis of national ideology in the socialist period to date, see Verdery, *National Ideology*.
71. Rose and Miller, 'Political Power'.
72. Burawoy, *The Extended Case Method*, 1.

I

PRIMITIVE SOCIALIST ACCUMULATION IN CLUJ

CHAPTER 1

PRODUCTIVE STATE APPARATUSES
Taking Over the Factories, 1944–1948

Whose City, Whose Factories? Rethinking the Communist Takeover of Industry

In the autumn of 1944, the Hungarian majority in Kolozsvár (Cluj) could still remember the joy experienced only four years earlier, when the soldiers of their motherland had been marching on the streets. The image of the soldiers waving at the people who gathered to celebrate the decision of the Axis to return Northern Transylvania to Hungary was still fresh in their memory.[1] During the war, the Hungarian population could hear the cadenza of their steps as a renewed promise that Kolozsvár would again be part of the Hungarian state, this time forever. At the same time, the Hungarian soldiers had been stepping over the Romanians' hopes that the city would remain part of Greater Romania, as decided by the victorious Allied powers in 1918–20. But the days when the Hungarian officers joined the Transylvanians at the tables of the elegant restaurants in the city centre, and smiled at the young girls passing by, were soon to be over. In October 1944, the Red Army entered the city, with the Romanian Army on its trail. Seen by some as 'liberation' and by others as 'occupation', the marching of Soviet soldiers on the streets was the sign that the old Transylvanian city was changing its masters for the third time in less than thirty years.

The Red Army soldiers descended the Feleac hill through the apple and plum orchards. Small two-room houses painted in blue and dark green guarded their passage through the Romanian, Hungarian and mixed villages that surrounded the city and supplied it with meat, vegetables, cereal, stone, wood and hay. At that time of the year, peasants' pantries were already full with jars of pickles and jam, pigs were being fattened for Christmas, hay was gathered inside the horses' stables, and corn was piled in the storage rooms. But the bountiful autumn was not peaceful. Firearms were heard everywhere on the trail of the Hungarian and German soldiers who were still fighting in the forest that separated the village of Feleac from the city. They were soon to be pushed northwards, and forced to retreat towards the train station, in search for an escape.[2]

The Soviet soldiers followed them into the city, entering from the South. They passed the Orthodox cathedral and the 1906 Secession building of the main theatre in the city,[3] and arrived into an empty city centre, where people were running away from the windows of their two-storey Habsburg-style houses. Women and children of all ages were trying to avoid the chaos unleashed by the Soviet troops in their victorious passage. The young servants of the Hungarian merchants had been long gone to their parents in the countryside, leaving their small rooms empty. Teachers opened the school basements for their pupils, while the Catholic and Protestant priests gathered their parishioners within the walls of the medieval and baroque churches that quartered the old city centre. Men were hiding, frightened by the rumours that the civilians taken by the Red Army never returned home. Shopkeepers locked the doors of their stores in the main street of the city, only to see them smashed hours later by hungry soldiers.

The entry of the Soviet soldiers into the imposing halls of the university building triggered new fears for the fate of the intellectual elites. Built in the latter half of the nineteenth century during the process of expanding higher education in the peripheral provinces of the Austro-Hungarian Empire, the institution had been recast by the post-1918 Greater Romanian government as the University of Dacia Superior, becoming a crucial space for the production and assertion of Romanianness in the interwar period. During the Second World War, after Northern Transylvania had been ceded to Hungary at the Vienna Arbitration, the Romanian professors and students had fled as refugees to Sibiu, and the university had been renamed 'Franz Joseph' by the Hungarian war administration of the city. Thus, in October 1944, only the Hungarian professors greeted the representatives of the Soviet Army. In only a few months, the Romanian professorial body was going to come back and re-centre the cultural life of the Romanian elites around the university once again.

In order to stop the retreating Hungarian and German troops, the Soviet soldiers split. Some of them fought their way towards the western part of the city. They passed the central library of the university, and ran along the corridors of the clinics where the soldiers' wounds were being tended. They headed West to check the Beer Factory for enemies and, according to oral accounts, depleted it of alcohol. Some of the soldiers crossed the river Someș/Számos into a marginal area inhabited by the

Romanians around Donáth Street – a picturesque combination of poor hovels and affluent merchant houses.

Other Red Army soldiers left the city centre and followed the road towards Mănăştur on the outskirts of the city, and inhabited by the Romanians. Integrated in the city at the end of the nineteenth century, the former village of Mănăştur had quickly become one of the strongholds of Romanian nationalism. The suburbs had preserved their rural image, with two-room houses and huge gardens, well known for the smell of their roses in the summer, and with small pubs scattered everywhere in the neighbourhood, offering cheap homemade food and local wine to the Romanian students.

Another group of Soviet soldiers headed north, quickly advancing towards the train station, which had been destroyed by Allied bombing in June. They would have searched the enemies on the corridors of the beautiful Marianum Collegium, the best Catholic confessional school in Cluj, which was preparing girls from all over Transylvania for teaching and administrative jobs. They probably searched under the red velvet chairs of Urania Palace, the most luxurious cinema in the city, before climbing the Fortress hill, where the Habsburgs had erected a garrison in the eighteenth century. They spread over the neighbourhood where the richest Hungarian merchants had built their houses in the nineteenth century, only to soon be mirrored by the local Romanian elites across the city. On the other side of the Fortress hill, the Soviet soldiers descended the winding roads between the railway workers' houses, with their low roofs and narrow yards.

As the Red Army approached the train station, the old synagogues in the area formerly dominated by Jewish population laid empty, silent witnesses to the deportation of almost twenty thousand Jews in the previous three years. The Jewish schools were now closed, some of them by the Romanian authorities in the late 1920s, some of them by the Horthyst administration during the war. Further to the north, the grounds of the Brick Factory had served as a ghetto for sixteen thousand Jews in 1944. The Soviet troops were going to find no more than eighty members of the Jewish community hidden by the local population in Cluj. Only fifteen hundred were going to come back from Auschwitz in the following years.

The soldiers left the central part of the city and rushed towards the north-east, beyond the railways, to get to the locally famous gardens of the *hoştezeni*, who were trying in vain to hide their food stuff.[4] For the time being, the *hoştezeni* had to forget their rivalry with the *mănăştureni* for supplying the city with the best products, and postpone their pub fistfights with the Romanian boys who had the courage to court their sisters. Many of the Soviet soldiers who remained in Cluj after their comrades followed the road to Berlin were accommodated by the *hoștezeni*, whose families had better houses and 'a lot of food and drinks to spare'. People would resent their presence, quickly labelling them as 'barbarians' in contrast with the 'civilized' and 'polite' Hungarian or German soldiers sheltered during the war.

During the war, the most important factories in the city had been organized for 'passive defence', with military and civil guards, and plans for the evacuation of the industrial equipment, which had accompanied a severe legislation regarding sabotage and stealing. Thus, in October 1944, many male workers were not at home, protecting the virtue of their wives and daughters from the Soviet soldiers, but in the factories. They were not fighting against the Red Army, but trying to prevent the dismantling of their industrial units by the Axis armies in retreat. As reported later by the newspapers, many workers resisted the Horthyst directives, which required the industrial equipment from the factories to be broken into pieces, and evacuated to Hungary.

This image of the workers defending their factories in front of the retreating Nazi armies was by no means unique. As shown by other scholars of Eastern and Central Europe, refusing to accept the dismantling of economic infrastructure was a powerful act of resistance of the workers from Zala County in Hungary or from Łódź in Poland. But in every case, this act was motivated by different forms of historical consciousness, and produced different effects. While the peasant-workers working in oil extraction in Zala acted from 'a desire to protect the local community'[5] and to return to the prewar 'normality' of American management and conservative politics, the workers in the industrial centre of Łódź explicitly articulated their resistance in terms of class struggle, but with a strong ethnic component. Like in Cluj (and elsewhere in Central and Eastern Europe), the factories in Łódź were 'a world of hierarchy and deference',[6] which was articulated both in class terms and in ethnic ones. The anti-German and anti-Jewish feelings in Łódź were rooted in historically established hierarchies of work and property. With the spectacular decline in the number of German and Jewish workers in the city due to pogroms, population exchanges and expulsions, the Polish labourers experienced a new sense of entitlement and empowerment in the immediate postwar configuration. They claimed factories as theirs both as workers and as Poles, and engaged on a road that was supposed to lead to workers' total control over their workplaces. The passionate relationship with materiality encapsulated in these stories of resistance in front of the Nazi soldiers was foundational for the postwar factory life in East Central Europe, but was directed towards different (indeed, opposed) goals: restoration of the prewar life and work for the people in

Zala country, revolutionary trajectories and a new sense of entitlement for the workers in Łódź.

In Cluj, the (mostly Hungarian) workers resisted the dismantling of the factories by the Hungarian and German armies in retreat, in spite of their national and political loyalties. It is no wonder that the postwar temporary local administration repeatedly hailed workers' political consciousness in front of war adversities. Nevertheless, their resistance can hardly be read as a sign of acceptance of the presence of the Red Army in the city, or as a sign of allegiance to whatever the new times would have brought forward. While the Soviet and the Romanian armies were approaching the city, the workers' attempt to protect the industrial equipment embodied both the hope of a return to the prewar 'normality', and the hope that this normality would (re)produce the factories' uncontested Hungarianness as experienced during the war. As this chapter will make transparent, it was impossible to disentangle control of the largest factories in the city – like János Herbák and the Railways Workshops – from the broader field of relationships in which the right to the city was negotiated.

The honour of protecting the factories with one's life was reserved for only a few male Hungarian urban workers, who lived in the industrial neighbourhoods. During the following few years, their commitment was to be recognized in various instances, especially when housing, employment or wage categories were being negotiated in the dire postwar conditions. It would deepen the fractures between this layer of core workers and other social categories – especially rural unskilled workers – who were going to enter the factory gates in the late 1940s and early 1950s.

While the workers in Cluj protected their workplaces, they never claimed the factories as theirs, and never explicitly questioned the owners' property rights. Immediately after the front had moved westwards, workers' councils were founded in every factory. They had a provisional character and the explicit function of maintaining production until the industrial units had been handed over to their owners, to their managers, or to the Office for the Management and Supervision of Enemy Assets [Casa de administrare și supraveghere a bunurilor inamice – CASBI]. The workers did not see themselves as leaders of the factories but as their keepers until someone else – someone who was 'entitled' to govern them – came forward. Interviews, archives, and local memory are equally and tellingly silent about this moment, which has never been perceived by workers as an easily missed historical opportunity.

Fast forward almost four years, the fact that the workers in Cluj did not see themselves as entitled to claim property rights over the factories, the fleeing of the former owners abroad, and the culture of deference in the workplace were going to ensure a calm nationalization of industry. The nationalization of the means of production and of the financial system was officially announced on 11 June 1948 as an epochal fracture between the 'dark times' of capitalism and a bright future, which could be brought into the now through an act of political will. This incident-free, almost silent character of the nationalization gave it a momentary appearance, marked by the party propaganda as the materialization of the fundamental socialist promise: workers' ownership of the means of production.

The eventful character of the nationalization has been unproblematically treated by the Romanian historiography as a change in property relations that essentially transformed the entire economic system in the second half of the twentieth century.[7] Nonetheless, the takeover of the factories was going to involve more than a legal act, and it affected a much broader field of social relations. This chapter will show why the nationalization cannot be understood simply as dispossession but as a complicated battle for the transformation of the factories into productive state apparatuses. It was this battle that was going to set the parameters for the long-term evolution of industrial socialism.

My perspective on this historical moment can be summarized in several points. First, the nationalization of industry needs to be seen against the background of a broader field of local relations in which the factories were embedded. In Cluj, this relational field was crucially shaped by the entanglement between class and ethnicity, against which the right to the city was negotiated. Second, nationalization cannot be understood as a radical fracture, but as a necessary step in a broader process of assuming control of the factories, which started immediately after the arrival of the Red Army and lasted for many years after 1948. Third, creating the factories as political spaces and simultaneously keeping them under control as productive spaces proved to be a difficult game to play for the new economic executives. And fourth, in the process, life itself – workers' bodies and their possibilities of survival – was firmly established as the political terrain on which the productive core of socialist industrialization was going to be negotiated for decades.

This chapter explores the nationalization of the means of production as part of a broader struggle to penetrate the postwar social fabric in Cluj. In the next section, I follow the struggles for the right to the city in between class and ethnicity, as part of the political transformations that marked the communist takeover at governmental level between 1944 and 1948. The second section investigates the attempts of the Romanian Workers' Party to form political allegiances in the factories through union and party membership. In the third section, I explore how workers' everyday lives and moral economies became a battlefield on which the communist takeover was played out. And in the last part, I turn to the June 1948 nationalization of the factories, which I explore not as a change in property relations but as a series of transformations on the shop floor that ensured the possibility of primitive socialist accumulation on the ground.

The Right to Cluj between Class and Ethnicity

On 23 August 1944, after a successful Soviet offensive in Moldavia, Romania declared a ceasefire with the Red Army.[8] King Michael removed the government led by marshal Ion Antonescu and broke Romania's allegiance to Nazi Germany, ending the Second World War alongside the Allied powers. Under Soviet guidance and control, unstable and fragile anti-fascist partinic coalitions took hold of the government. In the following months, three governments ruled the country in quick succession, built around the idea of unifying the political forces. Being outlawed during the war allowed the Romanian communists to carry the symbolic torch of anti-fascist purity in the face of the new times, and to use it in consecutive attacks against its main competitors: the historical National Peasants' Party, the National Liberal Party, and later the Social Democratic Party. On 6 March 1945, King Michael appointed Petru Groza, a member of the Ploughmen Front, to be the leader of the first openly pro-communist government in the postwar history of Romania.

In 1946, the National Democratic Bloc was formed through a protocol between the Romanian Workers' Party, the Ploughmen Front, the Social Democratic Party, a wing of the National Liberal Party (Tătărăscu), the Popular Hungarian Union, and the Jewish Democratic Committee. In November 1946, the coalition won the elections under the electoral sign of the sun. As historians have shown, the elections were marked by fraud and intimidation, and the campaign was manifestly violent and corrupt.[9] However, although the local party leaders were prepared to use bribes, beatings and creative counting to accaparate political power, they did hope to win the elections through a convincing political discourse and through an ever-increasing involvement in people's daily lives.

The end of the Second World War left Romania in a state of devastation and confusion. During the interwar period, Romania had been deeply integrated into the German economy, with the relationship between the two states being close enough to justify labelling the East European country as an 'intra-European German colony'.[10] Some regions had been placed under German political protectorate in the late 1930s, and had fully depended upon German capital. During the Second World War, these entanglements had been complicated by the integration of

Northern Transylvania in the Hungarian war economy. In 1945, this double dependency on Hungarian and German capital proved to be convenient for the postwar administration of industry, as most factories could be immediately placed under the administration of the Office for the Management and Supervision of Enemy Assets [CASBI], which controlled all movable and immovable assets belonging to the German or the Hungarian state, for citizens and residents of these states, and for German and Hungarian nationals.

War destruction had also taken its toll, and the reparations exacted by the Soviet Union put a lot of pressure on the economy. Between September 1944 and December 1946 alone, war reparations amounted to almost 50 per cent of the state budget. The Romanian–Soviet trade relations and the war reparations were managed through joint companies known as Sovroms, unequal forms of exchange that allowed the Soviet Union to provide limited technical assistance and capital for Romania's infrastructural projects in return for primary commodities and manufactured goods. They were organized around the exploitation of raw materials, manufacturing, transportation, trade insurance and banking.

Things were no easier for production. In 1945, the net output of industry was only 60 per cent of the 1938 level. With the war economy collapsing, factories had problems with their distribution and supply networks. As a result, many industrial units could not procure raw materials, production stopped for days at a time, and the management found paying wages a monthly challenge. The factories that had been central to the war economy suffered most, with heavy industry being especially hit by a lack of demand for their products. The lack of capital for the factories reached alarming levels in the autumn of 1946, just before the general elections. Agriculture remained in a desperate situation, traders experienced a chronic shortage of merchandise and foreign currency, key industrial sites were dismantled at the initiative of the Soviet councillors, and industry as a whole became chaotic and almost impossible to control.

The state seemed hopeless in its struggle against hyperinflation. The Central Bank of Romania was nationalized in December 1946,[11] with the explicit aim to obtain 'a real control over the production and distribution of commodities' and to guide the entire economic life 'according to national interests'.[12] Other measures were meant to further the control of the state over the financial system – but prices were still soaring. In April 1947, the American dollar equated to 900,000 lei, with the Romanian currency still in free fall. In July 1947, the price of a bread loaf was 165,000 lei, compared to 8.46 lei in 1944.

Consequently, a financial reform was implemented in 1947 by the Governmental Commission for the Recovery of the Economy and for

Monetary Stabilization.¹³ The reform established an exchange rate of 20,000 old lei for a new 'stabilized' leu and a new fixed price for gold. While industrial units could exchange a lump sum equivalent to the amount required to pay the wages for one month, commercial enterprises were required to declare all their existing stocks and were not allowed to exchange money at all, in order to force them to throw their merchandise on the market. As a cumulative result of these restrictions, only 27.5 billion lei out of the total of 48.5 billion available were exchanged, while the rest was blocked by the banks. The reform was part of a Europe-wide attempt to stop the postwar inflation through monetary stabilization, both in the West and in the Eastern bloc. In the Romanian case, it took the form of what economic historians called a 'mopping-up' operation, a combination between converting existing currency at deflated rates of exchange up to a cap, and freezing the remaining liquidities in blocked accounts.¹⁴

The monetary reform was accompanied by a series of anti-fascist purges, which led to the expulsion of the other political forces from the wheel of the state, under the accusation that they delayed financial stabilization and sabotaged postwar economic recovery. The historical parties successively came under a final attack, with their leaders imprisoned or executed. King Michael soon abdicated, and Romania was declared a 'people's democracy', establishing the Romanian Workers' Party as the unique official government force for more than four decades. The communists' ascension to political power was now complete, allowing the state to dramatically increase its grip on the economy.

The first reforms passed by the communist government had three aims: to increase centralization in the economy beyond the wartime level; to slow down inflation; and to improve the system of provisioning in the cities. These measures included forcing peasants to surrender variable parts of their harvest to support the industrial centres, reorganizing the 'economat' system (a network of cheap factory stores offering basic goods at subsidized prices), trying to control consumer goods prices on the free market, and unmasking anything that the state could label as 'economic sabotage' in order to limit profiteering and operations on the black market.¹⁵

Actions to ensure control over the financial system were soon followed by the establishment of the 'Industrial Offices' – fourteen organizational entities at national level, with the task of guiding and overseeing the economic activity of 750 industrial units from various economic branches, both state and privately owned.¹⁶ It is telling that the representatives of the industrialists interpreted the founding of the Industrial Offices as a de facto expropriation.¹⁷ The Ministry of National Economy was relabelled the Ministry of Industry and Trade, with increased attributions in the organization of production, the allocation of raw materials, the distribution of industrial products, the control of internal and external trade, and the setting of prices.[18]

At the beginning of 1948, foreign trade was already under governmental control, through the mediation of national trade companies for every industrial branch. In order to influence prices and to keep inflation under control, the state established department stores and local markets all over the country. In addition, state companies for collecting cereals, milk, fish and meat, as well as waste, had already been launched together with trade and supply companies for textiles, footwear and other types of consumer goods.

A less visible but crucial process was unfolding locally, with the leaders of the Romanian Workers' Party creating parallel state-like structures by infiltrating key institutions at all administrative and economic levels. In Kenneth Jowitt's words, the period under scrutiny in this book was a period of 'breaking through', understood as the 'decisive alteration or destruction of values, structures, and behaviors which are perceived by a revolutionary elite as comprising or contributing to the actual or potential existence of alternative centers of political power'.[19] Let us see what the documents of the local party organizations in Cluj reveal about these developments.

As the war front was moving further to the West, a period of confusion followed. The Soviet forces were simultaneously playing with three concrete scenarios regarding the region's future: that it would remain in Hungarian hands; that it would become again part of the Romanian state; or that it would survive as an autonomous multi-ethnic province. Officially, the situation changed on 19 March 1945, after the government led by Petru Groza was appointed and the Romanian administration was reinstated in Northern Transylvania. However, the Hungarians' hopes continued to feed a conflictual atmosphere for years to come.

This was the background against which the Romanian Workers' Party had to move from the status of a party backed up solely by the Soviet Union to the ideal situation of a party state benefitting from workers' support. Before October 1945, Romania had one of the weakest communist movements in what would become the Eastern Bloc. The Romanian Communist Party had become illegal in 1924 and its roughly 1,000 members had operated underground throughout the tumultuous 1930s and during the war. However, the postwar wind of change boosted the appeal of the party, which reached 710,000 members by 1947. No other communist party in the region had such a spectacular evolution. The increase in membership and the transformation of the party into a mass organization was possible due to the inability of the historical parties to respond to the new realities, to the radically changed electoral programmes of the RWP, to the RWP's uncritical acceptance of anyone who wanted to join, and to the febrile work of agitprop activists everywhere. But, as we will see, the most common reason to join the party was its increasing hold on workers' livelihoods and safety nets in the city. The 1945–47 period was thus marked by an intense struggle for legitimacy in the city, where the activists of the Romanian Workers' Party tried to become a ubiquitous presence. Gaining control over the unions, convincing workers to join the party, infiltrating the police and state institutions, and limiting the influence of other political forces were the main points on the agenda of the local cells.

In the city at large, communists appeared as the leaders of the postwar reconstruction effort. They were the most vocal in mobilizing local population to contribute to the repairing of roads, bridges, factories and administrative buildings, or to help with the reorganizing of firefighters and ambulance services. Linking the name of the party to the daily functioning of the city was imagined not only as an instrument for gaining legitimacy on the ground, but also as a first step in the construction of a prosaic form of 'stateness'.

Hunger, drought, a debilitating housing shortage, an epidemic of thefts and violent attacks, hundreds of refugee trains passing through the city, and the difficulties of replacing the Hungarian war administration with a Romanian one kept the first pages of the local newspapers. Although the government tried to secure exchange between the city and the countryside and fixed the prices for basic commodities, food, clothing and firewood were hard to find, and prices on the market were soaring. The city inflation surpassed that in the rest of Romania. Prices of most consumer goods increased by over 100 per cent, and some of them by more than 300 per cent, in just a few months. Many employees simply lived on credit.

The lack of industrial capital meant that supplying the population became a daily challenge. Since the rationing system was run and administered through the workplace, industrial employment provided access to a privileged food and clothing distribution system in which the 'economats' were central. Workers saw their livelihoods further threatened by inequalities in wages and access to benefits. Tax subsidies and aid for rent, salubrity or child support were allocated only to specific factories, depending on their size, centrality in the economic logic of the moment and managers' loyalty to the new regime. Soon, these forms of compensating everyday hardships were going to disappear, leaving space for standardized advantages for workers in heavy industry, who continued to be paid better than the ones in consumer goods branches for the whole socialist period.

With real wages permanently falling, workers earned very little and started to miss work. As production stagnated and the factories had to fire their workers, the number of people who could not find jobs grew. The twenty thousand unemployed in the city became a vulnerable category, whose fate was tragic precisely because, together with their wages, they lost access to the only reliable safety net in the city. As a consequence of growing poverty, the black market and crime were on the rise, and a climate of insecurity and fear penetrated every corner of life.

Due to their domination over the factory committees and the unions, deciding on people's employment became one of the most important sources of power for the communists. Endemic clientelism and the politicization of employment gave the party its first instruments for gaining allocative power and for securing precious positions for its followers. The party's hunt for members met people's need for jobs, to produce an employment regime that informally (but very explicitly) linked recruitment for work to recruitment for politics.

However, convincing the workers to support the party still proved to be a challenge. As the instructions for the party activists in the factory advised, their work had to be characterized by 'much brain and a lot of soul', in order to fight the workers' feeling that, as one party activist aptly put it, the economic situation was bad, but the political situation was similar.[20] 'Careful' and 'delicate' face-to-face interactions were the preferred method for increasing membership on a daily basis. The party had to take into account ethnic sensitivities, old feuds between foremen and their people, and the interests of the United Workers' Front, the political coalition the communists joined in 1945. Thus, intimate knowledge of workers' concerns proved to be an important advantage, which gave the party the instruments needed to deal with 'the undecided' ones.

Mobilized along ethnic lines in the city, and along the struggle for land in the countryside, women were the last to be convinced to support the party. Being responsible for the survival and for the well-being of their households, they were most affected by famine, drought, shortages and the imposition of agricultural quotas in the countryside. In Cluj, in January 1946, out of approximately eight thousand members only two thousand were women, and the situation was not going to change for almost a decade. This situation was consistent not only with the proportion of women in the workforce but also with their more vocal attitude against the party all over the country. Women dominated protests against the size and the price of the food rations in Baia Sprie, Dealul Crucii and Petroșani. In the streets of Cluj in 1947, thousands of women asking for 'bread' and 'justice' protested in front of the city hall, allegedly 'pushed by their men who thought women were less likely to be arrested'.[21] Their opposition against the party was rooted in the everyday battle for survival at home, and continued to be treated as an important political problem for years to come.

After 1945, Cluj became the nodal point of the Soviet provisional administration of the region, which allowed the party members to assume a crucial role in the consolidation of communist ideas and networks in the city. Every communist had an obligation to become a member of a mass organization in the factories and public offices, to check if the organization was keeping 'a communist demeanour line', and to keep an eye on those who 'did not follow an honest, democratic path'.[22] The university, the schools, the police, and the neighbourhood communities were all targeted in this encompassing endeavour of the party to ensure a step-by-step control of the city. It was the ethnic Hungarian and Jewish members who became central for infiltrating key institutions between 1945 and 1947. This was the direct result of their allegiance to communist ideals during the interwar period, due not only to their predominance in industrial settings, but also to the more inclusive position of the communist parties regarding the national question.

The founding of a communist cell at the Regional Police Inspectorate in October 1945 was a big step forward. The fact that the cell was largely Romanian in a city with a dominantly Hungarian population was another victory for the party. The communist cell of the police was designed to take care solely of the urban space, 'where all the reactionary instructions came from', and to counteract the excesses of the Hungarian Civil Guard that still patrolled the city.[23] It was going to be one of the strongest communist cells in the city, assisting the party with internal information about the opposition's electoral meetings and about the workers' state of mind (*starea de spirit*). They were often offering live updates on the conflictual situations in the city, when union workers could be quickly and sometimes violently mobilized against other social categories: nationalist Romanian students or the representatives of the National Peasants' Party.

However, the party membership of the ethnic Romanians remained a painful issue. Reports from January 1946 show that at the time it was impossible to bring more than 850 Romanians into the party, while 6,500 Hungarians and 600 Jews 'gladly joined the ranks'.[24] Finding Romanians who would agree to sign up for party membership became a daily task for the local organizations. Those party members who were fluent in Romanian were insistently asked to bring a Romanian comrade into the organization every month.[25] They were also advised to convince at least one Romanian soldier to join the party.[26]

The encounter between gender and ethnicity often produced political crises, like in the case of the Tobacco Factory, the only industrial unit where Romanian women constituted a majority of the workforce.²⁷ The Tobacco Factory was often called 'a chauvinistic nest' by the party activists in their reports to the City Committee. They complained about unsuccessfully counteracting workers' distrust, even after they managed to score some victories against the management. Already in the summer of 1945, the party pressured the union to contest the prewar regulations that required the workers to ask for a permit from their foremen to leave the shop floor, even for taking care of their physiological needs. They also contested the right of the security guards to search the workers for stolen goods every time they stepped out of the factory gate.²⁸ Only a few months later, the communist cell took action again, when the factory director decided to cut expenses by dismissing all the employees who had been working in the factory for less than two years. The party activists and the Local Union's Commission managed to change people's employment contracts, making them less vulnerable to arbitrary dismissal.²⁹ However, the workers still refused to join the party.

The other central stake for the emerging regime was the control over the unions. The interwar regional corporate logic of the unions – one guild for every historical region with a union of guilds serving at national level³⁰ – had been the first to be dismantled at the end of the Second World War, when the factory (not the craft) became the basis for unionization. Only a few months after the founding of the Local Unions' Commission in October 1945, the unions had already been reorganized around the industrial units, and comprised all the employees of a certain factory, irrespective of their profession. Manual workers and administrative staff became members of the same union and, in theory, they had to fight the same battle for increased production and for a better life. By just three years after the war, the interwar logic of unionization had completely disappeared, and was replaced by one based on the unions' central role in ensuring that factories could become effective redistributive arms of the state.

The party took rapid steps to break the solidarity networks weaved by the workers during the interwar years. As early as 1 May 1944, the communists joined the social democrats in the United Workers' Front, with the explicit aim to unionize the industrial workers. In early spring 1946, the unions in Cluj had over 32,000 members, of which 9,700 were women and 1,100 were apprentices. Although only approximately a quarter of the unionized workers were party members in 1946, the control of the party over the unions was already much more extended. The union elections turned into an important terrain for political struggle, and a good opportunity to assess the position of the party in various factories in Cluj. The resulting picture was mixed. At the Railways Workshops, the newly elected union representatives were all communists and the party declared a 'crushing victory', followed immediately by a series of purges to get rid of reactionary forces in the factory. However, at Dermata, the other stronghold of the party, the elected union representatives were perceived as being outside party politics of any kind, and were all Hungarians. Two social democrats and two communists on the list failed to get elected. The workers met the insistence of the party to elect an ethnic Romanian leader first with indifference, then with anger. When the factory committee requested the annulment of the results, the shop floor quickly became a turbulent space, beyond the control of the party for months.

Labourers' support for the United Workers' Front was generally enthusiastic, partly because of their prewar social democratic allegiances, and partly because of the sense of historical empowerment that the communists added to the political mix. However, the support was rather conditional and more directed towards the 'politics of one's stomach' than to bigger claims. While the workers did respond to the leftist call, and indeed grew more radical by the day, their demands addressed a field of social reproduction and provisioning that the party could not control. Issues like the workers' prewar debts towards the factories, or access to housing, food, electricity and heating, became not only expressive of the state's limits but also contentious, as the next section of the chapter will show.

Life as a Battlefield

In the factories, the party activists had the most difficult task as they tried to become simultaneously vocal defenders of workers' rights, overseers of the production process, political purifiers of the shop floor, and collectors of souls in their effort to expand party and union membership. Responding to workers' grievances related to food scarcity, famine and drought relief, rationed goods, lack of housing, forced evictions, and layoffs became a daily job for local officials, factory managers and party activists alike. A whole field of politics came to be articulated around workers' needs and around an increasingly inclusive notion of 'care'.

One of the fields in which the party was active from the start was the public fight against profiteering. Lucrețiu Pătrășcanu, at the time the minister of justice and a long-standing communist, showed that in 1945, in just one month, the Romanian courts judged 2,656 causes of saboteurs and profiteers, and 2,048 of these cases ended with a prison sentence. These statistics were the direct result of the coordinated action of the police, the Ministry of Justice, and the General Commissariat for Prices.

For instance, on 6 July 1945, authorities stated that the saboteurs and the speculants 'will be hit without mercy'. In Bucharest, the police organized more than four hundred policemen in 'control teams', who participated in several night raids in order to identify illegal actions in 126 bakeries and bread factories.[31] The fact that food stores were the first to be targeted by these raids shows the importance of these actions for establishing a connection with an impoverished and hungry population by manipulating a complex field of moral economy.

Rapid solutions became essential for preventing the always-in-the-air strikes, production stops and walkouts that dominated the world of Romanian labour between 1945 and 1947, especially around the signing of the collective contracts, the negotiation of wages and the activity of the economats. Workers gathering in front of the factories to protest against their low wages, against food shortages, and for the implementation or the renegotiation of the collective contracts were common occurrences in the postwar context.[32] They went hand in hand with the way in which trade unions and factory committees proliferated at local level everywhere in the country. However, the over-politicization of the shop floor did not mean that workers' bargaining on wages or working conditions was considered reasonable or legitimate. The party struggled with the initiatives of the factory committees and of the unions, which often failed to understand that 'the interest of the state is the interest of the workers'.[33] The possibility that workers would turn leftist vocabulary against the state on issues of wages and prices became a nightmare for the post-1945 communist-led governments.

The popularity of the party among the workers varied widely, according to the capacity of the factory cells to respond to mundane issues. Things as small as a successful rationing of flour pacified the factory space for several days, until another hardship made workers' raise their voices again. An alternating succession of quiet moments and outbursts of labour unrest dominated the factories until their nationalization. I illustrate it here with the sequence that took place in the spring of 1946, the year of the elections.

While the reports of the City Committee paint March 1946 as a calm month, a generalized scarcity of bread and corn escalated in the city in April. Simultaneously, production stopped in many factories due to shortages of raw material, leaving the workers unpaid. Workers' threats that they would leave their workplaces and the rumours of a general strike stopped in early May, when new lines of credit were opened for the industrial units, the economats ensured the basic food provisioning, and the necessary raw material was supplied by the Soviet Union so the production could restart. In mid May, labourers at the Railways Workshops promptly agreed to spend fourteen hours a day in the factory, when requested by their union's representatives to honour a request from the Red Army. The party immediately read the workers' readiness to work extra hours as the sign of a new social peace.

A general strike at Dermata at the end of the month proved them wrong. On 25 May 1946, 4,000 of the 4,500 employees of Dermata left their workplaces and gathered in front of the factory to protest against a reduction in their real wages. Other requests regarded the permanent lack of supplies at the economats, the inedible food at the cafeteria, and the horrid working conditions in some of the workshops, which they considered to be a breach of their collective contract, signed only two months earlier.

The next day, the party organization displayed an angry Manifesto on the factory walls.[34] It was titled 'What the Factory Did for its Workers', and listed all the 'gifts' received by the employees: the financial subsidy to workers' food in the cafeteria; the improved quality of the meals through the existence of a piggery, several milk cows and a vegetable garden; the coverage of workers' health insurance; the new tax exemptions; the 'generous' sickness compensation; the free sporting facilities; the summer colonies; the two free pairs of footwear annually; the nursery, the dentist and the medical emergency room in the factory; and the rise in the workers' nominal wages, without any mention of the soaring inflation. Where shortages and production stoppages were concerned, sabotage was blamed for the hard situation of the factory and for the ordinary moments when people were suddenly left without work or payment.[35] The fact that much of Dermata's paternalism was inherited from the interwar period went unacknowledged.[36]

The strike lasted for three days and completely stopped production. The situation was complicated by the fact that many of the strike's leaders were communists themselves. According to his own declaration after the strike, Kertesz Niculae, an old communist foreman, led the people in strike precisely because he took his communist creed seriously, and argued that 'real communists always fight against low wages'. A meeting was called and it quickly turned into an exercise in public shaming. The representatives of the party organization in the factory furiously reacted at the idea than 'one of them' was leading the protests. The main accusation against Kertesz Niculae was that, against the party line, he had discouraged workers from joining the party and advised his colleagues 'to work and have nothing to do with politics'. For him, the time of politics had passed.

The meeting was a clash of visions about the meaning of 'politics' in the new historical configuration. One of the activists, labelled by Niculae as one of those 'who discovered their communist sympathies only after 1945', furiously turned to the accused, condemning his 'arrogance'. He advised Niculae to 'remove his hat in front of the workers, and not to lecture them from a position of superiority'. Niculae's leadership in the strike was discussed in terms of 'treason of communist ideals'. His unorthodox ideas provoked other party activists to intervene and claim the necessity of an activity that would combine work and politics, in order to make a better future for all. The minute of the meeting reported little on Niculae's reactions, stating only that he was 'angry and unrepentant'.

Later in the meeting, Niculae was dismissed from the party. The following report accompanied the decision of the factory organization:

> Kertesz Niculae had been a member during the period when the party's activity was illegal. He officially joined the party in 1945, after an interruption caused by the war. In the beginning, he was very active, went to all meetings, and mobilized other workers into joining the party. Later on, he resigned and ceased to attend the meetings. When he was repeatedly asked to come back to the meetings, he wrote a letter to the factory organization, stating that until the recently trained members, the 'October communists' as he called them, become the leaders of the factory, he will not participate in any political activity. But when the strike started in May, he was the first to stop the machines and hinder production. Even those workers who wanted to work, could not. He listened to and applauded reactionary discourses. He was the first to say that the party should take care of the workers' interests, and the strike *was* in the workers' interests.[37]

The decision to dismiss Kertesz Niculae from the party was signed and had the rare mention that he could not rejoin the party even if his innocence was proven, indicating that workers with a genuine communist past had become a danger. Niculae was also fired immediately, with the stipulation that no industrial unit could hire him in the future. The representatives of the union in the factory signed both documents.

Niculae's story makes it clear that already, in 1946, a fracture had been created between the workers who had joined the Communist Party during the interwar period – when communist activity was deemed illegal by the Bucharest authorities – and the workers who joined the party after 1945. During the interwar period, radical notions of social justice had carried with them the danger of being imprisoned, beaten or killed. Even if only a few, some workers held genuine communist loyalties and resented their colleagues who joined the party after the war only because they felt the wind of change in the factory.

But the consequences of the strike at Dermata were much broader. At the request of the fellmongers' union and with the direct support of the party organization in the factory, 105 people were fired a few days later by the management, accused of sabotaging production and of encouraging other people to strike.[38] Some of them were arrested and interrogated. The insistence of the union's representatives that 'the guilty ones should be punished' seems to speak for the widely accepted idea that the unions acted from the beginning as controlling arms of the state and as part of the new logic of organizing class struggle from above. However, the fact that the leaders of the strike were also influential union members raises question marks about the idea that the total and actual control of the party over the unions was a fait accompli.

The attempt to appropriate the rights won by the workers themselves in prewar negotiations was not unique to the strike at Dermata. Work-related benefits were generally presented as the conquest of the communists (and residually of the social democrats) in the factory, even when they belonged to an older history of expanding the factories into the realm of social reproduction. But the way in which the party organization read the 1946 strike at Dermata clearly shows how the party's interest in keeping production going by any means and ensuring a stable basis for nationalization had already fractured its fragile alliance with the workers. Like in the case of Kertesz Niculae's dismissal from the party, workers' struggles for rights and recognition were by now silenced on grounds of illegitimacy, and the party officials in the factory were ready to make things clear: workers' voices could be heard only through their vanguard. The tension between the worker as producer and the worker as political subject was already rooted in the shop-floor realities, even before the communists had completed their quest for power.

As we have seen, the politicization of the entanglement between production and life was far from being unproblematic for the emerging party state. The daily negotiations between the party organizations, the unions, the factory committees and the workers reveal the fragility of a social project that, in order to function, needed to make workers' bodies its own – a move that simultaneously embraced productive and political reasoning. Although the Romanian Workers' Party concentrated many resources in colonizing the unions and attracting workers' in its attempt to control the factory space, they encountered countless difficulties when attempting to transform the factories in redistributive arms of the state. The short period before the official act of nationalization reveals the work/survival nexus as the most fragile node in the power relations that were articulated around the factory.

Nevertheless, this does not mean these efforts were for nothing. They would prove important for ensuring a mass of workers that was usable for political action, including for taking to the street to support the Romanian

Workers' Party or to silence other important voices in Cluj. These voices were fractured along class and ethnic lines, and openly struggled for their right to the city between 1945 and 1947. The supporters of the National Democratic Bloc frequently confronted the supporters of the National Peasants' Party in street fights, and many members of the agitation and propaganda sections of the Romanian Workers' Party learned the craft of activism by breaking the demonstrations of support for their opponents.

As people told me in interviews, the reasons for participating in these demonstrations were very diverse. Sometimes, the workers sincerely supported a measure of the government, like on 6 October 1945, when thirty-five thousand workers and artisans gathered to celebrate the distribution of the land titles for the peasants after the Agrarian Reform. On 17 October of the same year, almost eighty thousand people were waiting in the streets to cheer for Vasile Luca, a top party activist, Hungarian by birth, responsible for minorities issues, and perceived by the Hungarian population of the city as their representative in the party's top echelons.[39] Other occasions were good opportunities to escape work and join a popular celebration followed by music and dances. The workers quickly realized that passivity was no longer appreciated, and felt the pressures of the local party organizations to participate in mass demonstrations for securing employment.

In 1946, the elections year, workers' political participation got even more intense. The campaign was marked by violence, threats, and bribery of all sorts, while street manifestations became an almost everyday experience. The streets of Cluj seemed to be always full of people protesting or celebrating. In March 1946, forty thousand people took the streets for a communist demonstration. Only two days later, ten thousand women celebrated the 8th of March in the main square. On 10 March, fifteen hundred students staged a pro-monarchy manifestation in the city centre, carrying banners that read: 'Down with terror', 'Down with the terrorists', 'Freedom', 'Long live the King and the students', 'Long live the King and our country'.[40] The signs of the new times became clearer with the lavish parade for celebrating the First of May. Seventy allegorical cars, seventy thousand participants from all social categories, and cultural events all over the city could hardly mask the apathy of the crowd, which transformed the moment in 'an almost mute demonstration'.[41] The situation was different at the parade of the opposition on 9 and 10 May, when people celebrated King Michael's birthday. Although only eight thousand people – mostly students and intellectuals – participated in the events, the activists of the Romanian Workers' Party complained that the leftist counterdemonstration could not 'dominate the field', and the students succeeded in transmitting their 'chauvinistic, fascist' message.[42] In the view of the agitprop, this was a direct consequence of the fact that most workers refused to join the counterdemonstration and preferred to remain in the factories. To the party's joy, only five days later, on 15 May, ten thousand workers left their workbenches and joined a demonstration requesting the death penalty for the war criminals. On 19 May, twenty thousand peasants were brought to Cluj to celebrate the Congress of the Ploughmen Front, their main supporter in the government.[43] The following weeks stood under the sign of discontent, with small protests of the students, followed by arrests and beatings by the Romanian Workers' Party activists.

While the party was engaged in winning workers' loyalty, the university regained its central place for Romanian nationalism. During the interwar period, the Romanian students had held either conservative political sympathies for the National Peasants' Party, or straightforward far-right allegiances to the Iron Guard. The experience of refuge to Sibiu during the war, and the threat that Cluj would return to Hungary, triggered a new wave of right-wing radicalism among the students. The university became once again the symbolic infrastructure for political mobilization around the entwinement between 'Romanianness' and an elitist ethos. It stood as a counterpoint to the position of the unionized Hungarian workers, who were considered to be the most loyal supporters of the National Democratic Bloc – the coalition gathered around the communists, the social democrats, and the Ploughmen Front.

This tense situation culminated with the May–June students' strike. Although the reports relating to the protests in the city between January and May 1946 disappeared from the files, one declaration escaped the 'cleaning' of the archives.[44] According to an activist from the City Party Committee, on 28 May the students prepared a demonstration in the main square of the city to mark the beginning of the strike. The stated reasons for the strike were the harsh living conditions of the students, the need to depoliticize the university (read: to take communist politics out), and the necessity to separate the past of certain professors and students from their educational performance (read: in some cases, to ignore their fascist past). The strike was considered enough of a threat to make the party activists worried that they could not pacify the university for a long time and convince them to take radical measures.

At around 7.30 PM, a high-ranking police officer called the party committee on the phone to announce that a small group of students displayed a portrait of Iuliu Maniu, the leader of the National Peasants' Party, in front of the Local Unions' Commission. It was read as a clear statement of the antagonism between the students and the unionized workers. At the phone, it was labelled as 'an instigation to violence against the working class', and the police officer emphasized the need for immediate measures. He also declared that no police forces were available to help the party activists, so they should 'do [by themselves] as much as they can, as fast as they can'. As the students continued to gather in front of the university and in the main square, the police did send some troops to control the small crowd, and the party activists called the members of the local organizations at the Railways Workshops and Dermata to mobilize the workers. Only one day after their own strike ended, some of the Dermata workers responded to the call.

The workers were brought to the city centre by the factory lorries, armed with clubs, chains, knives and pistols. Since the students had already left the square, the workers followed them into the dormitory, and 'the lesson' imagined by the party activists degenerated quickly. The workers attacked the dormitory, destroyed the furniture and viciously beat up the students. After the students called the police in vain, they turned to the people from Mănăştur for help.[45] The police were amassed at the entrance to the city, preventing the Mănăştureni from joining the students against the workers. The conflict ended when one stone (or one bullet, according to other witnesses) hit a window of the Soviet headquarters across the road, and the officers threatened that they would shoot the whole crowd if order was not immediately reinstated.

The party activists quickly came to regret the amplitude of the event and the fact that the situation had not been solved 'by beating only a few students in the main square'. But the message was clear: the voice of the nationalist intellectual elites had to be silenced. Students' requests for better food and living conditions were labelled as a form of hooliganism, attacking national interest at its heart. Many were expelled, arrested and beaten by the authorities.

Although the open confrontations in the mid-1940s did not succeed in producing the simultaneously desired and feared unity of working-class 'interests' or 'consciousness', and did not immediately transform the workers into the party's object of action and representation, they succeeded in creating a form of ethnicized class awareness, which would fracture the city underneath a seemingly hegemonic internationalist discourse. The attack of the (Hungarian) workers against the (Romanian) students cannot be understood in isolation, outside a struggle for articulating the right to the city, or outside the moral economy of the workers in the mid-1940s. These forms were neither in conflict nor in consensus with the party's strategy, but rather syntheses of available political options, in a relational field where dispossession and disenfranchisement emerged differently for different social categories in the city. Never fully separated from ethnic struggles, this repertoire of contention was partly rooted in past struggles and in workers' narratives about themselves, and partly fed by a newly felt empowerment in their relation with the management and with the state.

On the one hand, the Hungarian nationalism of the factory met the Romanian nationalism of the university. On the other hand, the people in the factories faced the emerging intellectual elites as *workers* in a new situation of empowerment which, at least at a discursive level, functioned as a trigger to recognize class lines and smash them. Consequently, the Romanian intellectual elites saw their position in the city endangered by this new ideology, which stated the possibility that the workers, those 'Hungarians' living in the neighbourhoods where no honourable person would walk, could take over the city and make it their own. But the factories talked back. And, as expected, their voice was enthusiastically ethnicized and brutally classed.

Fast forward a few months after the two strikes narrated here, and the party summer reports were dominated once again by trust in workers' goodwill. In the last days of August 1946, however, the price of flour rose sharply and the economats could no longer supply the population with rationed bread.[46] The workers at Dermata and at the Railways Workshops immediately surrounded the party activists on the factory corridors and made them directly accountable for the bread shortage. The next day, exasperated party activists started to question the central strategy of the party regarding its communication with the industrial workers, and to reflect upon their fragile position in the factories:

> Our slogan, that we will raise wages without raising prices, was completely wrong. We imagined a campaign around this issue and we ended up ashamed. We could not find a just explanation when people came to confront us about it. We are weak at unmasking economic sabotage, so people's anger is unfairly directed against us.[47]

Party activists needed to keep a low profile for many days, hoping for the workers' mood to improve.[48] Rocketing inflation and the workers' impossibility to buy even the most basic goods on the market further continued to produce waves of discontent, which translated into the explicit menace of industrial conflict.

The union elections, the intensification of party recruitment, and the street fights preceded the general elections of November 1946. The victory of the National Democratic Bloc paved the way to subsequent steps towards a full control of the government by the communists. In 1947, the historical parties were going to be outlawed, the Romanian king was going to abdicate, and the coalition partners were going to be absorbed into the Romanian Workers' Party, which was going to become the unique political force in the country for more than forty years. These developments opened the possibility for the nationalization of the means of production, the collectivization of land, the further centralization of the economy and the implementation of Soviet-style economic planning. The last section of this chapter will analyse how the process of nationalization itself was grounded in the localized social relations explored so far.

'A Workers' Factory': Nationalization and Its Aftermath

As the previous sections have shown, the struggle over the shop floor was integral to the political developments of the 1945–47 period, and it continued in 1947–48, after King Michael abdicated and the Romanian Workers' Party officially monopolized political power in the government. The previous sections also showed that taking control of factories required the early establishment of new institutional frameworks and shop floor hierarchies, and increasing control over labourers' survival networks, all of them representing core infrastructure developments for the possibility of creating socialist accumulation on the long run. In what follows, I will show that after the nationalization, workers' everydayness continued to constrain the state's capacity to act simultaneously as a creator of socialist accumulation, as a planner of social production processes and as a political progressive force. The history of nationalization as a 'non-event' is important for understanding that although changing property relations was an essential act of primitive accumulation, it could not be equated with taking control of factories. On the ground, far from the central newspapers' propaganda, it was the latter that actually counted.

Although seen as the cornerstone of the socialist economic transformations, the nationalization of the means of production, of the financial system, of the mines and of the transportation network was surprisingly quiet at the time. The newspapers were completely silent about the forthcoming change. Even the party committee records in Cluj display an astounding lack of debate and discussion about 'the first act of socialist accumulation'[49] during the meetings immediately preceding 11 June 1948, when the nationalization officially took place. The reason for this silence was quite simple: by then, nationalization had been anticipated for a long time and it appeared as a logical consequence of a series of appropriations and negotiations for control over production in the Romanian industries.

Starting in 1945, many factories in Cluj entered under the administration of the Office for the Management and Supervision of Enemy

Assets. German and Hungarian citizens who had ownership interests in the factories had fled the country in the last days of the war, pushed by the advance of the Soviet Army.[50] The factories were suddenly without their Hungarian clients and suppliers but were still not reconnected to their Romanian markets. Transportation routes were interrupted and means of transportation were extremely scarce (party representatives were complaining that in 1945 there were no lorries or cars left in Cluj). The branches of Budapest-based banks had been closed and all the liquidities withdrawn. Emergency supplies from Romania were contracted through clearing arrangements, deepening the catastrophic situation of the Transylvanian firms.

The power void faced by the industrial units was soon to be addressed by the communist cells through a unified model of organizing production throughout the country: the factories came to be led by factory administration councils, combinations of former managers and notabilities of the city who could be trusted by the party. The most important factories in the city, like Dermata and the Railways Workshops, had an appointed Red Army officer, who rarely intervened in the daily matters of production but was quick to pressurize the factory administration councils whenever the products assigned to the Soviet factories or to the Red Army did not reach their destination.

Ideally, factory administration had to be in close contact with the factory committees, organisms formed by workers and union representatives, who were supposed to act as defenders of workers' interests and communicate their needs to the management. Factory committees were generally dominated by the communists and by the social democrats, the most attractive choice for the Hungarian workers in Cluj. In time, they would increasingly become vehicles for the will of the Romanian Workers' Party. Many factory committees relied on the so-called 'men of trust' – experienced male workers, generally married – who were at the same time respected by workers and considered not dangerous for the management. They represented a prewar legacy of shop floor hierarchy, and were rapidly instrumentalized as bridges between workers, foremen, the technical staff and the newly appointment administration councils in the negotiation of wages and social benefits in the factories.

Although some owners did retain legal rights over their business after 1944, the party organizations and the unions effectively prevented them from exercising actual control over the production process or over the workers. State regulations regarding the supply of raw materials, preferential prices for state industry, and prohibitions on employing apprentices hit small workshops especially hard. Many of them collapsed long before the nationalization. In the words of a party activist from the Cluj County

Committee in 1947, less than one year before the nationalization: '[T]he party does not touch private initiative. We even help it. But we also set its direction, so the ones who work will also profit from these initiatives'.[51] Actually, at the national level, the period 1945–47 witnessed a short-lived boom in the creation of firms. In 1947, there were over thirty-four thousand enterprises registered, with around 68 per cent created before 1940, 15 per cent related to the war developments between 1941 and 1944, and almost 22 per cent emerging between the end of the war and 1947.

In Cluj, financial control was made more difficult by the fact that on the territory of Northern Transylvania, Hungarian currency (pengö) continued to circulate, not only in trade but also in industry. Soviet roubles were also used in the city as legitimate currency. Officially, the Romanian leu replaced foreign currency in May 1945, but this led to endless problems. A part of the population continued to keep pengö for their anticipated repatriation in Hungary as well as for helping their families in the motherland. For the factories, the loss of foreign currency was often paralysing, as many of their commercial relations were negotiated in pengö. Moreover, the biggest factories in Cluj (like Dermata) had stores not only in Transylvania but also in Budapest and other Hungarian cities.

In June 1948, the Romanian government nationalized the most important factories in the country, the mines, the financial system and the transportation infrastructure. In Cluj Region, the first wave of nationalization targeted forty-eight industrial units belonging to the Ministry of Industry and to the Ministry of Mines and Oil, twenty-six mills and oil presses, six metallurgic companies, three electric companies, two mines, seven construction trusts, five timber factories, two graphic art factories, six textile factories, two leather and footwear factories, six chemical industrial units, six factories belonging to the food industry, and one insurance company. Some of these factories were simply too unproductive to be kept in operation, and were immediately dismantled. Some smaller firms were nationalized as well, but generally the decision was revoked within a few days, once contested by the owner.

A reconstruction of the administrative proceedings from 11 June 1948 shows how carefully the party prepared the day of nationalization. At five in the morning, the police were already guarding the most important factories in Cluj. The leaders of the party organizations were spread about in the workshops, in the cafeterias, and in the workers' locker rooms. At 5.30 AM, the agents of the Nationalization Commission started their work by sealing the cash safes and the documents for later checking. At 2.00 PM, all workers and the rest of the staff were addressed about the act of nationalization and its political significance. All speeches emphasized the need for continuity, and a renewed commitment to increasing productivity and fighting sabotage.

Factory directors received the news about the nationalization with calm, and readily lectured the workers about the benefits of being part of a factory that 'now belonged to all'. The factory managers of the 1945–48 period were generally long-term collaborators of the party – and many times were party members themselves. As a report of the regional party committee regarding the conditions of the nationalization process in Cluj shows, at the moment of nationalization the party had been de facto controlling the factories for at least two years. One of the important elements of this control over the factories was their top management, who had often played the role of a puppet in the hands of the local party organizations.

> Here, in Cluj, we have a somehow different situation compared to other cities, because the majority of the industrial units belonged to Hungarian, German or Romanian fascists who left the country together with the troops in retreat. Since then, the factories have been under CASBI administration. Basically, these factories have been under our leadership lately. The managers of these units were petty-bourgeois elements, party members, who took good money for doing nothing and were simply a burden for the factory budgets.[52]

As was soon to become clear, although some of the pre-1948 factory managers hoped differently and saw themselves as part of the newly emerging power structures, they were actually destined to occupy a transitory role in the takeover of industry.

The calm of the factory directors quickly turned into disappointment when the agents of the Nationalization Commission appeared accompanied by the new managers, all appointed by the city's party committee and approved by the regional and national echelons of the party. The agents reported on the disappointment of the former directors who were suddenly losing their financial advantages and status in favour of other party members. No act of resistance was recorded in Cluj during the proceedings but the tension intensified when the old guard was 'insistently' requested to help the new directors to understand their new administrative tasks. The situation was made even less bearable for the old administrative and technical staff of the factories as they were forbidden to resign or to ask for a transfer for at least three months after the nationalization. According to the law, the old managers had to stay in the factory until the new management was in place, and to help the new leaders with any needed information or advice. The situation would extend indefinitely in cases when a specialist was considered indispensable for the functioning of the enterprise. This second layer of technical management would de facto lead the industrial units for years to come, until a new generation of engineers of a 'healthy social origin' were prepared to take their places in production.

Factory documents reveal the fact that the party organizations in the factories had already made proposals for the appointment of new directors for the nationalized factories in April 1948. Their proposals tended to take into account work experience and technical expertise more than their 'clean social origin' and loyalty to the party. Some of these proposals are illustrated below:

> *The local electricity company*: Pentek Ioan, 42 years old, six years of primary education, a boiler stoker with 25 years length of service.
>
> Party member since February 1945. Honest, hard working, loyal to the working class. Good moral guide for the workers. Very popular among them. He is a good organizer of production and proves capacity for initiative. He is combative and vigilant against the enemies of the party. Although he does not have much political knowledge, he reads a lot and has good perspectives for growing into a dignified leader of the working class. Good worker.
>
> *The Ursus beer factory*: Vaidasigan Grigore, 41 years old, four years of primary school, 26 years length of service, locksmith.
>
> Employed at the Railways Workshops since 1922. Party activist since August 1944.
>
> Social origin: peasant. Party member since May 1945. Educated at the Cadres School in Constanța.
>
> Honest, diligent, disciplined element. The workers like him. He works well in teams. Sometimes he is slow and does not have enough enthusiasm for his party work. But he is thorough when he gets tasks from the party committee. He is not politically advanced. We can trust him but he is better fit to production than to political work.
>
> *The Victoria cooperative*: Zador Arpad, 50 years old, commercial college, private clerk, 33 years length of service.
>
> Social origin: petty-bourgeois. Party member since April 1945. He was not involved in any kind of politics before the war. Honest, devoted to the party and meticulous. He fulfils any task we give him and is very responsible. Generally apolitical, without much political knowledge, but striving to overcome these problems. We can count on him in production. He is diligent and totally reliable. He has the interests of the party at heart. He is an excellent accountant, skilled in all the fields of the administrative work. Very useful element.

Alongside workers who were core party members at their workplace, engineers, former technical managers and even labourers having a petty-bourgeois background were named as possible replacements for the pre-nationalization management. However, the Nationalization Commission rarely took their proposals into account, as they were considered 'not radical enough' for the new times. Those who ended up as the new leaders of the nationalized factories were mostly workers with a few years of education who had proved their loyalty to the party in the postwar years. In Cluj, forty-four of the new directors were workers, and only four were engineers who were 'loyal to the working-class cause'.

What about the workers? In their reports, the party activists contradicted the propagandistic voice of the newspapers which recounted the exaltation of the workers on the 11th of June, and remarked with sadness that the workers had not expressed 'an extraordinary joy' and 'were not deeply moved by the revolutionary act in itself, an act that opens bright future perspectives for the working class'.

> The class enemy tries by any means to compromise the act of nationalization. The County Committee helped the party organizations understand the cunning of these people, who use various methods to undermine our power. They launched a dangerous rumour, that the whole profit of the factory will be distributed amongst workers. They also promised a prepayment of 10,000 lei for every worker in the factory, and they encouraged the workers to request improvements in the social infrastructure of the factory, for their own benefits and comfort, like bathrooms, toilets, cafeterias and kindergartens.[53]

Like before 1948, the political atmosphere in the factories continued to vary along very mundane problems. In June and July, rumours full of hope were spreading in the factory, making the workers believe that the whole profit of the factory would be shared, that they were going to receive a large amount of money and were not going to pay anymore for social security. Some of the workers' informal leaders pushed things forward by saying that the workers should get better wages because the factory was theirs now. In August, when the workers realized that the nationalization had failed to materialize in actual 'collective property' and control of the factories, they started to murmur and to ask for 'at least' an income increase. In September, the workers from several factories grumbled that the piece-rate system had not been introduced everywhere and the salaries were still small. The possibility of a strike like the one in May 1946 at Dermata loomed large over the new economic executives.

Tensions escalated often, especially when the collective contracts were debated, since they were seen as a chance for the workers to supplement their income with access to food or to other types of compensation. The party activists complained that the workers proved unable to see that the collective contract remained the same 'only in form' but that 'in substance it was completely different from the one before the act of nationalization'. The collective contract was indeed going to fulfil a different role in the factory from the one the workers had expected in the first days after the nationalization. Its evolution was going to mark the transition from the negotiated local order of the postwar context to one that linked redistribution through the factory to a logic of productivity.[54]

However, like before 'the greatest historical act of the working class', shop-floor peace was going to depend on how the factory was able to function as an efficient redistributive node and to take care of workers' reproduction. Thus, a daily supplement of 250 grams of bread for the workers at János Herbák ensured a peaceful October; but it was not enough for November, when the workers protested vehemently and threatened to leave their workplace because of the systematic attempts by the factory management to downgrade their wages by placing them in a lower category of skill.

Workers' rumbles were not the only obstacle in transforming the factories into productive state apparatuses. The entanglements between the state economy and the private sector that were presupposed by the logic of primitive socialist accumulation came with their own tensions. Generally obscured by the memory of nationalization as a one-day historical event, the logic of the process was processual and somehow similar to the logic of collectivization. The Nationalization Law referred only to the financial system and to the large commercial and industrial units. Many industrial and commercial units survived until the mid-1950s to ensure pockets of flexibility in supply and demand in production, trade and services. Although for a much shorter period of time and to a different extent, keeping private enterprises in industry and trade alongside state economic units sprang from the requirements of primitive accumulation to keep the private sector alive and squeeze it until the state economy was strong enough to subsist without its capitalist exterior. As we will see in the next chapter, keeping peasants on the land for more than one decade after the nationalization was the other side of the coin, and came from the same rationale. Thus, a strange period started, with a partly controlled and partly chaotic market.

After the nationalization, the large factories in Cluj became the property of the state, received their credit from the State Bank and their production programme was laid down by the State Planning Commission in collaboration with the corresponding ministry or government office. However, they were connected in multiple ways to the private sector. Like most nationalized factories of its size, Dermata (later János Herbák) sold its footwear through its own stores, through state stores and through private ones. Until the mid-1950s, state industrial units employed private cartmen, many of them coming from villages around Cluj, whose survival depended upon their connections with the town. Carrier services had a price fixed by the state, but since they were in short supply, the factories were ready to pay much more, making cartmanship a very lucrative business for more than a decade. The same applied for the repairing of industrial equipment, which was often outsourced to the few hundred craftsmen who were still operating in Cluj until 1952. The artisans and craftsmen who were still working in their own workshops, the small tradesmen who ran their own stores, and the carriers and the carpenters who serviced the state factories were able to make factories pay a market price for their services, although theoretically the state imposed fixed prices for much of the private sector.

Although needed and kept for a long time as a necessary evil, small businesses faced pressures to organize themselves in cooperatives and to unify their networks. Already in 1945, the communist cells of the artisans in the city had been complaining daily that raw materials were being directed mainly to the large industrial units, and that the taxes imposed on them were suffocating. Small and medium workshops also had to deal with several waves of interdictions to hire labourers, who were badly needed in the larger factories; and with the introduction of the professional schools system through the new Education Law in 1948, which officially dismantled the old apprenticeship system, the artisans and the vendors in the city could not count anymore on apprentices either. Successive employment regulations of all sorts were meant to make their lives ever harder, until almost all shops were either unified in cooperatives or dismembered and included within larger industrial units.

In the case of service provision, many of these units were later transformed into cooperatives of production. This allowed their former owners to preserve some independence in the production process and in the organization of the workshops, including some of the former employees, now colleagues. These transformations are captured in the words of a tailor's daughter:

> My father had a lot of work. In the first years after 1949–50, when it was still allowed, he had a private tailor's shop right near our apartment, where there is a bar nowadays, right in front of the ambulance station. Later, when the nationalizations were made, he joined the New Road Cooperative with everything he had in his shop, including the employees. He was the master tailor there while the others used to sew, and I used to spend a lot of time there myself.[55]

Property relations might have changed after the nationalization, but the old hierarchies they embodied were thus preserved.

While the nationalized factories were still doing business with the privately owned ones, the idea that state factory managers could justify their choice of partners based on the logic of the market was dismissed as 'reactionary' and plainly 'dangerous' by the party activists. Choosing a private supplier was never a non-ambiguous solution. Generally, the state factory managers chose private supplies simply because their prices were lower and they were facing the pressures of decreasing production costs, which was no less a central trope of early socialist governments than it was for any capitalist firm. Nevertheless, these choices were also seen as providing fodder for the private sector and syphoning money from the state economy. Hence, deciding to sign a contract with a private workshop or supplier 'for the mistaken reason that the private print shop was cheaper' was not always considered a good idea, as the new director at Dermata was going to find out when a representative of the Economic Section of the Regional Party Committee stormed into his office to scold him and threaten him with dismissal for choosing a private printing shop instead of a nationalized one.

The situation of the large industrial units was not that clear, either. Some owners succeeded in negotiating their position with the party and kept their privileged positions until the beginning of the 1950s. One of the most informative cases is that of Blajiu Guban, the owner of Guban Chemicals, a small-sized footwear manufacturer, which would become famous during the socialist years for its specialization in luxury shoes. Adrian Grama describes the fascinating trajectory of Guban, who was, for a few years after 1948, a factory owner, a party member and a technical adviser to the Light Industry Ministry, all at the same time.[56]

In 1951, his footwear factory was still not nationalized, and the party officials started to worry that singling out Blajiu Guban would send the wrong message to managers and workers elsewhere. A *réquisitoire* describing the most pressing concerns relating to Guban chemicals was issued. The accusations concerned the fact that Blajiu Guban, as a public servant, 'was able to obtain raw materials outside the plan, without paying on delivery and thereby accumulating exorbitant debt', that 'he did not adapt his advertising strategy to the national market', and that he 'ignored labour regulations, paying his employees more than what was legally allowed, thus provoking the envy of those working for state factories'.

The boundaries between 'the state', 'society' and 'the market' not only disappeared in this case, but they were rendered more and more problematic as Blajiu Guban came to lend money to the local branch of the Metal and Chemical Trade Union and to the Financial Office of the city administration. In 1951, the situation got out of control when the Light Industry Ministry's investment plan allocated a budget for an expansion of the privately owned Guban Chemicals, and when Blajin himself bragged about the willingness of the state to invest in his own factory. The state investing in a privately owned factory and, on top of that, borrowing money from a private owner while controlling the banks, stretched the definition of what the 'socialist economy' was. The fact that this private owner was 'one of their own' introduced a tension into the notion of what the 'workers' state' itself stood for. Or, in the words of the party leaders in the above-mentioned *réquisitoire*: 'To prolong the current situation will only compromise the higher echelons of the party in the eyes of the workers; it will confuse the mind of the working man, incapable of understanding why a comrade from *ilegalitate* is an owner in the age of building socialism, and why the state backs him up'.[57]

An equally fascinating case was the business success of the foreman Luka Francisc from the Electrical Company in Cluj. Luka Francisc was employed as a foreman and promoted immediately as the head of the mechanical sector by the regional branch of the company. A 1951 report about the situation created by his alliance with the factory director showed that, before 1948, Luka Francisc had owned his own industrial unit, employing ninety workers and around twenty apprentices. Nagy Alexandru – the post-nationalization director of the regional branch of the Electrical Company – had been employed as a lathe operator at Luka Francisc's factory during the war. In 1950, the manager of the nationalized company offered a contract to his former employer, and made him responsible for the whole mechanical sector.

The 'alliance' could have gone unnoticed for even longer if the workers had not complained about his 'dictatorial attitude', manifested through the lack of empathy that betrayed the residues of his 'bourgeois mentality'. One day, he supposedly even slapped one member of the communist youth, and spat at him, shouting '*Zdravstvujte!*' No measures were taken against the foreman as the company director condescendingly dismissed the youngster's grievances.

The most important accusation against Luka Francisc was related to his 'refusal to understand the Nationalization Law'. After several years, the authorities discovered how his business, although nationalized, continued to operate to his advantage, and in much better conditions than before 1948. This is how it happened. Benefiting from insider knowledge, a few days before the buildings that sheltered his workshops were requisitioned, Luka Francisc had already moved all the industrial equipment into various factories. He hid most of it at the regional branch of the Electrical Company, which, like the other factories used by the former owner to hide his equipment, failed to list them in the inventory. The machines came back under Luka Francisc's own control once the company director employed him as a foreman and as the head of the mechanical sector. The private activity continued, and Luka Francisc used the machines 'like they were his own', asking his subordinates to work after hours, paying them from his earnings, and even offering them higher payments than the factory itself. Because it could not pay the workers directly, Nagy Alexandru took care to arrange important bonuses, which sometimes almost doubled their wages. To keep an eye on everything, Francisc refused any vacation and continued to work sixteen hours a day in the factory. Luka Francisc's employer, the Electrical Company, was one of his main beneficiaries and, according to rumours, the factory director received a share of the profit.

It seems that blackmail was not uncommon at the regional branch of the Electrical Company, where the director declared in private conversations that he needed to save the best positions for certain people because they knew many things about his illegal dealings. Nagy Alexandru himself summed up the intricate situation around the factory management when he stated in a meeting: 'I always feel like one of my feet is already in prison. But if I am going to prison, many will come with me'. Probably this is why the party could never find out the extent of the private production networks operating in the factory. Moreover, when the party organization tried to find out what was happening, its own members started to use blackmail as a strategy, trading information about the endemic corruption in the factory in exchange for access to housing or to better employment.

At the end of a tumultuous affair that kept the local party committees, the police and the Securitate busy for many months, the factory director, Nagy Alexandru, was charged with 'familialism'. It was stated that he paid his close collaborator in the factory a large amount of money in the form of higher wages and bonuses. He was excluded from the party, dismissed and later imprisoned. Luka Francisc was found guilty of sabotage, fired and spent several years in jail. Just by chance, I was going to find out something about his fate from two interviews with workers from Tehnofrig, a manufacturer of frigorific equipment for the food processing industry. According to their memories, after getting out of prison in the mid-1950s, Luka Francisc was employed at Tehnofrig and quickly became a foreman 'because he was a hell of a worker'. In the context of the generalized labour shortage that was going to dominate the unfolding of the First Five-Year Plan, his problematic political and legal past must have been forgotten.

Luka Francisc's case prompted the police and the Securitate to intensify their activity in the factories. In the following months, they discovered that at least two other foremen who 'donated' some equipment to the factory before June 1948 conducted their own small businesses from within the industrial unit. They sold their products not only on the black market but also to the state factories, which were always in short supply of everything. Like in the case of the Electrical Company, the party organizations in the factory seemed to have turned a blind eye to their illegal dealings, probably not only because their members had a share in the profits, but also because, in many cases, informal activity was precisely what kept the production going.

State factories also depended upon intricate connections with the rural economy. Besides supplying state industry with raw materials, and urban food stores with meat, grains and vegetables through forced deliveries to the state, peasants from the villages surrounding Cluj, as well as those around other Romanian cities, provided industry with supplemental raw material, food for their cafeterias, milk for their nurseries, fodder and manure for their annex farms, and firewood for their workers. In turn, factories were supplying peasants with consumer goods and agricultural tools through rural cooperatives, but at prices that were generally beyond a peasant's reach. But as we will see in the next chapter, the crucial dependency of industry on a non-socialist exterior was manifested in its desperate search for workers and in the daily struggle to expand labour that accompanied socialist industrialization for decades.

For many years, state factories needed to rely on the supply of a non-socialist exterior, made of a complex and politically ambiguous fabric of capitalist relations. If in the capitalist world 'the process of exchange between the capitalist and non-capitalist environment acts as a feeding ground of accumulation, and is a sine qua non of the existence of the capitalist economy',[58] the same can be said about the myriad of exchange threads between the nationalized and the private sector in early socialism. It was precisely the limited and contradictory reliance of socialist industry on a non-socialist exterior – mainly rural – that allowed the factories to function and expand in the 1950s.

The 'takeover' of the factories was neither simple nor unidirectional as generally assumed. It was not simply about building legitimacy either, as Mark Pittaway would have interpreted it.[59] Although largely unseen, the struggle over the control of the factories in the post-1945 period was fierce. For approximately four years, the complex transition of the factories from contested political spaces to state institutions entailed a battle to control labour and management alike, while keeping and even expanding the productive potential of the factories. It required the involvement of the workers in new forms of political participation, taking them out onto the streets to lead ethnicized struggles, while undercutting and reinterpreting their own moral economies and ideas of social justice. This transition had not yet been completed in 1948 when the most important means of production and the financial institutions were nationalized. It continued for years, as manifested in the many ways in which the state envisioned its subjects, and in people's countless responses to that vision.

Although the workers were going to benefit from an increased living standard in the following decades, and industrial order was going to remain the subject of mundane negotiations, the state was going to secure an ever-stronger hold on production. In this negotiation, the factories became fragile nodes of state power in which the need to manage production collided with an emancipatory projection of a better future, and with people's own struggles for existence and recognition. In the process, the boundaries between the workers and the state would be redrawn several times, and the shop floor would go through several waves of politicization and depoliticization, with control over production and everyday life being at stake.

Notes

1. The Second Vienna Arbitration. People from the countries that lost territories in the First and the Second Vienna Awards generally use the term 'diktats' to refer to the arbitrations.
2. The introductory reconstruction ended up being a highly subjective and fragmented narrative, mainly based on people's recollections and local histories, which in many cases tend to idealize the pre-socialist past of the city.
3. Hungarian until 1919, Romanian until 1940, then Hungarian again during the war.
4. The *hoștezeni* were living on the outskirts of Cluj and were supplying the city with fresh fruits and vegetables. Originally, they were a German-speaking population that had been brought from Central Europe by the Hungarian authorities in the seventeenth century, but later claimed no German identity and did not speak the language anymore. Their name comes precisely from *Hochstadt*, signalling their position outside the city walls. The *hoștezeni* survived the collectivization due to their crucial role in supplying the city with fresh food. However, after 1978, in just a few years, their gardens disappeared when the new neighbourhoods were built in Cluj. Many of them committed suicide when they were forcefully moved into blocks of flats.
5. Pittaway, *The Workers' State*, 30.
6. Kenney, *Rebuilding Poland*, 75.
7. Ionescu, *Communism in Romania*; Turnock, *The Romanian Economy*.
8. This schematic background of the economic and social transformations in Cluj draws on synthetic words on the history of Romanian communism. Cioroianu, *Pe umerii lui Marx*; Ionescu, *Communism in Romania*; Frunză, *Istoria stalinismului în România*.
9. Țârău, 'Campania electorală'.
10. Although they are not explicitly part of this inquiry, the continuities between the nationalized industry and the war economy are much more complex. See Grama, 'Laboring Along'.

11. The Law of Nationalization and Reorganization of the National Bank of Romania, M.O. 298, 28 December 1946.
12. *Scânteia*, 1 December 1946.
13. Reforma Monetară, Legea nr. 287, M.O. nr 187, 16 August 1947.
14. Gurley, 'Excess Liquidity'.
15. See Burtan, 'Principalele Transformări Economico-Sociale'.
16. Legea nr. 189, M.O. nr. 129, 9 June 1947.
17. *Liberalul*, 28 March 1947.
18. Legea 114, Înființarea Ministerul Industriei și Comerțului, M.O. nr. 89, 19 April 1947.
19. Jowitt, 'Revolutionary Breakthroughs', 7.
20. Arhivele Naționale Direcția Cluj (henceforth ANDC), Fund 2, CR PMR Cluj, Sectorul II, Raportul Organizației de Partid din sectorul II – July/August 1945.
21. ANDC Fund 2, CR PMR Cluj, Secția Educație Politică, Raportul politic al Comitetului Județean Cluj, August 1947.
22. ANDC Fund 2, CR PMR Cluj, Sectorul I Instituții, Celula: Prefectura Județului Cluj, Proces Verbal al sedinței celulei comuniste a Prefecturii Județului Cluj, 18 August 1945.
23. ANDC, Fund 2, CC P.C.R. Cluj, Regional Police Inspectorate, 21 October and 9 November 1945.
24. ANDC Fund 2, CR PMR Cluj, Secția Organizații de masă, Raportul pe luna ianuarie al secției organizațiilor de masă.
25. ANDC Fund 2, CR PMR Cluj, Secția Educație Politică, Circulară, Cluj, 14 August 1946.
26. ANDC Fund 2, CR PMR Cluj, Sectorul II, Raportul Organizației de Partid din sectorul II – 2 August 1945.
27. ANDC Fund 2, CR PMR Cluj, Comitetul Județean P.C.R. Cluj, Sectorul II, Celula: Fabrica de Tutun.
28. ANDC Fund 2, CR PMR Cluj, Sectorul II, Raportul Organizației de Partid din sectorul II – 2 August 1945.
29. ANDC Fund 2, CR PMR Cluj, Sectorul II, Raportul Organizației de Partid din sectorul II – September 1945.
30. Law 3,499, MO no 237, 12 October 1938.
31. *Scânteia*, 6 July 1945.
32. For an analysis of the labour conflict in the postwar period, with a focus on the collective contracts, see Grama, 'Laboring Along'.
33. *Făclia*, 19 April 1945.
34. ANDC, Fund Clujana, 80/1948.
35. At Dermata, production stopped completely for days: in 1945, 4–19 November and 20 November – 6 December; in 1946: 2 January, 6–11 March and 4 May. Isolated units of the factories in the city stopped multiple times, sometimes for more than a month.
36. For detailed discussions about varieties of paternalism, see Burawoy, *Politics of Production*; and Reid, 'Industrial Paternalism'.
37. ANDC, Fund Clujana, Report about Kertesz Niculae, department head of the Industrial Belts workshop at Dermata, Cluj, 10 September 1946; my emphasis.
38. Request to the Labour Inspectorate Cluj [Cerere către Inspectoratul Muncii Cluj], 1583/ 30 July 1946.
39. ANDC Fund 2, CR PMR Cluj, Sectia Educatie Politica, Raport politic pe luna Octombrie 1946, judetul Cluj.
40. ANDC Fund 2, CR PMR Cluj, Sectia Educatie Politica, Raportul Sectiei de Educatie Politica a P.C.R. Cluj, 25 February – 25 March.
41. ANDC Fund 2, CR PMR Cluj, Sectia Educatie Politica, Raport al Sectiei de educatie politica, luna May 1946.
42. ANDC Fund 2, CR PMR Cluj, Sectia Educatie Politica, Raport al Sectiei de educatie politica, May 1946.

43. ANDC Fund 2, CR PMR Cluj, Sectia Educatie Politica, Raportul Sectiei de Educatie Politica a P.C.R. Cluj, 25 February – 25 March.
44. The successive laws concerning the functioning of the archives allowed for the periodical disposal of certain categories of document. However, the employees of the archives claim that in 1965 the party decided to clean the archives of the most incriminating documents for the period between 1944 and 1965. The fact that the files still exist, and only the pages containing the reports and the declarations of the participants in the events were ripped, supports their memories.
45. People still remember how, after the leaders of the Romanian Workers' Party declared Romania a 'People's Democracy', a signboard appeared overnight at the entry of the suburb, saying: 'Democracy ends here, where Mănăştur starts'.
46. ANDC Fund 2, CR PMR Cluj, Raportul Organizaţiei de Partid din sectorul II, August 1946.
47. ANDC Fund 2, CR PMR Cluj, Raportul Organizaţiei de Partid din sectorul II, October 1946.
48. The factories in Cluj saw interruptions of production, spontaneous gatherings of the workers to claim their rights, wildcat strikes, and vocal complaints to their unions and factory committees. The events at Dermata in May 1946 were among the few labour conflicts in the country that could be properly labelled as general strikes – but explosive situations did emerge in Cluj, as they did in other important industrial centres like Bucharest, Arad and Reşiţa.
49. Preobrazhensky, *The New Economics*, 80.
50. Arhivele Naţionale ale României (henceforth ANR), CC P.C.R. Secţia Economică, 80/1945; Nistor, 'Constituirea si activitatea'.
51. ANDC Fund 2, CR PMR Cluj, Secţia Educaţie Politică, 142. It is telling that during the 1946 political campaign, the Romanian Workers' Party circulated a brochure titled 'The Communists and Private Property', trying to convince peasants, craftsmen and small traders that defending their property is crucial for the future of the country.
52. ANDC, Fund Clujana, 80/1948.
53. Ibid.
54. For an extended discussion on the collective contract, see Grama, 'Laboring Along'.
55. Gordeeva, Drancă and Orăştean, *Cluj-Napoca 1939–1960*, 31.
56. ANR, CC/PCR, secţia Economică, 169/1952, in Grama, 'Nationalization, Early Planning'.
57. Grama, 'Nationalization, Early Planning'.
58. Luxemburg, *Accumulation of Capital*, 426.
59. Pittaway, *The Workers' State*; Pittaway and Dahl, 'Legitimacy'.

CHAPTER 2

'More Precious Than Gold'
Labour Instability and the 'Stickiness' of Everyday Life

Planning Wages

In 1949, the new economic executives could read in *Class Struggle* that the historical possibilities opened by the implementation of the first One-Year Plan should make them happy to be the leaders of the newly nationalized industrial units. The 'luck' of running a socialist factory was contrasted with the hardships of a capitalist economy, where 'the anarchy of social production opposed the organization of production in each factory'.[1] But the experience of the Romanian factory managers was going to be quite different: in the emerging socialist economy, the anarchy of production in each factory conflicted with the organization of social production as a whole.

This chapter investigates this chaotic factory life as a direct effect of the exploitative mechanisms that preceded and accompanied the implementation of planning. It addresses the consequences of the state's systematic attempts to keep wages low and restrict workers' consumption on the ability to employ labourers. The chapter shows that the employment regime of the first postwar decade was marked by the impossibility of stabilizing workers and by unruly competition between factory managers. It further investigates two ways in which the workers responded to these attempts: a lack of commitment to their industrial units, and an incorporation of stealing into their daily strategies for survival. As it will hopefully become clear, these responses could hardly be understood in terms of either 'compliance' or 'resistance'. Both the workers' tendency to change their workplaces with astonishing frequency and the array of forms in which stealing and trafficking became equated with 'work' are treated here as forms of reappropriating control over the quotidian universe in which the factories were embedded. Since low wages could not shatter what I call the 'stickiness' of workers' everyday life, out-of-control informal labour markets proliferated and the anti-stealing campaigns that dominated the public discourse in the 1950s were rather fruitless. As we will see in Part II of this book, both the inability to 'fix' labour in place and the spread of thieving had further consequences on planning activity, which was predicated on the continuity of the production process.

These developments reclaim a deeper appraisal of the relationship between everyday life and the local, understood here as 'particular historical-spatial ensembles of relations of production and reproduction' made into concrete geographies of accumulation.[2] I am drawing here on subsequent developments of Alf Lüdtke's understanding of *Alltagsgeschichte*[3] to explore how these localized landscapes of accumulation go beyond a simple retrieval of small people's work and non-work subjective experiences. This 'stickiness' of everyday life in early socialism came precisely from the ways in which relations of production structured workers' social worlds in the 1950s within and beyond the factory walls.[4]

These particular dimensions of the relationship between labour and the state can be read in two temporal keys, each with its own corresponding level of abstraction: first, as the transition from a postwar fragile negotiation of industrial peace and political legitimacy towards a less equivocal form taken by class relations during the First Five-Year Plan; and second, as part and parcel of Preobrazhensky's primitive socialist accumulation, more concretely as a first planned stage of workers' 'self-restraint'.[5] In practice, the two entangled historical logics had the converging aim of lowering the cost of labour in the transition from the postwar penury and inflation-driven social contract to a wage system of Soviet-Taylorist inspiration that directly linked monetary incentives to workers' performance on the shop floor. This transition was realized through concrete measures of pressing the workers' wages down and restricting their consumption, which made the early socialist social contract between workers, their factories and the state rather fragile.

Equally vulnerable to workers' demands was the emergent Stalinist bureaucracy, which theoretically was trying to bring together the principle of hyper-rationality with a Fordist model of social reproduction, and to link them to the logic of ever-expanding productivity. In the process, the workers would lose the voice they shortly regained after the Second World War, and the Romanian Workers' Party would make the transition from an inconsequential political movement to a bureaucratic structure that would confound itself with 'the state' for decades to come. This would entail an ontological alteration of the state itself in the sense of a manager-state – a state that ran and created social production processes.

The socialist state apparatuses would be rooted in production and essentially connected to the establishment of a work/wage nexus that required both individualization and standardization. Consequently, they would be dependent on the specific form taken by the commodification of labour in state socialist regimes. In between these often-conflicting logics of the transition to socialist industrialism, the factory emerged as an almost impossible disciplinary regime, always chased after, always in the project, but never accomplished. It also emerged as a management object with blurred boundaries and porous walls, in which production and life came together in unexpected ways.

This should hardly come as a surprise for the reader after Chapter 1's exploration into how workers' lives and bodies became objects of state politics before and after the nationalization. In this period, although they were challenged in virtually every factory, wages continued to be set at governmental level (like during the war), and many prices followed the same controlled path. The end of the Second World War saw an explosion of small-scale protests around the negotiation of wages, collective contracts and norms. The erosion of factory owners' power, the revival of local trade unions and the establishment of factory committees constituted the terrain on which workers' demands for increases in wages, and for the management to honour the clauses of the collective contract, became a common occurrence – as did their endless stream of petitions to the Ministry of Labour, their presence on the streets, and their occasional strikes and violent outbursts.[6] These manifestations could hardly ease the dire consequences of the postwar penury, could not stop the inflationary wave, and could not force the state to renounce the policy of freezing wages. But they did constitute a negotiation space in which the workers were still able to pressure the state to concede at least some relief measures for the generalized scarcity.

Various components of workers' social wage functioned as compensations accompanying the state's efforts to keep workers' financial earnings low. Family allowance, winter help or monthly expensiveness bonuses represented such attempts to counteract the postwar inflationary effects. Industrial employment became the access gate to subsidized consumer goods through the economats. It also became the redistribution node for firewood, canteen meals and free food directly related to the nutritional requirements of the job: milk in toxic environments or pork fat for heavy work like mining and leather tanning.

These efforts against scarcity drew upon the interwar structures of provisioning around the largest factories. For instance, Dermata and CFR Workshops had built canteens, sport halls and showers for their workforce, and had been subsidizing dormitories for temporary male labourers since the late 1930s. During the war, most factories in Cluj expanded on this structure of provisioning by organizing vegetable gardens, piggeries and small farms. In the postwar industrial setting, the efforts of the owners, local unions and factory committees to ensure the smooth functioning of these redistributive forms were most of the time aggressively appropriated by the members of the local party organizations, who presented themselves as champions of workers' rights. Before its official ascent to power, the party tried to adopt, filter and subvert workers' voices by discursively connecting their sacrifices in the reconstruction effort to the activity of its local cells. After 1947, in preparation for nationalization and the implementation of planning, the official strategy was going to change, and workers' hopes and concerns were simply going to be silenced by absorbing them into a more inclusive notion of 'state interest'.

The financial reform implemented in 1947 by the Governmental Commission for the Recovery of the Economy and Monetary Stabilization represented the first clear attack against workers' social wages.[7] Its most important consequences were the suspension of the winter help, the abolition of workers' debts and the dismantling of the economats, in an attempt to extricate individual consumption from the finances of the factories. Even the smallest subsidies came under attack. For instance, before the financial reform, the workers at Dermata had benefited from being allowed to take home one pair of winter boots and one pair of shoes for free every year. The factory stores had also offered subsidized footwear for workers' family members. In 1948, the workers were still able to buy subsidized footwear for themselves but none for their families, and any mention of gratuity ceased. In October 1947, a circular announced to the workers at Dermata that they were also expected to pay for canteen meals in full.[8]

The National Bank established an exchange rate of 20,000 old lei for a new 'stabilized' leu and a new fixed price for gold. The population had one week to make the switch between the old currency and the new, but the law set a cap for the amount of money that one person could exchange: those employed in industry, services, administration, and liberal professions could exchange 3,000,000 old lei, while those who worked in agriculture could exchange 5,000,000 old lei, and an extra of 2,500,000 if they could prove they handed over the mandatory cereal quota from the last harvest.[9] Timing mattered. The day for changing currency was 15 August, and it was openly linked to the harvest period in order to offer an incentive to the peasants to bring their products to the city instead of withholding them for personal use or selling them on the black market. Industrial workers and functionaries would receive their wages directly in the new currency, making the transition easier to handle at the administrative level.

The monetary reform of 1947 was part of a long history of financial restrictions that started with the 1930s crisis and continued through the Second World War. These measures comprised austerity measures, wage 'sacrifice curves' for the state employees, and wage cuts in the private sector. Most broadly, the financial stabilization of 1947 was presented as a financial instrument meant to address poverty and the high level of inequality in the country. However, it was also explicitly framed in the language of 'class struggle' and in terms of restorative justice.[10] As a form of appropriation, it was openly directed against the bourgeoisie and against the well-off peasantry, as a step that preceded and eased the process of nationalization, as shown in the first chapter.

Consequently, the financial stabilization was accompanied by a spectacle of transparency: lists with official prices for everything from bread to soap appeared in every newspaper and in every corner of the cities and villages. In Cluj, groups of people gathered every day in the city centre to see the lists and, armed with this knowledge, proceeded on their daily hunt for food, firewood or clothes. Party activists often complained that these were the first spots where spontaneous protests against the government and the party ignited. All over the country, the raids organized by the General Commissariat for Prices against 'saboteurs' and 'profiteers' initiated a wave of requisitions against small stores and workshops, which were immediately nationalized, even before their owners had been found guilty by law. These raids often had a performance-like character and unfolded with the aid of an angered population, either because people were called to identify and denounce 'the profiteers', or because they were called to be part of the judicial proceedings. Nevertheless, while the setting of prices at state level, the tighter control of the supply of the population's food and basic items, and the attack against corruption and embezzling might have soothed the urban population for short periods, the state could do nothing against inflation itself, nor against the party's hopes and promises that 'less money on the market' was necessarily 'good money' – the kind of money with which people can make long-term plans because it was not going to lose its value.[11]

The monetary stabilization was also meant to strengthen the provisioning system connecting the city and the countryside. Again, the measure can be read in a double temporal key: in the short term, it addressed the horrid consequences of the famine that was affecting the Romanian population in the postwar years; in the long run, it was going to support the first wave of socialist industrialization under the propagandistic trope of 'the alliance between peasantry and the working class'.

However, in the months following the financial stabilization, the documents of the regional party committee in Cluj were full of complaints from the local executives, exasperated by the fact that peasants continued to refuse to bring their products to the city. 'Hard-working people' getting angry when finding the stalls empty also featured prominently in the newspapers.

Price scissors also had their own unintended consequences on the ground. As a party activist from the regional party committee decried in a meeting, peasants generally felt 'that the prices of industrial products were higher than the prices of food', which discouraged the 'exchange' between the countryside and the city. Of course, food was to be found on the black market, together with other types of consumer goods, so prices went up and inflation retook its ascending path almost immediately. By comparing the lists of official prices at local level to the prices on the black market, he showed how, while the price of an egg was set at 2.50 lei, it was sold on the black market at 10 lei, and one kilo of pork was sold at 300 lei although the state set its price at 90 lei. Workers' wages were soon to prove insufficient once again.

Read in a long-term temporal key, the significance of the financial stabilization of 1947 was different. By connecting the possibility of exchanging money to specific social categories, the reform was a step towards a world in which money was going to reflect a productive effort, and those outside wage-earning would be left behind. It was linked to the establishment of a new wage system, which constituted the foundation of the state's wage policy until the end of the First Five-Year Plan.[12] Through its insistence on the generalization of the piece-rate system, the new wage system was an important first step in the process of transforming the wage itself into a direct expression of productivity. The piece-rate system was going to be introduced 'everywhere it was possible' on the basis of 'scientifically set' technical norms, which would take into account a worker's skill level and the difficulty of the operation, and would be established through a classical Taylorist decomposition of tasks and chronometric measurements of each component. Following a centralization of the results for the most representative industrial units, production quotas would be set by the government for an entire industrial branch.[13]

As shown by dozens of articles in the most important newspapers of the time, this move was an explicit struggle against the levelling system of wages that had dominated the postwar years, and against the consequences of this levelling for labour productivity. The new wages would appear as a combination of two factors: skill, and the industrial branch in which the worker was employed, classified according to the priority given by the state to that branch in the early stages of socialist accumulation. Between 1947 and 1949, the ratio between the wage of an unskilled worker and the maximum salary of a factory director was of 1 to 5. In 1949 the ratio changed to 1 to 8.4, and more wage differentials were introduced.[14]

If we take 1938 as a baseline – like the first communist governments always did, since it was considered the starting point for the war economy – real wages in 1955 represented only 67 per cent of the prewar ones and were the lowest in Eastern and Central Europe.[15] This was a meagre comparison, since the life of an industrial worker in 1938 was far from easy. A 1938 survey of the living standards of the industrial workers in Cluj shows that collective contracts were rare and the level of unionization low, so workers were generally forced to accept the arbitrariness of the interwar labour relations. More than three-quarters of the workers were employed through individual contracts, which kept their wages low – and their living conditions appalling in many cases.

Against the law, workers' working days were long. Almost 85 per cent of the overtime for the skilled workers, and almost 100 per cent for the unskilled ones, went unpaid.

In addition to these hardships, almost 40 per cent of the skilled workers and 35 per cent of the unskilled ones had, at the time of the survey, experienced unemployment at one point in their lives.

Table 2.1 1938 wages in Cluj. Industrial skilled vs. unskilled workers.

Romanian lei	Skilled (%)	Unskilled (%)
Under 1,000	20.75	21.77
1,001–2,000	40.25	64.45
2,001–3,000	23.25	12.45
3,001–4,000	9.25	1.33
Over 4,000	6.5	–

Table 2.2 Hours worked per week for the industrial workers in Cluj in 1938.

	Skilled (%)	Unskilled (%)
Under 48 hours	16.25	6.67
48 hours (legal time)	67.25	72.89
Over 48 hours	12.25	10.66
Variable	3.50	4.89
Unlimited	0.75	4.89

Source: Bindea, 'Conditiunile', 8.

But compared to 1938, the decrease in workers' real wages and the soaring prices made everyday life even harder in the 1950s. Behind the tropes of betterment that accompanied the monetary stabilization and the implementation of the new wage system, the real cost of living is more obvious when we compare the average working time that needed to be spent by an industrial worker in order to buy one kilo of bread in 1953: 40 minutes for rationed bread, 80 minutes for bread bought in a state shop, and 195 minutes for bread bought on the black market.[16] The evolution of the hours worked for a weekly subsistence basket is even more telling for the increasing pressure on workers' real wages during the First Five-Year Plan. While one worker worked on average 7.7 hours for a subsistence basket in 1938, he or she worked 10.05 hours in 1951 for the same quantity of products, 10.5 hours in 1954, and 11.0 hours in 1955. But this then went down to 9.45 hours in 1956, after the implementation of a new wage system at the end of the First Five-Year Plan.[17]

The wage system established in 1947 was going to structure workers' planned 'self-restraint' during the First Five-Year Plan. Other administrative measures at the end of the 1940s reflected the same reasoning. The most important was the transformation of the ration card, which not only gave access to a much longer list of consumer goods than before, but was also an inscription of employment directly rooted in an accumulation logic that privileged heavy and extractive workers over those employed in light industry.[18] Essential for the logic of double-dwellers, which will be discussed in Chapter 3, landholders were completely excluded from access to rationed items.

The 1938 industrial survey in Cluj also showed that piecework was not generalized before the war, when half of the skilled workers and almost 57 per cent of the unskilled ones in Cluj were still paid by the hour.[19] Hence, the wage system of the late 1940s represented a radical move towards linking the possibility of survival to money and wage. Its 1949 modifications can also be read as successive attempts to increase productivity and further favour the introduction of piecework.[20] The distance between the base wage and the total wage – what the worker could earn by adding norm fulfilment, norm breaking and bonuses for quality and raw material savings – was supposed to function as an individual incentive to work more, better and faster. Keeping the work norms low as a general rule, and introducing progressive piece-rates – which meant the workers earned more for breaking the norms than for reaching them – further foregrounded the productivist logic of the state. It was a key moment that pushed Romania into the broader transition to a piecework system as an intrinsic part of the Taylorist managerial strategies that dominated labour relations after the First World War in almost every industrializing society. In 1953, in the middle of the First Five-Year Plan, more than two-thirds of the workers were integrated in a form of payment-by-result work: approximately 75 per cent in metallurgy and in light industry, and around 60 per cent in construction works.[21] The generalization of piece-work during the First Five-Year Plan was telling for the roots of early socialist accumulation, which was firmly located in workers' efforts rather than in capital investment or technological advancement.

The new economic executives would further use the base wage to calculate production costs, work norms, overtime, enterprise benefits and labour productivity. From this point of view, these politics of calculability were central in a process of labour commodification, which, as Martha Lampland convincingly shows, lived a crucial moment in socialism.[22] The next two sections will show how the direct relationship between the possibility of survival and industrial employment was established in Cluj, and why the analysis of this relationship cannot be separated from workers' own responses to the violence of abstraction behind the monetarization of their reproduction.

Analytically, the commodification of labour refers to the abstraction of decoupling labour power from living labour, or as the artificial separation between people's mental and physical capacity to work and the actual waste of their bones, blood and sweat in the act of work itself.[23] This work of objectification has been seen as fundamental for the possibility of selling one's labour power and for all the consequences that follow: setting a price for labour, defining a labour market, and calculating the demand for workers. As such, the lines of separation between labour power and living labour on which the capitalist managers and socialist planners alike calculated production costs and wages played a constitutive role for the evolution of global industrial modernity. Of course, these lines are imaginary, but this does not mean that they have not produced real historical effects. To assess them, we need a deeper understanding of how the fictitious separation between labour power and living labour have been pushed forward to produce imaginative forms of exploitation, how responsibility for life and its prerequisites have been negotiated, and how the two dialectical moments presupposed by the notion of 'free labour' have been played out historically.

In the opening of the sixth chapter of *Das Kapital*, Marx identified labour, or labour power, as the only commodity whose use-value is in itself a source of value. Understood as the totality of intellectual and physical abilities of a human being that can be exercised whenever people work, labour power appears as the only commodity whose consumption creates surplus value. But for labour to appear as a commodity, two conditions are necessary. First, the seller and the buyer have to meet in the market as 'equal[s] in the eyes of the law'.[24] In order for this legal equality to be preserved, the workers can only alienate their labour power temporarily, otherwise they would become commodities themselves, instead of possessing their labour as a commodity. The *legal* separation between the worker and their capacity to produce is thus achieved. Second, once the workers can temporarily dispose of their labour power without any legal proscription, they should be compelled to sell it by creating specific historical conditions: labour power has to become their only means of production and subsistence. It must fully depend on their wages.

With irony, Marx shows that since capital accumulation is dependent upon this historical encounter between 'the owner of the means of production and subsistence' and 'the free worker … as the seller of his own labour power',[25] capitalism as a political and moral arrangement finds its foundations in this sphere of commodity exchange to become 'a very Eden of the innate rights of man'.[26] The whole notion of citizenship that crosses Western modernity appears then to be centred around and marked by four notions: Freedom, as the legally unconstrained possibility of the buyer and the seller of labour to seal a contract; Equality, as they meet in the market as owners of commodities that are exchanged as equivalents; Property, as both the buyer and the seller dispose of their own possession in this exchange; and 'Bentham', because individualism, selfishness, and financial gain are the reasons behind these encounters.

Of course, planned economies were not that 'very Eden of the innate rights of man' ironically evoked by Marx. They were certainly not the realm of Freedom, Equality or Property in the above-mentioned sense. Property in socialism was defined as collective property, so the boundaries between who was buying labour and who was selling labour were discursively blurred. The worker (as the seller of labour power) met the state (as the buyer) in a highly regulated environment, in which employment was theoretically both universal and mandatory. Moreover, in the Romanian process of proletarianization, to 'free' labour had an ambiguous meaning.

First, from a legal perspective, although it did refer to an individual right to work, the right to be hired by different employers was severely limited. In order to work where they wanted, the workers had to be recognized as 'free workers' and stamped as such by the state. In the first year of planning, factories were obliged to publish in the local press and to display at the factory gates their job openings. But the rule, both for the factories and for the prospective workers, was clear: 'Only *free* workers, whose payroll card states that their last factory consents to their being hired elsewhere, can be employed. The Office for Labour Force Planning will be informed about all the hirings'.[27] This dimension resembled more a feudal card of passage then the capitalist notion of 'freedom'.[28]

Second, according to the legal provisions of the postwar years, the worker had not only the right but also the obligation to work. This obligation to work is still alive in people's memory. It repeatedly emerged in our conversations in the form of a story, always the same but with different characters: everybody seemed to have a neighbour or a lazy cousin coming from the same village, who was caught wandering in the streets, taken by the police and immediately led to an employment office. Although much more inefficient than police action, visits paid by the union leaders and by the members of the local party organizations to workers' homes followed the same line, trying to convince them to come to work and to pressure them to become conscious productive subjects of the socialist state.

Third, the fact that, in state socialism, labour power was sold and bought as a commodity requires some specifications. On the one hand, labour power did enter the calculation of prices for every product manufactured in the factories, traded between economic units, or bought by people in commercial stores. On the other hand, the price of labour was fixed by the state. However, it was far from being homogeneous. There were significant differences in payment between heavy industry, light industry and trade cooperatives, deepened by a hierarchical distribution of incomes within each industrial branch. Both differences reflected the developmental logic underlying the economic priorities of socialist construction in a backward country, but in specific ways. Wage differences between industrial branches were an expression of the centrality of heavy industry for economic growth and socialist accumulation; however, the differences in wage categories corresponded to a ladder defined by the government and designed to encourage workers' skilling. Nevertheless, in most cases, the work was the same. Many of the workers whom I interviewed executed the same operation, on the same machine, for almost all their working life, but their wages went higher and higher as they moved up on the skill ladder. Financial gain represented an incentive for undergoing a process of self-transformation through education and skilling, which were supported by the state, ran through the factories, and were basically free for all workers. As such, professional education was part of the mechanisms of (re)producing labour power twice: first as free public service, and second as financial reward once completed. Seniority and stability were also recompensed financially, as a measure of workers' loyalty to the factory. Thus, wage differences in state socialism did not express a difference in the difficulty of the operation itself. It was not execution but labour power as a combination of the costs of its reproduction, skill and seniority that entered the production costs of the manufactured goods.

Fourth, as this chapter will show next, intense labour shortage, governmental employment regulations, and managerial coping strategies defined a historically specific labour market in which workers were 'more precious than gold',[29] and the competition for labour was fierce. One of its main characteristics was the disequilibrium between the demand for workers and their availability. The other was the fact that although the relationship between supply and demand did not determine the price of labour power like in the neoclassical model (does it ever?), it did influence the possibilities of earning more or less within local negotiations over wage categories. Further on, this localized competition and mobility of labour represented the space where people could imagine and pursue survival strategies, negotiate their worth, and acquire forms of rationality expressed in monetized forms.

'Fixing' Labour

Like in most European cities, unemployment plagued the city of Cluj during the first years after the war. Queueing for work at the gates of the largest industrial units in the city became a daily reality for thousands of people. With the collapse of war industry, factories lost their military contracts and it took them years to regain some of their prewar markets, sometimes just before being nationalized. Economic networks were broken, raw materials and industrial equipment were in short supply, and reorienting production towards civilian use required time and inexistent resources. Unemployment was aggravated by the return of soldiers, refugees and war prisoners, and by the large-scale population exchanges between Romania and Hungary.

The beginning of industrial expansion quickly reversed chronic unemployment. Already by 1947, the factories found themselves in short supply of labour. An out-of-control instability of the local workforce accompanied the endemic labour shortage. Hunger, lack of shelter and a generalized penury pushed people to accept any kind of work, but also quickly pushed them out of the factory gates with the loose hope for 'something better'. For the leaders of the Romanian Workers' Party, workers joining and then leaving the factories, sometimes in a matter of days or even hours, was a chaotic movement that carried with it dangers of sedition and sabotage. For the city administrators, labour instability meant health hazards, ethnic conflict, homelessness, and an unstoppable wave of criminality. For the factory managers, this unprecedented labour instability equated with a disaster. Production often stopped, calculations of labour costs were not reliable, and productivity plummeted; thus the postwar executives could feel the combined pressure of the Red Army officers, of the local party organizations and of the factory committees.

No matter how much pressure the ministries and the party organizations were going to exercise over the factory managers, labour fluctuation remained exceptionally high throughout the First Five-Year Plan.[30] Low wages and the chance to earn money in the private sector, or simply to return home to the countryside whenever they needed, continued to drive people away from the factories and to make them consider industrial employment as one among many possibilities to survive in a rapidly changing world. From this angle, the issue of employment appears as immediately connected to localized livelihood structures within and outside the factories, and it becomes an important key for a deeper understanding of people's survival strategies in early socialism.

From the beginning, the 'rational reallocation of the workforce' became a top priority for the newly installed government led by the communists.[31] In 1947, less than one year after the elections that marked the official change of the regime in Romania, the eighty-eight branches of the Central Commission for the Rational Reallocation of the Labour Force were founded as regional calculation centres, specialized in compiling statistics about the necessary and the available workforce at a given time. Their founding was preceded and followed by rounds of lay-offs, meant to reveal the hidden unemployment in the factories.

The suspicion that hidden unemployment plagued the Romanian factories was rooted not only in comparison with the prewar situation but also in relation to the Soviet experience of the 1920s, when growing unemployment coexisted with labour shortages due to the unequal distribution of industrial and construction projects all over the country. This ideal type of revolutionary chronology must have been important in the Romanian scenario for nationalization, so the Romanian party officials proceeded according to the concrete Soviet experience, and tried to 'guard the gates of the factories'[32] even if the need for workers was growing continuously. The Romanian government was forced to ignore the follow-up of the Soviet story, which continued with huge labour shortages in the next decades. They could also make little use of the parallel experience that accompanied the beginnings of the socialist industrialization in Hungary or in Poland.

The idea of 'hidden unemployment' was also rooted in the suspicion (often justified) that factory managers were hoarding labour and refusing to 'free' it for other industrial units that really needed it. Their justifications – that workers were getting sick, were joining the Army or were needed for large construction projects all over the country – were generally considered to be 'excuses' for avoiding the 'more rational solutions' that were 'surely available to them'.[33] Thus, most of the time, requests for more workers received a negative answer, like the one the factory managers from János Herbák read at the beginning of 1949 in a note from the Light Industry Ministry: 'The annual fund calculated for wages cannot be exceeded by any means in any industrial unit because this would lead to economic losses. We refuse to pay for any increase in production costs'.[34] However, the factory managers ended up employing people anyway, knowingly facing the anger of the higher echelons of the party and of the ministries.

By 1949, their stubbornness in ignoring government instructions became a nationwide issue and came to be extensively discussed in the party meetings. An entire conference was dedicated to *hozraschot*, the Soviet system of accounting that established enterprises as autonomous economic entities, with independent balance sheets, costs and benefits. The system of accounting was supposed to verify if economic life was governed according to the 'principle of thrifty economy' [*principiul gospodăriei chibzuite*] at the level of production unit. The cost of labour associated with manufacturing became one of the main concerns in the overall struggle for rationalizing industry.

The opening speech, later published in *Probleme economice* (Economic problems), started with complaints against the factory managers, who knowingly tried to push the limits of their privileges by employing more workers than they were allowed to.

> We still have cases when the leaders of an industrial unit estimate the production plan figures but forget to send us their financial plan. They employ more workers than they should, use more money for wages than approved and get into trouble. Then, they need new credit for continuing activity.
>
> Workers and technical staff are here today, there tomorrow, wandering from one place to another. Factories even steal people from each other. We have to allocate the labour force better. We need to put a stop to this instability – us, the party and the unions together. We also need to bind the workers to the factory by offering them incentives that are correlated with the production indices, so they don't feel like changing their workplace and disorganize everything all the time.[35]

This passage illustrates a whole range of problems that factories ran into for not being able to secure a stable workforce: productivity declined, financial production targets were not met, and their further functioning depended upon the allocation of more resources. It also points towards the fact that an illegal competition for workforce between the factories was emerging.

On the ground, while competition between enterprises for attracting labour force was legally prohibited and the upgrading of the existing labour force's skills on the shop floor was preferred, factory managers faced the other economic executives in a harsh unofficial labour market dominated by big players from heavy industry branches, who were overbidding for workers by offering them higher wages and access to housing. The records of the 1950 meetings of the Cluj Regional Committee – gathering all factory directors from the region – help us to map the consequences of this competition.[36] In his address, the prime secretary deplored the way the workers were 'stolen' from their workplaces and lured into other factories, and further advised the new economic executives:

> Labour fluctuation is not the problem of a single industrial unit. We need to work together constantly to keep our people. Comrades, we have these difficulties but we need to be careful not to use unjust methods like telling people to leave their workplace and join another industrial unit. These are not healthy methods! We need to follow the path of growing our own people if we need them. We have wonderful results at the Railways Workshops, where they manage to transform an unskilled worker into a specialist in six to eight months. All factories have to follow their lead. This is the best way to create cadres in all fields.[37]

He further complained that when outsiders were offered incentives to join a factory, more senior workers often felt their position was threatened and so left in order to get better advantages elsewhere.

However, against what the prime secretary wanted to convey, the example of the Railways Workshops was telling for the inequality of resources between industrial units. Being the largest factory in Cluj and belonging to a key heavy industry branch, the Workshops' workers were better paid and thus more interested in preserving their workplace. The factory benefited from an extended social infrastructure inherited from its interwar paternalist development. Most importantly, its workforce contained a core of experienced urban workers around whom a solid network of apprenticeship had been constituted. On its foundation in 1948, the largest professional school in town emerged.

In the following hours, the defensive speeches of the factory managers showed precisely that: stabilizing labour might have been a regional problem, but every factory faced it differently. At the Electrical Company, the workers were leaving en masse, and new workers refused to enter the factory gates because the company were not offering any possibility for piece-rate work. The labourers felt they could not control their earnings and, as a result, not even the unskilled workers wanted to work there. At János Herbák, there were almost five workers leaving the factory for every newly employed one. Locksmiths and turners were the first to leave because being employed in a footwear and leather factory they earned less than their comrades employed in heavy industry. So, they were often leaving the factory, sometimes even preferring to work far from home or to leave the city altogether for towns like Reșița or Brașov, where heavy industry was more developed than in Cluj. In an interview, the director of Armătura bitterly recounted how he met one of the six drivers who left the factory without notice, and learned they were leaving the factory to join the Danube–Black Sea Canal. The reason was simple: at the canal, they could earn as much as 40,000 lei a month, in a period when a skilled worker at his factory only made around 7,500 lei. Industria Sârmei, a large wire plant in a small city near Cluj, was one of the few to report a surplus of labour and no problems with raw materials, due to its access to an important pool of rural workers and local resources, and virtually no competition from other large industrial units in town.

At Breiner Bela, a small textile factory in Cluj with a preponderantly female workforce, the workers were quitting because they were being forced to work three shifts, although women were legally exempted from working late at night. To plea for the elimination of the night shift, the director invoked childcare and women's safety. However, he felt compelled to add that the night shift was 'first of all inefficient' because women's work was poor and productivity was lower. The consequences could have been dire as the factories supplied by Breiner Bela risked being left without the needed materials. This double logic – of care and efficiency – was going to dominate the requests for workers, or for the improvement of their lives, in the factories over the following years. It reflected the way in which labour faced the state simultaneously as a subject of care and protection and as a productive resource. The two would not be disentangled until the 1990s.

Legal measures to stabilize labour continued to flood industry for a number of years, but failed to become more than empty promises. For instance, in 1951, all factories in the country received governmental instructions for the implementation of a decree that specified regulations for employing, transferring and firing personnel.[38] The instructions emphasized the importance of the 'continuous strengthening of the socialist organization of labour' for the development of the national planned economy, and tied this organization with the 'conscious and freely consented discipline of the working people in the production process'.[39] The document also underlined the fact that 'conscious work discipline was the result of a process of educating and re-educating the masses who were now freed from exploitation'[40] and that this process would take a long time. Labour competitions, the 'patriotic initiative' for fulfilling the 1951 plan in eleven months, and the new wage system were rhetorically considered equal incentives for promoting a 'new attitude towards work'. The battle against those who had produced damages to the national economy through their acts of indiscipline – including absenteeism and fleeing to a better workplace – was proclaimed.

Positive measures against labour turnover were specified in the above-mentioned 1951 instructions: higher pensions for the workers who could demonstrate continuity at the same workplace, facilitated access to apartments and credit for housing, and an annual financial bonus awarded for continuity in certain industrial branches – coal, mining and non-ferrous metals.[41] Through a classical carrot/stick move, the instructions also emphasized the legal sanctions against those who left their workplace without the explicit approval of the factory director. Only health, pregnancy, childcare and the necessity to follow one's life partner to a different geographical location were considered 'justified reasons' to leave employment. Transferring people within the same industrial unit without governmental approval was also prohibited. Doctors 'who help[ed] the backward elements to skip work' or get transferred faced serious penalties, while the factory managers even faced the threat of imprisonment for a period of between three and twelve months if they facilitated an illegal transfer, or if they employed workers who left their previous job without written consent.

These measures seemed pointless. In the middle of the First Five-Year Plan, labour turnover was escalating everywhere. The 1953 reports from János Herbák were more than ever flooded by complaints, and even the representatives of the local party organization seemed hopeless when showing that enforcing discipline, especially with regard to labour fluctuation, was an impossible task. In August 1953, around 16 per cent of the workers at the leather and footwear factory missed work daily, and 7 per cent never justified their absence. A report showed that the factory had started the year with 3,880 industrial workers. During the year, they hired more than 900 workers but approximately 950 left the factory. Among those who left the factory, 19 per cent refused to renew their employment contract; around 3 per cent were cases of illness or disability; almost 11 per cent retired; around 45 per cent left the factory by request; almost 9 per cent left to continue their education; and 14 per cent were fired.[42]

The workers who resided in the countryside could not be convinced to see the factory as their primary workplace.[43] The factories sent their representatives out into further villages, trying to persuade peasants to work in Cluj to complement their income. But because many factories had already introduced the piece-rate system, the newcomers were not qualified for their work, they produced little and could not meet the planned quality standards.[44] Moreover, due to endemic shortages of raw materials, the workload was massed at the end of the month and the workers could see neither the logic of coming to work 'just to stare at the walls for days' nor the logic of working 16 hours a day at the end of the month for very low wages and no benefits. Even members of the agitpro started to complain that, when earning such low wages themselves, they 'could not convince anyone to come to work anymore'. Workers' consequent low earnings made them go back to the countryside or find activities that required less precision or dexterity. During the several severe bread crises that affected the city until the early 1950s, not only peasants but also urbanites left to work in the villages in exchange for wheat.

For party members, the mistake of skipping a work day was seen as a betrayal of their political goals. Comrade Oltean from the tannery at János Herbák was excluded from the party for missing work in order to sow some lease land in his home village, where he was also the secretary of the local organization. In a factory newspaper article, proletarian anger was directed against his 'attitude towards work discipline', which was 'intolerable'. The last line of the article was intended to plant the seed of mockery in the minds of his colleagues: 'Look how comrade Oltean understands the struggle for strengthening our popular democracy regime: being an employee of our factory, he helps the *chiabur* to gain fat'.[45]

The consequences of labour instability were more severe for newly opened factories like Tehnofrig, which did not benefit from a prewar core of skilled and stable workers like János Herbák or the Railways Workshops.[46] In its first years, Tehnofrig not only had to face the same problems as the other factories when it came to semi-proletarian and seasonal work but also got all the workers who were fired from other industrial units for political reasons or for severe indiscipline. As a result, Tehnofrig failed to fulfil its plan for 1953. When confronted with the possibility of being fired or directly accused of sabotaging the national economy, the exasperated outbursts of the factory director turned into aggression against the staff. They were sugar coated in the reports of the party organization as 'talking more energetically to the workers', but on the shop floor his attitude produced a wave of complaints that he was 'dictatorial and he distanced himself from the working class'.[47]

The impossibility to stabilize labour was also related to the difficulty of ensuring continuity in production because of raw material shortages, bad weather, broken industrial equipment, or bad coordination of the plan figures. The introduction of the piece-rate system and the successive renegotiation of norms almost everywhere in Cluj made life impossible for the workers during those months when the production stopped for days and they could earn nothing. Thus, heavy rain became fatal for the brick factory and lack of wood was lethal for the furniture factory. A shortage of copper was blamed for the workers' low earnings at Armătura, where manifestations of anger erupted all the time. In 1954, after the work norms had been raised and workers' real wages fell again, one of the factory managers declared:

> There are even manifestations of distrust in the measures taken by the government and by the party regarding the raising of the work norms. For instance, Comrade Kálmán, a communist, told us in the meeting that the party promised that workers' earnings won't be lowered, but they were. For more than a month he could not earn more than 380 lei. He cannot find food or clothing in the state commercial stores so he has to buy everything on the black market. The prices on the market are too high compared to the workers' earnings. He declared in front of everybody that he would leave the factory if the work norms were raised again. ... Then other people stood up to tell us they could not fulfil the plan because they didn't have raw materials to work with. Workers don't earn enough and prices go higher and higher all the time. For example, they cannot find shoes in those stores that sell consumer goods on ration books. But the shoes they find outside the system cost 400 lei, so no worker can buy a single pair of shoes from his salary.[48]

For the consumer goods industry, the situation was even worse. At János Herbák, severe shortages of raw materials stopped production for months in 1954, although the Light Industry Ministry had already planned for the factory to run at only 40 per cent of its capacity in order to avoid bottlenecks. The management could not ensure continuity in production, and needed to watch their workers waiting in vain for their wages and anxiously hoping to run through the factory gates. The consequences for workers were dear as the average wage fell from 375 lei in September 1953 to 230 lei in October 1954. But these averages expressed nothing of people's despair, especially during the winter months when production stagnated for almost 75,000 hours and 223 workers earned nothing. Because they could not leave the factory without written approval, 22 per cent of the workers missed their work for more than a month in February 1954, intentionally forcing the management to fire them and thus free them for jobs in other places.[49]

A special commission from the Central Committee of the Romanian Workers' Party came to Cluj and declared the situation at János Herbák an 'emergency'. As a result, the factory managers took the following measures: many workers were sent on unplanned vacation; some of the workers were temporarily transferred to other workshops at János Herbák, and some to other factories and cooperatives in the city; and some new models of footwear were introduced to absorb more of the workforce. But the main concern was to convince people not to leave the factory, as their close friends and neighbours who were working in other places were quick to report to their foremen about the difficulties of János Herbák. Through these kinship and friendship networks, many of the workers from János Herbák were persuaded to quit their factory and work somewhere else, in more advantageous situations.

As countless factory reports show, the situation failed to improve during the First Five-Year Plan, and actually deteriorated towards its end. The most important reason for this failure was the need to keep production costs and wages low. In a memoir regarding the impossibility of paying the workers in August 1954 at János Herbák, the circumstances surrounding labour turnover received a lengthy treatment. Analysing the causes of the truancies and the difficulty of hiring new workers, the leadership of the factory came to the following conclusions: (1) the differences between wage systems in various industrial branches and the decision not to improve the wage system for the leather and footwear sector led the workers to move towards those branches that had more advantageous wage systems; (2) the slow rhythm of agriculture's transformation compared to industrial development and growth did not free up as much manpower as was needed by the continuously expanding needs of the industry; and (3) some of the absentees were leaving the factory for seasonal and occasional work, especially in the private agricultural sector where they could earn 30–40 lei and food every day, while in the factory they could not earn more than 15 lei.[50]

The 'solution' – of a purely propagandistic nature – was also presented in detail:

> To strengthen discipline, the leaders of the factory, together with the party organization and supported by the factory committee, formed comradely collectives who visited the absentees at home. The collectives tried to explain to the workers how wrong their attitude was, telling them how many difficulties they were causing in production – bottlenecks, low productivity and, finally, falling earnings for all the others. However, since the absentees were found at home doing various kinds of work that provide a much higher income than their factory wage, our actions were useless.[51]

Useless as these actions were, the grim images painted by the pleas of the 'comradely collectives' were true, as the same memoir shows. The wages in the leather footwear industry failed to attract workers in the factories and mobilize them. Almost 50 per cent of the workers at János Herbák were included in the lowest three categories of payment, earning between 176.80 and 210.40 lei. Even the good workers from these categories, who exceeded their norms by 50 per cent, still earned less than 300 lei monthly and were tempted to leave the factory for a few days, just to earn money somewhere else.

But the truancies had a devastating domino effect in the factory, leading to more and more unaccounted absences daily. In the memoir it was presented in a sequential manner, almost like in a movie.

> In the beginning, those who were unjustifiably missing work belonged to the first and the second wage categories. Because they were missing all the time, we needed to reorganize the existing workers to ensure the continuity of the production process. The regrouped workers, not having the skills to execute all these operations, earned very little, so they did not come to work anymore. This induced irregularities in the rhythms of production and the plan was not fulfilled. The income of the workers from the fourth and the fifth categories fell. Consequently, the key workers, the highly skilled ones, started to have many absences, provoking more and more bottlenecks and leaving the workers from the next operations without work.[52]

Because of these problems, the plan for August 1954 was not fulfilled. As shown by the memoir, the income of the piece-rate workers drastically dropped, which affected the political atmosphere in the factory strongly enough to pressure the Ministry of Labour to intervene on behalf of the workers. The ones who worked for a fixed salary were soon paid, after the government had issued a derogation from the law, admitting that the factory had not been to blame for the situation created.[53]

The administrative staff and the foremen – who were paid according to the percentage of the plan fulfilled during the previous month – bore the sanctions and saw their earnings cut almost by half, although the factory managers tried hard to place the blame for their failure outside their industrial unit. They argued that the sanction was not deserved since the administrative staff actually worked more during those months when the plan was not fulfilled, as the factory had to send innumerable extra reports and memoirs for justifying the 'catastrophe'.

The most serious problem was posed by the foremen, who threatened to leave the factory en masse if their salaries, including the overtime, were not paid. The memoir pleaded their case, describing how in the summer months, when workers' absences sky rocketed, the foremen were the ones keeping the factory alive: 'The foremen started to execute multiple operations in place of their key workers. They moved frantically from one machine to another, staying extra hours in order to prevent the complete stopping of production. Some of them executed more than two norms every day'.[54] Since their requests to leave the factory was not approved, the foremen requested to go back into production as skilled workers, in those workplaces where their dexterity and their will to work two norms in a day would pay off.

Like in Hungary or Poland, foremen were key workers who found themselves a world apart from the peripheral ones. They were recruited from the most loyal workers with 15–20 years' experience in production, and were known by the factory leadership to be responsible and reliable. Although they earned less than many of their most skilled workers, and complained endlessly about it, foremen were generally still willing to get their job done. Although harshly exploited during the first years of planning, later in the 1950s the foremen re-emerged as a labour aristocracy, as the possibility of losing them for other factories and the knowledge that no good worker would wish to become a foreman in these conditions put management in an impossible situation. This conjuncture placed the foremen in better positions to bargain their way to a better life, sometimes at the expense of other categories – especially the unskilled, the inexperienced, and, often, the women.[55]

Far from becoming more controlled, the competition for hiring more workers (and the best ones) exploded in 1955, at the end of the First Five-Year Plan. In a plenary meeting of the City Committee, Comrade Szekely, director of János Herbák, presented the problems of his factory:

> I don't know how the problem of discipline is solved in other places, but if we had the discipline we had two or three years ago, we could produce 10–15 per cent more. Two years ago, 15 to 20 workers were missing work daily. Today, 150 are missing. They are using this tactic to get fired in order to find work somewhere else, because legally we cannot sign their transfer. At the soles factory the situation is dear. We need workers but we cannot transfer people from other workshops because they simply don't want to go, saying that they would be better off not coming to work the next day than to work there. And it is not only about the money, it's the working conditions, too. I demand that other factory directors promise nothing to our workers! They are learning their skills in our factory and then leave us to earn more somewhere else![56]

Since increasing wages was not in his power, Szekely proposed the building of a new hospital for the industrial plant and other infrastructural improvements, so the workers would appreciate their workplace more positively, even if their wages were low. His requests were accepted in principle, but the Light Industry Ministry failed to introduce the financing of these projects in the investment plan for another four years.

Although inequalities between heavy and light industry were significant, differences in payment were not confined to those between economic sectors. There were huge disparities between the local cooperative production and state industry regarding the wages, the technological process and the working conditions. One of the party ethnographers who spent a few days at the small textile factories of Centrocoop reported in a 1955 note:

> The workers from the textile factory Victoria Cluj are unhappy with the fact that the wages situations was not solved. Their wages are extremely low, their equipment rudimentary, and still they produce the same goods and have the same work norms as at Varga Katalin, which is part of the Light Industry Ministry. Varga Katalin has better machines and the women there earn around 500 lei, or even more. ... This is why there was a large fluctuation of workers at Victoria Cluj. For instance, in 1954, 140 of our 240 workers left the factory only 3–4 weeks after they were employed. This turnover compromised the plan because the newcomers had to be initiated in their tasks, hence they were not efficient.
>
> For instance, while we were there, Vincze Gizella requested a raise in her wage because she doesn't have money to feed her child. Her income is simply not enough for buying bread and milk. She does not have the strength to work anymore because she is malnourished. Other women told me the same thing: they cannot work because they don't eat enough.
>
> They also complained that the director shows contempt to them when they complain about money or about problems with their children. He also ignores them when they recount how they are attacked by depraved men in the street at night because the factory does not want to solve the illumination problem.
>
> If things continue like this, the cooperative will dissolve soon.[57]

The fact that many of those working in the cooperative system were women did not help their situation. Although the regime proclaimed equality between men and women, the experience of the postwar generation was going to be quite different from the official discourse.

Until late in the 1950s, reports about sarcastic responses from the factory directors when presented with 'womanly' issues were common. This included requests for employment, for pay raises, and for exemption from working at night. As we saw, transferring people from one workshop to another was a handy solution for many problematic situations. Minutes of the factory committee meetings at Armătura, the Railways Workshops and Varga Katalin show that, following open expressions of discontent from the workers over low wages, women were asked to occupy the worst-paid positions because they were not the heads of their families, or because, as young unmarried girls, they did not have to support their children. Generally, the economic executives did not go as far as forcing them to move to these workplaces but rather tried to persuade them by presenting the new workplace as 'safer' or 'easier'. If forced transfers happened, they were not visible in the reports for the local party committees.

Not all women had a weaker negotiating power compared to that of men. The field of battle for labour was obviously gendered, but it was highly differentiated. The position of the women who worked at János Herbák, for instance, could not be compared to the position of the women who worked in the same industrial branch but in cooperatives or in smaller industrial units. Larger factories like Armătura, Carbochim, the Railways Workshops and János Herbák often employed families, with husbands and wives working together, sometimes even in the same workshop. People who brought their spouses into the factories were more likely to be part of the skilled and stable workers in the factory. So, although not directly readable in the reports, their requests probably weighted more than those of others.

'No Factory Ever Went Bankrupt Because of a Sledge': Some (Not So) Ethical Dilemmas around Stealing and Everyday Life

As the previous section showed, early socialism was marked by high instability in the labour force, which produced labour shortages, bottlenecks, and great difficulties in controlling the factory space. For a long time, government officials continued to complain in vain about how many workers were being employed without the factories having the means to pay them. However, their complaints proved futile and had the appearance of a rhetorical artifice. Factories needed to function, so their leaders were in fact allowed to use a wide range of informal practices in order to secure the production flow. These informal practices opened a space in which a rough competition for workers produced localized and contradictory labour markets, within a field of forces dominated by the permanent failure to stabilize and discipline labour.

When analysing factory documents and political speeches in the 1950s, one can easily see that factory (in)discipline was not a unified field of battle for the party. At the most general level, stealing, truancies, fighting, drinking and producing poor quality work were all understood as the outcome of a temporary failure in the historical process of controlling labour. But some acts of indiscipline bore very different sanctions, had very different political consequences and produced different alliances and fractures in socialist factories. There was a clear demarcation between stealing and other misdemeanours, and a further emphasis on misbehaviour that hindered productivity. And there was a further distinction between those acts that stopped production and those that did not. As they were simultaneously played against notions of politics, legality, and everyday life, these separations were never easy to achieve in practice.

Because it was possible to be legally framed as 'sabotage' or 'acting against the national economy', serious theft from the workplace was understood immediately as a form of political action. Years in prison, forced labour or even death followed. Stealing was not the only misdemeanour that stood on this slippery legal and political terrain. Serious accidents or the deterioration of the industrial equipment could easily be framed as 'conspiracy against the security of the Romanian Popular Republic', treason or 'working for the enemy'. After 1949, all these acts carried the punishment of death. Failing to denounce these criminal acts was indictable and it could lead to five to ten years of forced labour.[58] Moreover, things as different as accidental fires, stealing, destruction, technical mistakes, failing to direct production as set by the plan, or 'instigating the workers to issue *unjust* claims' came to be labelled as 'sabotage' when the party needed a scapegoat.[59]

The special place stealing and sabotage had in the disciplinary and legal logic of the state was manifest in how the sanctions against them were communicated within the factory space. In Cluj, circular letters coming from the Central Committee of the Romanian Workers' Party or from the ministries repeatedly emphasized the harsh penalties that stealing and sabotage brought with them.[60] These letters needed to be posted in every corner in order to be 'understood and absorbed' by the workers. At János Herbák, lunch was an especially preferred time for reading them aloud, not only because all the workers were together but also because relating these announcements to biological functions like eating transformed fear into a bodily experience. As a measure of prevention, the potential consequences became literally inscribed on their bodies. But playing the threat card was never easy, as the atmosphere surrounding the implementation of the death penalty for economic offences that could be considered 'sabotage' reveals.

A report of the Cluj County Committee for January 1949 shows that the newly introduced death penalty not only produced 'fear and conformity' but also made people angry. They got to frame legal situations in unexpected ways, quite far from what the party wanted or anticipated. While fear and distrust might have been important for breaking shop-floor solidarities, they also needed to be controlled, so as not to become disruptive for production politics in the factory.[61]

> The Reaction tried to use all the laws passed by the National Assembly against the party and against the regime. They used the death penalty against us and told people that it was strange to introduce this law exactly when it was being abolished in the United States. They tried to show that this law would be used against any workers who made even small mistakes in their work. At the

> Railways Workshops, the party organization did not do a good job in explaining the new laws to the workers. The factory management got instructions from the court of law, and the party did not even know. After we had been onto the shop floor to explain things again, the political mood got better. But there is also a rumour that we introduced the death penalty because the war is coming.[62]

Workers tended to link the introduction of the death penalty with their experience of the shop floor during the war. The fact that the factory disciplinary regime could easily slide into the legal one, and that socialist legality bore uncanny resemblances to the war juridical restrictions, made workers uncomfortable, fearful and avoidant of party politics for months.

Their fears were not ungrounded, as discursive lines were hard to draw between 'small mistakes' and acts that could be framed as 'reactionary' or 'endangering socialist economy'. In general, stealing and sabotage (or accidents framed as sabotage) brought with them truly severe sanctions only when they stopped production. Some missing leather, a few nails or an accident in the foundry could quite easily be hidden and overlooked by the factory management if production had not been directly or immediately affected. If production did stop, the party organization in the factory was the first to know.

Nonetheless, the way its members acted upon this information was not homogeneous, and it quickly became a problem for the higher bureaucratic echelons. Many times, the party organization acted as expected and immediately communicated the issue at hand to the Economic Section of the Regional Party Committee. But towards the end of the second One-Year Plan, alliances between factory managers, members of the factory committees and party hierarchy were exposed more and more as being the source of most of the factory's problems under the label of 'familialism'. For instance, a 1950 report on the activity of János Herbák showed how the secretary of the party organization and the secretary of the factory committees (two brothers) 'do not use the critique against the factory director but rather hide each other's mistakes'.[63] Anti-stealing and anti-sabotage campaigns thus became instrumental in breaking cross-hierarchical forms of solidarity within the factory.

This was the overture of an ongoing struggle against thefts that the party initiated in the factories, which culminated with a huge national anti-stealing campaign in 1952, and was connected to a new monetary reform and to a new wave of internal purges. In this context, the 1952 campaign was instrumental in creating fear and distrust, and weakening the social fabric in the factories and in the villages. The disappearance of employees accused of stealing and sabotage, who were imprisoned or executed, were followed by the appearance of new ones – people coming from other parts of the country or employees who were known to be loyal to the party. The anti-stealing campaign was also important for purifying the system of various politically untrustworthy 'elements', effectively accompanying the most radical purges of the Romanian Workers' Party.

Although they involved both legal and propagandistic actions, the anti-stealing campaigns were not a success story. Against the party's efforts and higher prosecution numbers, thefts multiplied every year and it was not long after the end of the First Five-Year Plan that everybody could see that the battle against stealing had been lost. Thus, at the end of the First Five-Year Plan, the failure to limit the number of thefts led to the introduction of a new law which (following a Soviet model) reframed stealing as 'violation of public property'. But instituting harsher penalties, heavy fines and increased jail time also proved incapable of stopping this endemic phenomenon. According to Bottoni's figures, between 1957 and 1959 alone, 150,000 people were caught stealing – and numbers went even higher after 1960.[64]

If the anti-stealing rhetoric and legal measures were such failures in moral and juridical terms, one might wonder why the party continued to emphasize them so much for years to come. Why, or rather when, was the act of stealing really problematic for the newly nationalized factories? As this section has shown so far, the anti-stealing discourse was crucial throughout the nationalization of the means of production and the implementation of planning after 1948, not only because thefts abused state property but also because they were painful indicators of the state's lack of control over the shop floor. Thus, anti-stealing campaigns became essential for drawing not-so-clear boundaries within the factory space between repression, discipline and the rule of law, and for communicating to workers and factory managers alike that they were continuously being watched and assessed.

It is my interpretation that the anti-stealing campaigns, both legal and political, were even more importantly related to the efforts of the new economic executives to create a socialist regime of efficiency in which the continuity of the production process was central. As the factory documents show, the most important line of demarcation for deciding if a theft was serious or not was production stoppage. From this perspective, the anti-stealing battle became part of a broader endeavour to create permanent and continuous movement on the shop floor, and to ensure the circulation of commodities. Planning and accumulation depended on that.

At an even more basic level, stealing had become an intrinsic part of the social fabric of the city. In the factory, this translated into an implicit acknowledgement of the fact that workers would steal to live, and the factory would become an extension of their survival space. Thus, instead of operating with straightforward legal or categorical distinctions, the new economic executives dealt with rather practical separations, like those between small and large thefts, or between stealing for personal consumption and stealing for profit.

While more serious acts of stealing were punished by imprisonment, forced labour or death, the fight against small generalized theft was mostly discursive. Small thefts – like the ones of the protection equipment that people wore at home or sold on at the Sunday fairs – were generally noticed only in passing, as a problem of people still lacking 'the advanced consciousness of the proletariat'.[65] Sometimes, financial sanctions or a request to cover the cost of the stolen goods followed. However, most of the time face-to-face meetings with members of the local party organization, factory disciplinary commissions, or newspaper articles were used to convince people that because industrial units were state property and the socialist state was a workers' state, they were not stealing from the factory but from themselves.

As David Ost showed for the Polish case, this impossibility to escape a position of interiority within a self-declared workers' state had definitive consequences for how the workers could imagine and frame their claims, and for how the state could respond to them.[66] For the workers, it meant to be unwilfully made part of the same structures of power that exploited them. What was central to the functioning of the socialist states was their need to permanently (re)create a double bond between power structures and the people, both as *workers* and as *political subjects* within the factory space. Although the modernization project animating the socialist project from the beginning was theoretically founded on the necessary collapse of the boundary between production politics and state politics,[67] the direct double determination of its subjects made the socialist state strong and vulnerable at the same time.

Supposedly, workers themselves manipulated the idea of collective ownership of the factories to fight against the harsh sanctions of the management and of the party when caught stealing. A legend started to circulate in Cluj in the 1950s about a man who stole a piece of equipment to use it at home. He was caught by the guards, and a few weeks later he was brought in front of the disciplinary commission of his factory. When accused of stealing, he denied the theft by saying: 'I did not steal anything. Everything is the property of the people. The factory is ours'. Supposedly, the members of the disciplinary commission were baffled and could not say a word. No sanctions were issued against the worker. Depending on the person interviewed, the worker was from Tehnofrig, from János Herbák, from Carbochim, or even from CUG – an enterprise that opened only in the 1970s. The hero of the story was always a man and, depending on the age of the workers interviewed, he was a member of the 1950s or the 1960s generation. But the recurrent story was surprisingly similar, and all my interviewees ended it with a clever smile on their faces, which showed much pride for 'their' fellow's deeds. His cunning, real or not, still produced satisfaction for turning the logic of the state upside down.

Of course, stealing was often framed not as an administrative or even as a legal problem, but as a political and moral issue pertaining to the domain of the 'proletarian ethics' and 'proletarian morals'. And this framing was directed precisely towards the rowdy and fluid rural–urban population that the factories needed to rely on. The moral effects of employing temporary workers were often brought forward at the party meetings. The party activists from the Cluj Regional Committee and government officials often asserted that besides breaking the law when employing temporary workers, the factory managers risked introducing 'unknown and unhealthy elements', who created disciplinary problems.

At first glance, the reports from the factories seemed to confirm the relationship between temporariness and problematic behaviour. They emphasized the tendency of the temporary workers to do poorly at work, to sleep during the night shifts and to walk away the minute they did not like something.[68] They were perceived as a risk for the security of the factory, and many unsolved thefts were considered to be their deeds. But again, it is hard to assess if there was indeed a difference between temporary and permanent workers' practices when in the same report we find complaints that the thefts had become generalized, and even security guards and firemen were being caught stealing. Most probably, discipline in this context was just a rhetorical artifice meant to establish geographical fixity, permanent work and the feeling of belonging to a factory as desirable, yet wandering around as a social danger.

A synthetic look at the factory reports shows that workers were rarely fired for indiscipline, even if the law required the termination of their employment. The 1950 Labour Code itself specified very lax provisions for discipline. Article 20 stipulated that the individual work contract could be terminated if the employee did not exercise his or her duty for one month without a good reason. Women could be fired if they failed to return to work for more than three months after their maternity leave had ended. All employees could be laid-off if they were unable to exercise their duties for more than three months for medical reasons or if they were incarcerated for more than two months. Any penal sanction related directly to their work or to their activity in the factory could be sanctioned by terminating their employment, but the precise conditions under which this could happened were left open.

My interviews with two former factory managers at Armătura confirmed that, for decades, the directors of the industrial plants in Cluj had faced a lot of pressure when considering firing someone. First, labour shortages made them aware of the low probability that they would find a better worker than the one they were firing. Second, an understanding and tolerant factory director was an important bidding element in the competition for attracting workers. Third, the party explicitly demanded that the new economic executives kept workers happy, even if this meant placing the responsibility for workers' mistakes on someone else. Fourth, the party organizations and the unions often exercised their right to influence management decisions; they were most of the time against harsh penalties in order to ensure party popularity among the workers.

So, instead of being fired, workers were typically moved around. It was certainly easier for a director to justify this solution than a decision to fire a worker; so transfers under false reasons, within the same industrial unit or between factories, were the preferred way to deal with problematic situations. Since drawing the line between a disciplinary transfer and a regular work transfer was difficult, employees who faced transfer as a sanction benefited from the same rights as the others, and even received an allowance to help them with travel and moving expenses.[69]

'Everybody should earn a bread' was a leitmotif in the interviews I conducted a few decades later, which confirm the emergence of the 'director' (*directorul*) as an embodiment of paternalistic care for the labourers. This embodiment functioned both as self-identification, and as part of workers' imaginary. The factory managers of the 1950s I interviewed always talked about 'their' workers when referring to the factory's productive employees. For the workers of some factories in the city, summoning the figure of the director triggered respect and even tenderness. In some scenarios, *directorul* functioned as a condensation of power, respectability and care, sometimes expressed in a semi-eroticized language. In many interviews, female workers from Armătura remember the long-term successful factory manager as 'always respectful', 'always greeting every woman on the shop floor and on the corridor', 'always wanting to see things with his own eyes', 'taking care of everything', 'taking care of everybody', and being 'such a beautiful man, walking through the factory in his white suit, like a French actor'.

Former factory directors and several workers told me during the interviews that the preferred strategy for dealing with slackers or with people who could not do their job properly was finding a new workplace for them, where 'they could be useful', or at least 'not hamper others' activities'. Former managers interpreted this strategy as a form of caring for 'their people' and of ensuring their well-being, even when workers proved incapable of doing so themselves. The workers agreed in some cases, like Armătura or Carbochim, but strongly mocked the idea of management 'caring' for them in factories like Tehnofrig.

Transforming a moralizing rhetoric into a set of practices and rules about workers' conduct was going to be an almost impossible historical mission, and factory directors were about to learn that the transformation of the capitalist industrial units in 'socialist' ones required them to adhere to a very specific vision of the factory as a management object. The newly appointed managers knew very well that nothing happened solely on the shop floor. Piece-rate, socialist competitions, Stakhanovism, or wage categories made no sense outside a relational field in which the transformation of iron into ploughs or of leather into shoes also required the transformation of human hearts and minds. As new people flooded through the gates, it became impossible to imagine the factories as bounded isolated objects. Their porous and transparent walls made poor boundaries for a space that needed to be defined and regulated, but nobody could actually say where it started, where it ended, or who participated in it. And what to do with those bones, muscles and blood, with those needs and hopes that emerged 'outside' the factory but were actually incorporated in every nail, in every piece of silk and in every book that was produced on the shop floor?

Thus, many factory managers articulated a very different moral stance towards workers' thefts and refused to take for granted the delineation between 'factory's interests' and people's lives. Their 'working-class solidarity' and their 'mistaken notion of being sympathetic to the workers' went much further than the party wanted, and a new difference between 'stealing' and 'eating from one's workplace' became the expression of the emerging informal arrangements between industrial employment and workers' reproduction.

These limits of the struggle against everyday thefts were made clear to me in an interview with a former factory director at Armătura:

> Nobody wanted to upset the workers. The party was always there to watch us. Sometimes the party organization took our side, but generally they supported the workers because, you know ... the whole thing with 'the working class' [he laughs and then stays silent for a while]. Actually, I think we also understood people from our factory well. They were poor, uneducated, and they worked a lot in very hard conditions. It was not a problem for us when they took two faucets to use them at home. The factory had given them credit for buying the land for those houses anyway. We just closed our eyes and left them alone. In other factories they were controlled at the door all the time.

But maybe this was later, I don't remember when [he pauses again]. Yes, we knew they were stealing some materials but we did not care too much. It was not a big loss at such a quantity. You cannot imagine, there were mountains of iron pieces in the factory yard! Mountains! And anyway, what would you say to a worker who achieves his norm in these harsh conditions and at the end of the shift makes a sledge for his little girl with the factory's materials? What would *you* say?

Asking this, he looked at me as his question was not rhetorical but one that required a concrete answer to a real moral dilemma. I tried to refrain from having a personal opinion, and discussed the fact that after 1989 everybody talked about theft as a generalized phenomenon in socialist factories. Asked what he believed about the postsocialist discourse, he shrugged his shoulders. He stood silent again for a while, then spoke softly: 'No factory ever went bankrupt because of a sledge'.

Notes

1. *Lupta de clasă* [*Class Struggle*], Seria a V-a, June 1949, 95. *Class Struggle* was the most important programmatic journal of the time.
2. Kalb, *Expanding Class*. See also Warde, 'Industrial Restructuring'. For how geographies of accumulation are also always geographies of social reproduction, see Meehan and Strauss, *Precarious Worlds*. For a discussion about the necessity to factor East Central European experiences in the historical practice, see Bucur et al., 'Six Historians'.
3. Lüdtke, 'Introduction: What Is the History of Everyday Life?'; Lüdtke and Templer, 'Polymorphous Synchrony'. For an anthropological perspective on the relationship between class and Lüdtke's concept, see Sider, *Culture and Class*; Kalb, 'Frameworks'.
4. For a congruent interpretation, see Eley, 'Labor History'.
5. Preobrazhensky, *The New Economics*.
6. For the best account to date on the relationship between war regulation of factory life, postwar scarcity, and the struggles of labour in Romania, see Grama, 'Laboring Along'.
7. Reforma Monetara, Legea nr. 287, M.O. nr. 187, 16 August 1947.
8. ANDC, Fund Clujana, 0/1949, 14.
9. Decision 4.322/1947, Ministry of Industry and Trade.
10. The Romanians had already been acquainted with austerity measures, wage cuts, a falling living standard, and the experience of inflation. The consequences of the Great Depression had dramatically affected the everyday lives of the Romanian people. In 1933, the general index of the nominal wage represented only 63 per cent of its 1929 value. Between 1930 and 1934, the wages of the state employees underwent several rounds of significant cuts, called 'sacrifice curves'.
11. *Scânteia*, 5 September 1947, no. 914, 'Perspective după stabilizare' [Perspectives after stabilization].
12. Modified by Decree 118 in 1949 and again in 1953. A new wage system would be implemented in 1957.
13. There were explicit attempts to theorize this relationship at the time, like in Lascu, *Minimum de existență*. The impact of this monetarization on the accounting system of the factories was also analysed; see Boc, *Întreprinderea și contabilul*.

14. Vasile, *Politicile culturale comuniste*.
15. HU OSA 300-60-1, 300 RFE/RL 60 Romanian Unit, Box 410. Of course, much of the decrease in workers' real wages was due to war and the postwar situation. However, during the First Five-Year Plan, they continued to drop. While in 1951 they were at 76 per cent of the 1938 level, in 1955 they were only at 67 per cent.
16. Thomas, 'Les travailleurs roumains'.
17. The weekly subsistence basket contained various quantities of bread, flour, potatoes, sugar, beef, milk, eggs, butter and other fats.
18. Law 308, MO 115, no. 200, 1 September 1947.
19. Bindea, 'Conditiunile de munca', 8.
20. The 1953 modifications favoured the consumer goods industry more than the 1947 and 1949 legal stipulations. Generally, this is interpreted as part of the regional 'new course' after Stalin's death, and as a reaction to the workers' protests, especially in East Germany. However, in the Romanian case, the 'new course' was rather mimicked and had a specific character, which for space reasons cannot be discussed here.
21. Thomas, 'Les travailleurs roumains'.
22. Lampland, *The Object of Labor*, and Lampland, *The Value of Labor*.
23. Marx, *Capital*.
24. Ibid., 271.
25. Ibid., 274.
26. Ibid., 280.
27. MO 12 July 1947.
28. Employment offices were not new to the Romanian factories. To prevent unemployment and to solve the problem of the allocation of labour in a more efficient manner, the Law for the Organization of Labour Placement was issued in 1921, followed by the founding of the 'Placement Offices' in 1922. The measure had as much to do with industrial employment as with the national problem and with the effort to form a Romanian workforce in the cities. Before the First World War, the Old Kingdom was an immigration country where 'things went so far with using foreign labourers that the popular language was changed and people used to say "German" instead of "mechanic", "German woman" instead of "governess", "Serbian" or "Bulgarian" instead of "gardener", and "Hungarian" instead of "servant"' (Ministry of Labour 1940: 197). The ministry synthesized the problem: 'A disorganized movement of the manpower from one part of the country to another followed traditional routes and was complemented by the waves of foreign labourers who always found the borders open. This was the "organization" of employment in Romania. The results of this 'organization' was that the foreign workers earned a gratifying living by occupying the best-paid jobs, while the Romanian workers had to live a modest life' (Ibid.: 178).
29. The expression was used by a factory manager I interviewed, when explaining why he could not fire workers for disciplinary reasons.
30. Actually, as my interviews with factory managers and personnel officers from the factories show, labour fluctuation was going to remain endemic in the 1970s and 1980s.
31. ANDC, Fund 55, CO P.M.R. Cluj, 1/1951.
32. Goldman, *Women at the Gates*.
33. ANDC, Fund Clujana, 24/23/1950.
34. ANDC, Fund Clujana, 33/41/1949, 93.
35. Conferinta Vasile Luca, 'Despre Organizarea Întreprinderilor de Stat pe Baza Gospodăriei Chibzuite' [About the organization of state enterprises according to the principle of the thrifty household], *Probleme economice* (November 1949), 1–19.
36. ANDC, Fund 13, CR P.M.R. Cluj, 8/1950.
37. ANDC, Fund 13, CR P.M.R. Cluj, 8/1950, 152.
38. Decree 207/1951.

39. ANDC, Fund 13, CR P.M.R. Cluj, 27/1951, 105–10.
40. ANDC, Fund 13, CR P.M.R. Cluj, 27/1951, 105.
41. ANDC, Fund 13, CR P.M.R. Cluj, 27/1951.
42. ANDC, Fund Clujana, 14-28/1955.
43. ANDC, Fund 55, P.M.R. Cluj, 3/1953.
44. ANDC, Fund Clujana, 31-18/1953.
45. ANDC, Fund Clujana, 31-18/1953.
46. ANDC, Fund 13, CR P.M.R. Cluj, 132/1954, 32.
47. ANDC, Fund 13, CR P.M.R. Cluj, 132/1954.
48. ANDC Fund 55, CO P.M.R. Cluj, 374–76.
49. ANDC Fund 55, CO P.M.R. Cluj, 246.
50. ANDC Fund 55, CO P.M.R. Cluj, 20 September 1954, 59.
51. ANDC Fund 55, CO P.M.R. Cluj, 20 September 1954.
52. Ibid.
53. Derogation from art. 5 of H.C.M. 1156/1954.
54. ANDC Fund 55, CO P.M.R. Cluj, 20 September 1954, 59.
55. For a comparative perspective on the role of foremen in establishing authority in the West European factories, see Eeckhout, *Supervision and Authority*.
56. ANDC, Fund 55, CO P.M.R. Cluj, 1/1954, 269–70.
57. ANDC, Fund 13, CO P.M.R. Cluj, 230/1955, 150.
58. Law 16/1949 introduced the death penalty for crimes against the state's security and against the national economy.
59. ANDC, Fund Clujana, 33/105/1949.
60. ANDC, Fund Clujana 0/1949.
61. ANDC, Fund 3, CJ P.M.R. Cluj, 103/7, 1–16.
62. ANDC, Fund Clujana, 33/105/1949, 3.
63. ANDC, Fund Clujana, 33/105/1949.
64. Bottoni, 'A sztálini "Kis Magyarország" megalakítása'.
65. ANDC, Fund 55, CO P.M.R. Cluj, 1/1951.
66. Ost, *Solidarity*.
67. Burawoy, *The Politics of Production*.
68. ANDC, Fund Clujana, 24/23/1950.
69. Ibid.

CHAPTER 3

'Workers', 'Proletarians' and the Struggle for Cheap Labour

Accumulation Rhythms and the Labour Regime of Early Socialism

The transformation of social relations on which primitive socialist accumulation rested restructured not only industrial life but also the countryside. Like in the Soviet Union in the late 1920s, the Romanian collectivization of land was loudly announced as a solution for multiple problems: the dismantling of capitalist exploitative relations in the villages; the escape of Romanian agriculture from backwardness; the modernization of rural communities; and the release of some labour force, necessary for the expanding state industries. Scholars of Romanian socialism addressed these transformations by showing how the relationship between industry and agriculture produced an ever-increasing population of 'workers', which grew steadily and transfigured the landscape of labour.[1]

This chapter will challenge the categories behind these numbers and will show that at a closer look, what statistics simply mention as 'workers' becomes an uneasy conglomerate of people from different class backgrounds, from different places and with different ways to understand their belonging to the factory. Mapping the workforce of the early socialist factories in Cluj reveals an intricate tapestry of employment forms and corresponding logics of using wage labour in everyday life. A core of experienced urban workers – mainly Hungarian – shared the shop floor not only with newcomers in the city, but also with commuters and temporary labourers – mostly young Romanian men and women from nearby villages and from the outskirts of the city, teenagers brought in for summer work by their parents, army soldiers, former prostitutes, intellectuals of the old regime and prison inmates.

My findings join the rich literature on socialist urbanization, which has convincingly shown that it was not 'the proletarian' but rather the peasant-worker who sustained accumulation in early socialist factories.[2] Like in other East Central European countries, Romanian industrialization was accompanied by the phenomenon of under-urbanization, which means that 'the growth of the population falls behind the growth of urban industrial and tertiary sector jobs',[3] and the infrastructural investment remains low in comparison to industry. Under-urbanization has been regarded as a characteristic feature of socialist urban transition, which distinguished East Central European industrialization from other semiperipheral developmental efforts.

This chapter offers a new reading of the daily presence of 'double dwellers' and of 'urban villagers' in the Romanian socialist factories, in which the imbalance between industrial development and urban growth represents a top-down, strategic delay in the process of urbanization. In what follows, I explore the encounter between a top-down strategy for industrializing an agrarian country by keeping labour cheap, and people's own rethinking of their lives, worth and opportunities. Starting from the truism that early Romanian industrialization lacked proletarians, I raise two questions about the relationship between state-organized production and people's own struggles for survival. Who were the employees of the early socialist factories in cities like Cluj? And, what forms did their employment take? In other words, to whom did the arms that built socialism belong?

In her analysis of urban transformation in Budapest, Judit Bodnar has already noted that double dwelling can be imagined as a 'highly flexible multiple-source income-earning strategy' or as 'a powerful element in combined survival strategies'.[4] This also holds true for the case of Cluj and its hinterlands. A better understanding of the place of wage labour in a broader economy of subsistence shows that the basic categories of rule of early socialist regimes – 'worker' and 'proletarian' – could hardly be recognized as such on the ground. My findings directly confront the practice of taking for granted these central tropes, which are here questioned as conceptual abstractions that had little to do with local economic or social realities.

Accordingly, I set myself a straightforward task: to analyse how industrial work structured the field of biographical possibilities for the generation of people entering the factory gates at the end of the 1940s and during the First Five-Year Plan in Cluj. I argue that while the newly nationalized factories were confronted with a severe labour shortage, the state strategically postponed proletarianization by relying instead on a particular rural–urban fabric, which produced various forms of labour: wage labour, forced labour and temporary or seasonal labour. Preobrazhensky's strategy of 'starving of the rural household' was adopted within limits, so peasants would be motivated enough to complement their income through industrial employment, but not necessarily driven to despair and leave the village en masse in search for a better life in the city. This way, the price of labour could be kept low, and a flexible workforce could be used according to the necessities of the industrial units.[5]

The functioning of the industrial centres on which early socialist accumulation rested was completely dependent upon an increasing availability of labour. However, although socialist industry did rely on attracting a predominantly rural workforce into the factories, it could not afford to welcome them into the cities. As long as the state could not provide housing, food or transportation for all, people still needed to take care of a large part of their lives. It was convenient and necessary to rely not only on proletarians – be they old urban labourers, former craftsmen or peasants made into workers – but also on a flexible workforce, who could take care of their own reproduction and would swing daily or seasonally between the city and the countryside. They would use their 'free time' to work on their small lot and allocate their wages to the maintenance of a rural household that was systematically impoverished by agricultural quotas, expropriations and price scissors.

The slower tempo of the collectivization of land in the countryside functioned as an essential temporal fix within this logic. While the nationalization of the factories was completed around 1952, the collectivization of land unfolded in waves and ended only one decade later, in 1962. This way, those who counted as 'workers' and contributed to the accelerated industrialization of the country also ensured the reproduction of their rural families in times when they would not otherwise have survived. So, while the state officials discursively decried the behaviour of a not-fully-urbanized labour force, they had to rely on categories of population who were not completely 'free' from their means of production or subsistence. The ideal form of modern employment in the Fordist tradition, which involved workers' total dependency on wages, an insurance system and the factories' social infrastructure, had to wait for an indefinite future.

The peasant worker remained the crucial pillar of Cluj industry until the end of the 1960s, when the city saw a massive boost in housing construction, and industry benefited from increased technological investment. Even after that date, the radical programme of urbanization that dominated the 1970s would only partly solve this situation. With all the techniques of stabilizing and expanding labour in an urban environment, the entanglement between rural and urban life would continue to be fundamental both for workers' own reproduction and for the functioning of industry until the collapse of the regime.

The dependence on the countryside for the development of the city included the reliance on a workforce that could make use of both rural and urban resources, thus allowing for a partial externalization of labour's reproduction costs.[6] Socialist accumulation in the 1950s appears as a combination of workers' forced self-restraint (one of the easily forgotten dimensions of Preobrazhensky's primitive accumulation), directly unpaid labour and externalized reproduction costs for a flexible but unruly rural–urban workforce. Planning labour was central to these mechanisms, but it cannot be understood outside a class logic that pushed peasants to reproduce themselves qua peasants in a changing world.

The next section of the chapter offers an overview of the territorial logic of early socialist industrialization, which was placed at the intersection between a long history of uneven development, a specific modernization project, and the pragmatic requirements of production and social reproduction. The third section focuses on the implications of welcoming the newcomers into the city, not only in terms of housing and infrastructure, but also with regard to their interactions with the denizens of Cluj. In the fourth section I move on to commuting as an encounter between the state's strategy of keeping the price of labour low and people's strategy to use wage labour for reproducing their lives in the countryside. I conclude with a mapping of the other categories of 'workers' that populated the shop floor of the early socialist factories in Cluj, and discuss the problems of including these other 'arms that built socialism' into the factory life.

Shrinking Life and the Territorial Logic of Socialist Industrialization

The implementation of the first one-year plans prompted the Romanian economists to link the fundamental economic law of socialism – satisfying the material and cultural necessities of the working people – to the idea of even development. As a political and economic vision, even development stood in firm opposition to the distribution of the productive forces during the capitalist period, and to the ways in which capital structured the Romanian landscape.[7] Through planning, new materialities were going to produce a new territory, an ordered reality understood as *kosmos* against *chaos*, or as enlightenment against a pre-rational historical phase.

Following the nationalization of the industrial units in 1948, planned territorial allocation of the productive forces was meant to develop the regions that had been 'left behind' during the interwar period, and to attract all the available labour and natural resources in the economic circuit. The state sought to minimize the physical distance between sources of raw materials, manufacturing centres, distribution networks and urban markets. New industrial towns were to be created, some villages were to be remade into small industrial suppliers, and manufacturing was to be encouraged through the founding of cooperatives and small productive units all over the country.

The plan was supposed to redefine territory through the social dependencies created by production itself. This territory appeared then not as a pre-given container of the economy, but as the direct outcome of material relations, jobs, infrastructure, factories and housing. As always in the making of a political project, it was going to emerge within an essential relationship with a working population, which was both the final aim of this project and its condition of realization.[8] This relationship was discursively condensed into the mantra of progress for the socialist period: 'In a socialist society, the task of satisfying the material and cultural necessities of the working people lays at the foundation of the territorial allocation of the productive forces. The fulfilment of this task becomes possible only if we ensure the even economic and technological development of all regions, the uplifting of those left behind to the level of those who are economically and culturally in advance'.[9]

The Romanian politicians described this image of progress as a coherent sequence in which the fast industrialization of the 'left behind' regions would lead to urbanization and to cultural advancement. It would produce economically complex regions, coherent entities within which agriculture and industry would complement each other harmoniously. Their focus had 'both an economic importance and a political one, because creating industries in these regions not only aids their economies but also increases the number of jobs for workers, which further means the political elevation of the population'.[10] Since nationalism was considered the result of historical class domination translated in ethnic terms, this political advancement would have represented a solution for the national problem as well.

The relationship between the city and the countryside was central to this notion of even development. Theoretically, the territorial systematization that was going to accompany socialist industrialization was the mixed region, with industrial centres, small industrial towns and an agricultural production capable of sustaining them. Although the regions were going to specialize around a central industrial branch, they also needed to develop small units of local industry to cover the immediate consumption needs of the villages, and to maintain the agricultural production at a level which (ideally) would suffice for the basic food supply of the industrial centres.[11]

The principle of proportional territorial distribution of the productive forces represented a clear recognition of the political potency of neglect, and a full affirmation of allocative power as the spinal column of state socialism. Its imagined function was to link centres of production, distribution and life into an organic whole. Spreading factories all over the country was equated with bringing life in dead organs, while biological terms like 'pulsating' were used to describe industrial rhythms.[12] Economy was not just compared to life; it *was* life itself, as revolving around production and reproduction. The organicist vision of the party followed the developmental ideal of a society where 'the individuality of the whole grows at the same time as that of the parts'.[13] Socialist construction was predicated upon a new form of social cohesion, arising out of an understanding of economy as shared life, a structure of common experiences, which further constituted the ground for new disciplining techniques and for different forms of moral regulation. The organic solidarity of early socialism was not understood simply as the outcome of differentiation and interdependence in a world increasingly centred around the factory, and it was not to emerge spontaneously. It was the result of a coherent political project, which advanced 'class struggle' as the key to a deeper understanding of all social fractures and as the path towards the formation of a new historical consciousness.[14]

Nonetheless, this vision of even development hardly described what was happening on the ground during the period of primitive socialist accumulation. In practice, economic efficiency was the most important criteria for allocating investments. In the actually existing territorial logic of socialism, labour was considered a highly mobile productive force, while capital had to be fixed in the proximity of natural resources and transportation lines.[15] This tension between the need to polarize resources and the need to evenly distribute jobs, infrastructure, and 'culture' in the broadest sense was an everyday reality of early socialism, but the general tendency was to further develop the existing industrial centres while financially starving other regions.[16]

The First Five-Year Plan was the one that focused most on the more advanced regions, concentrating investment in the metallurgical and engineering centres like Hunedoara, Reșița, Bucharest and Brașov.[17] Seven industrialized counties received 58 per cent of investments, although containing only 22 per cent of the population. Per capita investment in the least industrialized counties was less than a third of the national average, with the exception of those areas where untapped natural resources could sustain primary commodities export.[18]

Table 3.1 Migration destinations in 1966.

	Urban population (%)	Investment per head (national average = 100 %)	Industrial production per head (produced value, compared to the national average)	Rate of migration per 1,000 people
Wave 1*	63.8	133.6	164.2	7.96
Wave 2**	36.3	100.7	100.1	-1.32
Wave 3***	25	75.8	60.3	-3.87

Notes:
* Regions from Wave 1 – post-nationalization investment: Banat, Brașov, București, Hunedoara.
** Regions from Wave 2 – capital investment in the late 1950s: Bacău, Dobrogea, Galați, Maramureș, Ploiești.
*** Regions from Wave 3 – heavy capital investment after the mid-1960s: Iași, Argeș, Mureș, Cluj, Crișana, Oltenia, Secuime.
Source: The figures are calculated on the basis of *Anuarul Statistic* 1939–1940 and *Enciclopedia României*, Vol. II.

Creating industrial agglomerations and neglecting peripheries was not a Romanian phenomenon. It reflected the constraints faced by the socialist governments elsewhere. In Hungary, between 1949 and 1953, 44.7 per cent of the new jobs in Hungarian industry were created in Budapest.[19] Between 1951 and 1960, Krakow and Łódź cumulated 54 per cent of all industrial investments in Poland. Like in the capitalist world, polarization was the rule, not the exception, so several cities in Eastern Europe became industrial super concentrations: Budapest hosted 34 per cent of all industrial jobs in Hungary, Sofia 16 per cent of those in Bulgaria, Katowice 20 per cent of those in Poland, and Bucharest 16 per cent of those in Romania.

The development of industrial super concentrations further reproduced a process of uneven proletarianization, with migration flows tending to follow the three large investment waves of the Romanian socialism.[20]

As the first investment wave was directed towards old industrial regions like București, Brașov, Hunedoara and Banat, people from other areas started to knock at the doors of their factories. In the mid-1960s, approximately 32 per cent of Romanians had been born elsewhere than their current place of residence.[21]

As argued in the first section of this chapter, the nationalization of the means of production and the collectivization of land were not only a historical turn in property relations but temporal strategies that proved essential for primitive socialist accumulation. More concretely, their different rhythms were going to benefit the factories by ensuring a flexible, easy to move around and cheap labour force that kept a foot in the countryside. While nationalization of the means of production was more or less completed between 1948 and 1952 (with a concentrated momentum in June 1948), collectivization was a longer process that was not going to end until ten years later, on the onset of the third industrialization wave. Thus, in the 1950s, collectivization did not represent an essential tool for making proletarians, but a strategy of temporization that relied on a gradual shrinking of life in the countryside.

This shrinking of life refers first of all to the employment possibilities in the rural areas. Before the war, peasants who were landless or had too little land to ensure the survival of their families found daily or seasonal work on the domains of the local landlords or on the land of the better-off peasants. Those who were at an 'easy distance' from the towns became carriers or apprentices in the artisans' shops. Young Hungarian girls from the Transylvanian villages easily found work as servants and kitchen maids in Cluj, Oradea or Târgu-Mureș. These forms of employment persisted for a while after the war, but they rapidly dwindled under the pressure of nationalization and with the decline of the urban and rural interwar elites.

Immediately after the war, poor peasants received some land in the 1945 Agrarian Reform in order to encourage them to develop a more positive view on the pre-1947 communist-leaning governments. However, the size of the plots was not enough to make them economically independent – they still needed to work for someone else, thus basically preserving the class relationships in the rural areas. The Land Reform of 1945 took around 1.5 million hectares from the remaining large landlords, from smaller landowners who did not work the land themselves and from the German population. The land was distributed to some of the newly formed state farms, to 400,000 landless peasants, and to another 500,000 'dwarf' peasants, whose plots were considered unviable. Additional land was confiscated in 1948 and 1949 from the royal family and from landowners with more than twenty hectares, but this land was directly transformed into collective and state farms. At the agricultural census of 1948, half of the adult population held some agricultural land, but only 2.3 per cent of them held plots larger than ten hectares. By banning all sales and leasing of land, as well as sharecropping, the Land Reform was relatively successful in stopping the double tendency of fragmentation and polarization of land holdings that had dominated the interwar period. However, more than half of the plots did not provide enough for the survival of the peasant households in the late 1940s.

In March 1949, the Central Committee of the Romanian Workers' Party made a historic decision on the policy for the socialist transformation of agriculture. Peasantry was split into five categories, or 'classes', each bearing important economic, political and symbolic implications: *chiaburi* (kulaks), including those hiring labour on a regular basis; large landowners, owning over twenty hectares of land; middle peasants, owning five to twenty hectares; poor peasants, owning less than five hectares; and landless peasants. The 'alliance' between peasantry and the working class referred explicitly to the middle peasants, with a 'leaning on' the poor and landless ones, and with a stated need to 'contain' the kulaks.

The disappearing employment, as well as the postwar famine and drought, were complemented by almost impossible forced deliveries for peasants. In 1949, agricultural taxes were fixed at rates between 7 per cent (for incomes of 12,000–15,000 lei) and 37 per cent (for incomes of 400,000 lei). Anyone who held more than ten hectares of land or who hired labour could be declared *chiabur*, and local councils could claim another 20–50 per cent of their incomes. There were further attempts to replace seasonal or daily employment on their lands with permanent contracts. Accordingly, agricultural labourers could no longer be discharged off season and had to be paid a monthly wage of at least 3,300 lei. This regulation of rural employment basically prevented most peasants from hiring labour. It is no wonder that youngsters, mainly men for this generation, left the countryside for the city, or started to commute daily, simply not to face brutal hunger and to take pressure off their families.[22]

Increasing the share of large land holdings would have allowed a more rapid mechanization of agriculture, a direct form of controlling the rural sector and a more reliable supply source of food and raw materials to support industrial and urban growth. Large-scale agriculture to support rapid industrialization was the final aim of the collectivization process but there was disagreement on the sequence of these historical processes.[23] Two positions were represented at the top in the Romanian Workers' Party between 1946 and 1952. Ana Pauker, the party secretary for agriculture, and Vasile Luca, the minister of finance, supported a collectivization process that would have encouraged the peasants to voluntarily join the cooperatives and would have gradually led to an increased productivity of agriculture through mechanization. As the head of finances in the new socialist government, Vasile Luca argued for price parity between agriculture and industry, and for a balanced development of heavy and light industry, specifically for supplying the countryside with retail goods.[24]

The second opinion was that rapid industrialization led by the development of heavy industry with the help of a subordinated agricultural sector and a sweeping collectivization process had to be the agenda of the government for the first decade of planning. Gheorghe Gheorghiu-Dej, the prime secretary of the Romanian Workers' Party, gradually came to support the latter position. His view came to the forefront of the debates on collectivization in the early 1950s, once the state officials realized that the continued attempts to attract peasants into collective farms were being met with fierce resistance.

As peasants refused to make their product available on the market, the price of food rose steeply and the bare necessities of one's table were often out of workers' reach. Those who did bring products to the city markets and sold them to the state, accumulated cash reserves and set up a regime of saving that kept liquidities out of circulation, which further amplified the inflationary tendency that marked the first postwar decade. The destabilization of the countryside had a negative impact on the trade balance because Romania, unlike other countries in the region, was an exporter of agricultural products and raw materials. It also had severe consequences for the provisioning of the cities, where workers endlessly murmured about the lack of food and its price. Since a fragmented peasant economy proved impossible to control, shortages of agricultural products, volatile prices and rampant inflation pushed the state towards more forceful solutions.

Hence, further pressures were added to the 'scissors' that cut deep into rural lives with the announcement of the financial reform of 1952. Money from the better-off peasants was confiscated, utilizing a partly similar rationale that marked the 1947 monetary stabilization.[25] The 1952 financial reform was explicitly directed to stem the rise of prices for agricultural products and consumer goods on the free market, while the controlled prices for industrial commodities stayed the same. Its logic was unambiguously stated in the preamble of the Law. The financial reform of 1952 was aimed to strengthen the Romanian leu, to increase workers' real wages and to improve provisioning. The reform tied the Romanian leu to the Soviet rouble instead of the US dollar, 'which [wa]s an unstable, inflationist, crisis-hit currency, whose purchasing power [wa]s continuously falling'.[26]

The reform came at a moment when the socialist sector already dominated industry (95 per cent), transportation (85 per cent) and trade (76 per cent). In agriculture, only around 13 per cent of the land for cultivation was owned by the state or included in collective farms and against the logic of 'squeezing' the rural, two-thirds of the state's budget came from accumulations produced in the socialist sector. The legislators decried the fact that 'capitalist elements in the cities and in the villages' manipulated prices by hoarding food stuff and not bringing it onto the market. In the five years since the 1947 monetary stabilization, the price of food on the free market had risen more than three times, while the prices of industrial goods had stayed the same. The state failed to requisition enough food in order to influence prices on the free market and to ensure workers' provisioning through ration books. Primitive socialist accumulation was in danger as profiteering led 'to the weakening of the exchange between the city and the village', which was 'the economic foundation of the alliance between the working class and the working peasantry'.

The exchange of the old lei for the new ones privileged workers and poor peasants by offering advantageous conditions of exchange only for small amounts of money and for small savings bank deposits.[27] The rationale behind this progressive rate was clearly expressed in the preamble of the Law: 'The conditions of exchange will hit the capitalist elements in the cities and in the villages, especially the *chiaburi*, who profited from the increase in the food stuff prices on the free market and sabotaged the fulfilment of acquisitions plans. They will have, with the occasion of the monetary reform, to give what they accumulated illegally back to the state of the working people'.

Alongside Bulgaria and Poland, Romania was one of the three countries that failed to stop the inflation of the 1940s, and had to appeal to the population's liquidities once more in early 1950s. With the 1952 monetary reform, the socialist government finally managed to stop the inflationary tendency that started with the Great Depression, went through the Second World War and then dominated the postwar era. The financial anti-inflationary measures joined the other twenty-three monetary reforms that took place in both Western and Eastern Europe between the autumn of 1944 and mid-1952.[28] Like in other Eastern European countries, bank deposits were treated more gently then individuals' holdings of banknotes in order to encourage saving and to decrease the speed of money circulation. In order to secure workers' goodwill and to fit the lower level of liquidities, the implementation of the Reform was accompanied by a price drop in basic consumer goods like bread, meat, sugar, pasta, wine, textiles and cigarettes. The government aimed to reduce hoarding and excess liquidities in the hope that it would curb the demand for goods. They also sought to induce workers (especially semi-proletarians) to take their wages and industrial work more seriously.

The resounding failure of the agricultural policy of the socialist government was denounced and politically instrumentalized in the most important wave of purges in the history of Romanian communism. In 1952, two hundred thousand members were expelled from the party in a matter of months. Gheorghe Gheorghiu-Dej, the secretary of the party, blamed his political rivals, Ana Pauker and Vasile Luca, for the failure of the first wave of collectivization, rampant inflation and appalling living standards. Subsequently, the process of collectivization proceeded slowly and carefully, which had important consequences for the constitution of a reservoir of cheap and flexible labour for the socialist factories. The expropriation of the kulaks and the slower disintegration of middle peasantry during the thirteen years of the collectivization process further narrowed the structure of life possibilities in the countryside.

The foreign trade deficits, the fear that workers' unrest would catch fire in Romania like in other countries in the socialist bloc, the internal pressures generated by labour shortages and fluidity, and the incapacity to coerce the peasantry into ensuring the necessary supply for urban and industrial growth forced the communist government to accept further corrections of course. The Party Plenum of August 1953 took place after Stalin's death and marked the beginning of a four-year shift in the state's strategy of investments. The consumption fund grew, the total investment fell below its 1953 level in absolute terms, and previously underfunded economic sectors received a long-awaited-for boost. The annual increase in employment also fell from 220,000 in 1950–53 to 32,000 in 1953–58.[29]

The pressure over the countryside also diminished, as the purchase prices for agricultural products were raised and the terms of trade between the villages and the city became less exploitative for the former. Compulsory deliveries were basically abandoned in 1957 and replaced by more advantageous state contracts that would function as incentives for the peasantry to sell their products through the socialist trade system. The peasants' joy was short lived, though, as a last wave of collectivization at the end of the 1950s and the beginning of the 1960s finalized the Romanian collectivization process.[30]

On the whole, although Romania was a cereal exporter and the modernization of agriculture was discursively supported by the state, only 10 per cent of the investment total during the First Five-Year Plan was directed towards agricultural production. Agriculture was left as a residual, mostly seasonal employer. It remained a labour-intensive sector, which in the last decades of socialism was kept alive with the contribution of schoolchildren, students and soldiers, and with the input of the industrial workers themselves, still embedded in their rural world, helping at the collective farms during the weekends and working their gardens after exhausting factory shifts. This was going to be a long-term trend, which kept the Romanian countryside in a relatively backward and dependent state.

Wages in agriculture continued to be much lower than in industry for the whole socialist period. In addition, they were partly paid in kind, which gave peasants less access to liquidities to buy goods and forced them to chase an extra income from the cultivation of their private lots.

Table 3.2 Average monthly income (Romanian Lei).

Year	1950	1955	1960	1965	1970	1975	1980
Wage earners	337	499	802	1,028	1,289	1,595	2,238
Collective farmers	172	381	416	506	589	1,018	1,388

Source: Ronnås, *Urbanization*, 72. Average monthly income (real wages) for all those who worked on salary or wage. For collective farmers, this is a nominal income in kind and in cash.

Although slightly decreasing, the disparity between retail prices in urban and rural areas was maintained for the whole period. In the mid-1980s, retail prices in the countryside were still 10 per cent higher on average than in the cities. The 'alliance between peasantry and the working class' was built around the impossibility of the former to become workers themselves on the collective farms. Pensions for collective farmers were introduced as late as 1971, while individual farmers got access to pensions in 1977. Both were much lower than for industrial workers.[31] Allocations for children in the villages were also introduced later but were approximately two-thirds of those in the cities.

With life in the villages under increasing pressure, wage work did become a safety net for young workers and for their families. But the planners were 'anxious to avoid the heavy costs to families forced to move into urban growth centres in conditions frequently unsatisfactory, and considered such levels of inter-regional migration undesirable'.[32] Commuting and not transforming peasants into urban workers came to be considered the strategy for covering the necessary workforce, for keeping labour cheap and for solving the housing problem.[33] It met with peasants' historically produced 'stubbornness' to reproduce their lives qua peasants – not through the so much commented upon conservative thinking and resistance to change but through the incorporation of new resources and possibilities into a life they knew.

It was thus a sign of success that migration as a whole indeed declined sharply, from 20.9 per thousand inhabitants in 1956 to 14.5 in 1964. short-distance migration routes became prevalent, and commuting became the preferred way to bring workers from the rural population into the factories.[34] Cities like Cluj, which were administratively 'closed' because of the paralysing lack of housing, were following this trend from the beginning. The solution adopted by people from other regions who wanted to work in Cluj was to settle in the villages surrounding the city and commute daily from there. A suburban belt was created, one that offered people the possibility to live in individual houses, grow vegetables in their gardens, and raise animals in addition to their factory work. It was an explicit attempt to 'enable rural dwellers to combine the advantages of cooperative farm membership and rural amenity with a salary derived from industrial employment, and also enable the state to limit its urban housing programme'.[35]

This strategy that connected territory, population, capital investment and employment in specific ways represents the background against which the fundamental acts of primitive socialist accumulation – the nationalization of the factories and the collectivization of land – unfolded on the ground. The labour regime produced within this nexus was dependent on the gradual 'shrinking of life' in the villages, which preceded and accompanied collectivization of land for more than a decade. As the rest of the chapter will show, this labour regime brought together on the shop floor experienced industrial workers, former artisans and craftsmen, newcomers to the city who had to become proletarians overnight, a large number of commuters who functioned as both a permanent and a temporary workforce in the factories, unskilled women who needed to complement the income of their households, soldiers, children and prison inmates.

Vinituri at the Gates

Although factory managers sent daily requests for more workers to the Office for the Rational Allocation of Labour Force, they could do little to offer shelter to the newcomers. The cities were simply unable to welcome this much-needed workforce due to a paralysing housing shortage. Between 1948 and 1955, the urban population in Romania increased by 225,000 every year, while less than 150,000 dwellings were built in the cities in the whole period.[36] In Cluj, between 1944 and 1946 alone, the city population officially rose from 120,000 to 160,000. The neighbourhood around the train station remained practically uninhabitable for a long time because of the heavy bombing in the summer of 1944. Many private houses had been converted into official institutions or into headquarters for the Soviet soldiers in the city.

Waves of refugees joined the lines of the hungry, unemployed and homeless people in the city after the drought of 1946, when famine became tragic. The older generations still remember people from Moldavia and from the southern part of Romania 'invading' the city in 1946 and 1947, in their desperate attempt to escape dying of starvation and thirst because of the terrible drought in these areas. The geographical origin of the *vinituri*[37] was sometimes hard to assess by the old Clujeni. But wherever they came from, it was clear that these people were not seen as the kind of 'good people' who formed the population of the old city.

Even worse, they were entering a city dominated 'not by class struggle, but by the struggle for food and for our stomachs', as a former worker, a teenager then, told me. While many families offered them shelter and water, to share the square pieces of *mălai*[38] with the newcomers made people see them as the ones 'who were taking the food out of [their] children's mouths'.[39] The refugees were often placed in marginal neighbourhoods, far from the city centre, and were 'slightly despised by the city centre inhabitants who considered themselves city dwellers and saw the others as peasants'.

Many of the newcomers, especially people coming from remote regions, were considered a health danger for the city population.[40] Local authorities required special hygiene measures, and factories were made responsible for educating people to go to the hospital when they were sick or giving birth, to wash themselves and their clothes more often and to prepare their food in a certain way. The party activists complained bitterly that people who came to Cluj from remote areas still used charms and incantations when in need of medical assistance.[41] Special conferences about hygiene and communal living took place in the factories, while the experienced workers were asked to actively become models to be emulated by the *vinituri*.

Working-class families also came to live in horrible conditions, sharing a very small space in which sanitation became increasingly problematic. Local officials declared that during the First Five-Year Plan, things got worse than before the war, when the situation was dire. According to Bindea's survey, almost 86 per cent of the unskilled workers, 81 per cent of the skilled ones, and 91 per cent of the clerks lived in rented accommodation in 1938. Less than 13 per cent of the skilled workers' houses and less than 9 per cent of the unskilled ones had canalization, and basically no working-class house or apartment had an indoor bathroom. Less than half of the skilled workers' houses, and less than 17 per cent of the unskilled ones', had electricity.[42]

Given the lack of private property among the working class, and the additional war destruction, the party committee got daily reports of scandals because of the lack of space. Cases when three families with eight to ten members shared one room and a tiny kitchen were so frequent that the local authorities started to worry that an epidemic was simply inevitable.[43] Some parts of the working-class neighbourhoods slowly transformed into veritable slums where overcrowding was accompanied by the poor state of the roads, by the lack of gas, electricity, water pipes and sewerage, and by the increasing degradation of the walls. These spaces remained pockets of extreme urban poverty for years. The party activists often complained that the inhabitants of these slums could not see any real improvement in their lives long after other social categories had enjoyed the benefits of the communist takeover.

A 1955 memoir of the Regional Party Committee painted the grim picture of the housing situation in Cluj at the end of the First Five-Year Plan. The population in Cluj rose by 72 per cent in ten years: from 105,000 people in 1945 to 180,000 in 1955. Between 1945 and 1955, around 600 houses had been destroyed but only around 130 had been built. Around 800 buildings, initially allocated to housing, had been occupied by industrial units and institutions. Eighteen new factories had been added to the city industry in this decade, many of them employing over 500 workers, and two of them – in the construction sector – over 1,000 workers. The number of workers in old factories like János Herbák, Menajul, Unirea and the Railways Workshops grew by more than 5,000. Sixteen trade cooperatives added more than 3,000 people to their prewar workforce. Ten institutions of higher education, two operas, three theatres, forty-one schools, ten professional schools, twenty-nine day-care centres for children, forty-one kindergartens, three museums, six cultural houses and several libraries were located in the main buildings in the city centre. The party committees and several state institutions occupied several of the most imposing buildings in Cluj, previously used for housing, now expropriated.[44]

To add to the impossible situation, the early socialist development of Cluj was chaotic. A general plan for the city's development could not be drafted at the time. The first synthetic vision of what the city of Cluj 'should be' was encapsulated in a 'Project of Systematization' as late as 1959–60. The project brought together the economic functions of the city with its cultural and administrative ones. Housing only started to feature prominently in this late-1950s vision of urban development, which was going to be part of the second and the third waves of industrialization.

During the First Five-Year Plan, the living space ratio in Cluj was 4.1 square metres per person instead of 8 square metres – the health standard imposed by the law. This calculation was optimistic because many people were not registered as living in Cluj but still rented a room somewhere, sometimes in houses without bathrooms or kitchens, sometimes sharing them with four or five other families. Until 1955, almost ten thousand requests for apartments had been registered at the office for housing of the City Central Committee of the Romanian Workers' Party and less than two thousand had been solved.[45] More than 4,500 students of the over 8,000 enrolled in the two universities in 1955 were housed in people's homes as 'tolerated in the family'.[46] There were also three thousand workers living illegally in the city, paying a monthly rent that varied between 70 and 200 lei.

For people on the outskirts of Cluj and for those residing around the continuously growing factories, transforming tool huts into small rooms and renting them became a supplemental – sometimes crucial – source of income. The lack of space and the disappearing intimacy even for families who had enjoyed it before the war was worsened by the lack of basic amenities. As Reka recalls:

> In the 1950s, most of my colleagues used to share a flat with another family. It was a flat with several rooms, a kitchen and maybe a bathroom; few people even had a toilet because each family had one room and the toilet was at the end of the hallway. In this house, for example, there were fifteen families, each with one room, and there were only two toilets: one up and one down. When they started building blocks of flats, there were apartments with four rooms in which two families lived, sharing a bathroom and a kitchen. This was until '62–'63, and then each started living separately. We used to live in an old building called Korda Palace, across the Conservatory, on the first floor, and we had no sewerage, no toilet in the apartment, no running water. Almost everyone lived like that and we didn't even think it could be better. And then in 1960, the university needed that building because half of the building was already occupied by classrooms and the other half by apartments for teachers. When the university evicted us, everyone got apartments in Mihai Viteazu Square, and it was like heaven on earth, because you had a bathroom with a toilet, and a shower, and warm water, and cold water, and central heating; and we no longer had to worry about gas or, like before '52, wood, when we used to carry wood from the cellar up the stairs.[47]

Many workers whom I interviewed lived in this kind of rooms, with an outdoor toilet – even after they got married and had their first child. The wet autumns, the freezing winters and the choking smoke coming from their improvised installations for heating and cooking are still vivid in the memories of their youth. The introduction of methane gas through voluntary and forced labour was considered little short of a miracle.

In the period under scrutiny in this book, the local officials' achievements were measured rather in fixing and solidifying existing infrastructure than in further expanding it. Much of the city's infrastructure was legally, economically and politically connected to the materiality of the factories. In the socialist cities, pipes, heating and electrical systems, roads, hospitals, cultural events and sporting facilities were financially supported or entirely dependent on industrial units. Although continuous efforts were made to compensate for the lack of comfort at home with the help of the factories' social function, their infrastructure remained underdeveloped for many years after the war. Showers, toilets and hot water were never enough, food at the cafeteria always seemed to be insufficient or of low quality, and work clothes came to look awful as poor workers also used them at home and in the street.

Moreover, as the allocation of flats became increasingly connected to one's workplace, the factories needed to take over the entire issue of accommodation and meals for their workers. Families with children were given priority to both factory and People's Town Council flats. The young male workers coming to the city for work from outside villages or other cities were accommodated in shanties or dormitories where twenty to thirty people were crowded together, in conditions that resembled those in the army. The memories of life in these rooms are bittersweet. In our interviews, one man, who later became a foreman at Tehnofrig, fondly remembers his encounter with the nineteen-year-old peasant who became his lifelong friend; another one still feels the joy of having a warm-water shower in the morning and an indoor toilet; and a former unskilled worker at the Railways Workshops smiles as he recounts the feeling of freedom when he could invite a girl – his future wife – out for a coffee and a cake, paid for from his own salary.[48]

Some memories are different, as people recount the occasional fights between young Romanian and Hungarian men, the 'Hungarians' stubbornness not to learn the Romanian language', or the loneliness and confusion when they left their villages. They remember their coming to town not as a path to freedom, individual autonomy, or a better life, but as an existentially painful fracture, forced upon them because 'in the village there was no future left'.[49]

Although coming from a peasant family himself, Ion, a worker employed in 1949 at János Herbák, described his shock when confronted with the 'chaos' of male sociability in the factory dormitories. He compared those 'animals' with his 'serious family' of middle-peasants from a village around Bistrița, with a religious mother and a non-drinking and non-violent father, who worked 'from dawn till dusk' and 'never said a bad word to anyone'. After just two months of 'despair', although money was tight and he wanted to save as much as possible, Ion rented a room on his own and moved out from the crowded room. He lived there for another year, until he got engaged and needed to find a room to accommodate both him and his wife; but it was not until 1962 when the family was assigned an apartment by the factory. By then, their son was nine.

A new wave of ethnic tensions travelled to the city with the Romanian and Hungarian youngsters moving to Cluj. The encounter between their experience and the nationalism of the urban workers was going to shape the factories as ethnicized spaces for years to come. Workers' tendency to be segregated along ethnic lines was harshly criticized by the party activists but their comments had little to no importance for the local situation in the late 1940s or early 1950s. A report of the Cluj Regional Committee of the Romanian Workers' Party about the persistent 'national problem' in the city and in the nearby villages clearly showed the tendency of the Hungarians and Romanians to live separate everyday lives.[50] The choir of the Railways Workshops had no Hungarian or Jewish members. The workers' theatre at János Herbák was purely Hungarian and the members refused to stage any play in Romanian. When the factories were decorated, only the red flag of the communists appeared on the corridors, while the Romanian national flag was nowhere to be seen. Both Romanians and Hungarians endlessly complained when their own language was not being used during meetings. Although the Romanians understood Hungarian and vice versa, everybody claimed that the discussions at these meetings were suddenly beyond their linguistic competence.

Nevertheless, the ability to speak both languages and to be tolerant about the use of Hungarian in everyday life and at the workplace often united Romanians and Hungarians in their identification as 'old Clujeni' against '*vinituri*'. As Gyula, a Hungarian worker from János Herbák between 1945 and 1995 told me, when someone was upset about hearing people around them speaking Hungarian, 'he failed the test of being a real Clujean'. Although ethnic tensions remained important for years, the fracture between 'real' Clujeni and *vinituri* was going to become more and more important in the battle to dominate the city and the factories.

When talking about his own nationalism at the time, Lászlo, a former worker born in 1937, recalls:

> I have always been a nationalist. [He pauses]. You are Romanian, but I have to tell you this. I have always been a nationalist. But I must explain this! [He starts to walk around the room, in a state of agitation]. You know, Cluj was a Hungarian city. I believe it was Hungarian until Ceaușescu came to power. But I was never against the Romanians. Never! I had Romanian friends; there was never a problem with them in the city. We all spoke Romanian and they spoke Hungarian. But when these newcomers [*vinituri*] came, we all had a problem. They did not speak Hungarian, they did not wash themselves, they were aggressive with our women, they fought, they spat in the streets. They were peasants! The Romanians who lived in the city before the war also hated them. So I have nothing against the Romanians. I have a problem with these scums [*scursuri*] who invaded us. And most of them were Romanians.

Many of the younger people, including the Romanians, still charge the boundaries around the notion of 'real' urbanites with emotion when discursively defending it against *vinituri*.

Interviewing a younger Romanian woman, born in the 1950s, reveals the same positioning towards the peasants becoming workers in various rural–urban migration waves. Georgia, the daughter of an activist who joined the party in 1945, and a quality controller at the Brushes Factory herself, emotionally remembers the stories of her parents about the city, and concludes:

> You know, communists did some very good things. I don't feel guilty that my parents were party activists. They really believed people's lives should be improved. And they loved their city. They loved Cluj so much! Even when I was a little girl, the city was like a garden, like an orchard. When they [the Romanian Workers' Party] started to build the new neighbourhoods, they tried to keep them like this: with grass, trees, flowers and the river down there. … But they also brought the peasants into the city. This was the end. It is true that they received houses and jobs and they were very poor. They were really poor… For them, it was better. But this was the end of the city as I knew it. I can still see these peasants in my block of flats behaving worse than in their father's field [*pe moşia lui taică-su*].

The fact of bringing peasants into the cities to work or to live did not mean they became workers overnight; this was clear not only for people like Georgia and Laszlo but also for the party activists themselves. They knew not only that this transformation was going to take time but also that it could not be simply framed as a 'cultural' or an 'ideological' problem. Economically relying on newcomers as a 'workforce' and politically transforming them into 'comrades' would prove to be a challenge for decades.

In-Betweeners: Commuting to Cluj for Work

In 1955, at the end of the First Five-Year Plan, an analysis made by the Ministry of Labour concluded: '[T]he development of our national economy has led, even by the end of 1949, to the exhausting of the skilled and unskilled labour force in the industrial regions of our country'.[51] The most important solution was to expand the activity of the Office for the Reallocation of Labour Force into the countryside in order to find workers ready to commute, and to direct them towards the factories that needed them. The national campaign's outcome was a list of 65,874 people who were willing to work in the cities and commute daily. Of these, 46,112 workers were distributed immediately to the factories. At the end of the campaign, 19,762 people were still available, but in less than one month not a single worker without a contract could be found on the list.

While there was at least a propagandistic expectation that those workers who managed to move to Cluj despite the housing shortage and the restrictions of settling in the city would go through a process of self-transformation that would make them into the ideal subject of communist politics, party activists and new economic executives alike weaved no illusions around the commuters' integration. The commuters' special position on the shop floor brought many problems in its wake. From the factory and Party Committee documents we know the commuters were rowdy, left their workbench whenever they wanted, and talked back to their foremen if something bothered them.

Factory documents are full of complaints about the impossibility of disciplining labour because a large number of the workforce were 'all sorts of people', who did not consider working in the factory as their main activity. Commuting came to be understood as one of 'rural versus urban' mentality and, even more explicitly, as a lack of crystallization of the working class.

> Work indiscipline comes from the fact that these people have an old mentality. They see themselves as seasonal workers, like in the countryside, working in many places just to earn more money. ... These comrades have a careless attitude towards work and no class consciousness, because *we do not have only industrial workers here but all sorts of people*.[52]

Or, as a report from János Herbák for the City Party Committee in 1953 shows:

> The party could not convince the workers from rural areas that their first task is to work in the factory. This is why they continue to work in their villages. Even our comrades who live in the city often go to the villages to work for wheat, flour or vegetables. Many workers at János Herbák are young; they could work a lot and we would not need extra workers. But the Youth organization does not educate young people to be disciplined; they could not convince them to have a just attitude towards work.[53]

We know from the production reports that the commuters were able to endanger or even stop production for days during the summer months, when their labour was needed in their villages. It seems impossible though to find a single mention of their actual number in the 1950s. How many commuters were employed in the factories in the 1950s was a difficult question to answer, not only for scholars on rural–urban migration but also for government officials at the time.

Not knowing exactly how many temporary workers and journeymen were employed in a factory at a given time was related to factory managers' efforts to defend commuting as a category of flexible employment. This flexibility referred both to the limited and problematic possibility of expanding and contracting the labour force in the factories according to the shifting requirements of production and to the fact that this category of labourer allowed factory managers to exercise a certain degree of financial control within the limits set by the plan. This was possible because many of the peasants who came to work for a few months in winter and then disappeared were paid not from the wage fund of the factory but from other sources. However, production costs, wages and long-term investments were planned in detail, which theoretically left little freedom to the factory managers to handle the finances of the enterprise. One of the tools at their disposal was the director's fund.

The director's fund was established as a means to improve the working and the living conditions of the employees – housing, workers' clubs, kindergartens, summer camps, health facilities and cafeterias.[54] Leaders in production and Stakhanovites were supposed to be financially rewarded with the help of this money.[55] Cultural and leisure activities also had to be partially covered from the director's fund, especially the ones that were supposed to create a sense of community in the factory, like parties, Sunday trips, and sporting events. How the factory managers actually used this fund was, however, very different. Mostly, they used it to solve issues related to the workers' payment.

The importance of this source became apparent from the first year of planning. In debt and chronically underfinanced, the newly nationalized factories fully depended on the ministries' decision to extend their credit. With the implementation of the first one-year plans in 1949 and 1950, many of them were in a very difficult situation, not being able to pay their workers for months. The state immediately covered the wages of the permanent employees, in an attempt to secure their good opinion about the nationalization and show them that, in a workers' state, their work would always be rewarded. Nevertheless, other overdue payments were dealt with differently. Temporary workers were simply left to the goodwill of the pre-nationalization leadership of the factory, who had no power left to honour their financial promises. The post-1948 directors were not held responsible for these payments. This way, the state could easily 'forget' some payments and release a small part of the nationalized industrial units' debt burden. But there was something more fundamental to this decision behind the simple attempt to save some money in the process of nationalization: it was a clear statement about how the responsibility for various categories of labourers was going to be split between the state – in its official, legal form – and the quasi-informal arrangements of the socialist factories as productive state apparatuses. The state made it clear that it was not going to support temporary work financially, and that the factory managers were responsible for covering the external labour by using the limited funds available to them. When the director's fund was established as a financial instrument in every factory, this situation became the norm.

The number of commuters in the factory fluctuated so much that it was simply impossible to follow these workers' trajectories with the weak statistical apparatus the factories had at their disposal. What we do know from the production reports is that they were considered 'temporary workers', whose activity was unproductive and thus represented a hidden production cost. Commuting was also considered a form of encouraging people to continue searching for better jobs elsewhere. Nevertheless, the difference between the time spent in the factory by the temporary and the 'permanent' workers could not have been very big in the first years of planning in conditions of huge labour turnover. Except for very few workers – generally skilled Hungarian males from the old factories from Cluj and their wives, who spent decades in the same workplace – the distinction between 'temporary' and 'permanent' was blurred. Sometimes, workers with a permanent work contract left the factory during the summer months to work somewhere else or to take care of their parents' crops, but many never returned. Sometimes, young girls entered the gates of the factories just before they got pregnant. They used the child benefits and the paediatric facilities of the large factories but then switched to another job just before their maternity leave ended. Considering a job as 'temporary', although it was defined as 'permanent' in their employment contract, was common practice among unskilled workers, who were always in search of something better.

Most commuters came from the villages surrounding the city: Feleacu, Chinteni, Apahida, Florești, Gilău, Sânnicoară, Vâlcele or Dezmir. Some of them owned gardens or small plots of land themselves or together with their families. Others worked as day labourers for other people and they were better paid than in most factories. Most importantly, they had access to food in a period when scarcity and even famine dominated life in the city. Having vegetables on one's table was simply a luxury when the most common meal of the workers consisted in a big slice of baked polenta. Even the workers who were living in the city sometimes worked in the countryside in exchange for milk, potatoes, eggs and vegetables. In addition to the food scarcity, urban workers were extra motivated to occasionally perform work in the countryside because their earnings were very low even when they exceeded their factory norms by 50–80 per cent. Shortages, assaults in production at the end of the month, discontinuities, overtime and penalties for low quality output worsened the situation even more. Workers simply left the factory to work their parents' land in the countryside, and returned only when the need for cash surpassed the advantages of staying home. Therefore, factory managers knew very well that the indiscipline of the commuters was less an issue of backward mentality and careless work ethos than a direct result of the state's unwillingness to pay them decent wages.

The prevalence of semi-proletarian and unskilled work transformed some economic sectors in seasonal activities, which barely functioned during the summer. For construction work, for instance, it became a catastrophe, since construction yards were dominated by unskilled workers, who earned little and had few reasons to stay in a fixed job. The increasingly worrying situation forced the party to place construction work in superior wage categories for stopping labour fluctuation. Construction work became one of the best paid sectors of the socialist economy but it remained for decades the one sector that could never keep its workers. In 1961, it still had the highest share of commuters of all economic sectors – 63.5 per cent; this was followed by manufacturing 21.4 per cent, agriculture 35.7 per cent, and transportation 30.6 per cent.[56]

Women who wanted a good financial situation dreamed about marrying a construction worker. But there was also a price to pay, as one former worker told me about her best friend's marriage:

> The construction workers were better paid. Women had more money, their children had nicer clothes. But these men were also scoundrels. My friend was married to one. He drank half of the money before he brought his wage home. She was lucky that he was sluggish and so he did not beat her. But many were hitting their wives. They were jealous, you know? Because they spent so much time away, drinking, surrounded by brutes coming from everywhere. When they came home, they were also drinking and there was always scandal.

Because of their frequent job changes, construction workers were less flexible when it came to their wives' factory work. They became known as a category of workers who were to be avoided by young girls, even though 'they could buy them nicer presents' and provide for their children.

From the beginning, the legal treatment of the commuters made staying for long in a workplace an unattractive option. There were many differences between the social rights of the workers residing in the city and those living in the countryside and holding a small piece of land. The commuters did not have the right to cards for rationed food or to consumer goods from the economats, and could not receive credit from their factories. Successive legal provisions encouraged – or not – the factories to financially support the transportation of their workers from the countryside, but it was subject to continuous negotiation. As this increased the prices of commodities, the government refused to pay for it in an attempt to pressure factory managers to find a local labour force instead. But because this was impossible, the commuters had to walk several kilometres every morning in order to get to work. The lucky ones were biking to work, but having a bicycle in the 1950s was uncommon because they were expensive and out of reach for most workers. However, by 1950, the rampant labour shortage forced the government officials to reconsider their position and to allow state institutions to pay for the transportation of their employees if they lived between 5 and 45 kilometres from their workplace.[57] The payment was confined to those who could prove that they could not find housing closer to their workplace and that the factory could not find the needed personnel in the locality. The factories submitted the necessary documentation, and some of them immediately bought buses for their workers.

The commuters themselves faced 'the rural mentality' in their villages, especially the women. Although young girls from the surrounding villages had worked as servants in the middle-class homes in Cluj before the war, factory work was different because it escaped parental control. Thus, working in the city was not a popular option for girls who had been born in the 1930s and 1940s. As Lampland shows for the Hungarian case, 'control of labour was in the final analysis a male prerogative, which extended not only to his own labour, but to that of his wife and children. Women could never fully achieve mastery of self, no matter how hard they worked as managers of the family household'.[58] As controlling one's labour became key to the social hierarchies in the village, the increasing possibility to go to town for work had the side effect of increasing gender inequalities in the countryside. Women themselves could contribute little money to a rural household; in a generation when they were still not absorbed into industry, the possibility of being employed as servants in the cities was shrinking every day, and working for kulaks or for landlords was virtually disappearing. The fact that women of the 1950s generation became much less mobile than men completed their experience of being the crux of reproduction for the household economy in the village. This partly explains their strong, and often violent, reaction to the dispossession resulting from collectivization.[59]

The gender line was going to structure the rural for a long time. Female labour in agriculture increased from 54 per cent in 1956 to 63 per cent in 1977, as well as the mean age of the active population employed in the agricultural sector. The division of labour in the countryside also changed. While men took jobs as mechanics, tractor drivers and agricultural technicians, women stayed as collective farmers, and their earnings remained way below their husbands'.[60]

Another generation would pass until young girls from the countryside would force the factory gates. This transition, which took place mainly from the late 1960s onwards, can be related to many factors: the precariousness of life and the quasi-impossibility to practise subsistence agriculture for families with many children after the land had been appropriated; the ever-shrinking employment within the village boundaries – including for day labourers; the weak chances of finding a suitable husband and the attraction exercised by a marriage outside the village; the hard work on the collective farms, where the labour force became increasingly feminized and aged; the newly built flats in the city and the promise of a separate home from both the husband's parents and her own; and the universal mandatory education, which drove both boys and girls far from the remote villages and into larger localities.

Propaganda accompanying recruitment in the countryside increasingly targeted women when the reservoir of male labour was exhausted. As my interviews with female workers revealed, it met with fantasies in which the city was represented as a world of openness, freedom, wealth, security, easier life, and love. However, it was not earlier than the mid-1970s when women felt that going to the city for work became 'the possibility of having a future or nothing'.

The fact that people I interviewed repeatedly referred to their coming to town in search of 'a future' or because 'there was no future in the villages' does not mean that the Romanian villagers had had brighter perspectives before the war. Extreme poverty, illness, illiteracy, lack of electricity, roads and transportation, and an extremely poor diet were everyday realities for most peasants in the historical Romanian provinces. Thus, this lack of 'future' in the postwar era must be understood rather as people's growing impossibility to reproduce themselves *as peasants*, in the sense of reproducing the production relations they were part of and within which they could see, think and imagine their survival. It must be understood from the perspective of class.

Although impossible to meet agricultural quotas, high taxes and the expropriations of land led to a radically shrinking of life in the villages, and although peasants increasingly needed to take factory employment to be able to support their households in the village, labour shortages continued to escalate everywhere. The situation was only going to get worse in the following years, and it led to a full-blown crisis of employment at the end of the First Five-Year Plan. Thus, since bringing peasants into the factories was not enough to ensure the functioning of industry, more workers were called upon to build socialism.

Arms That Built Socialism

As we have seen in the previous section, the slower tempo of the collectivization allowed peasants to use wage labour as an additional support for reproducing a permanently threatened structure of livelihood in the village. It also allowed the state to keep the price of labour low by partly externalizing the costs of its reproduction. The case of commuters is the most revealing because this category of workers can be traced in an explicit developmental strategy that shaped the relationship between territory, population and labour. However, the drive to move the costs of reproduction outside the realm of the state touched other social categories as well.

Urban women were the first ones targeted for industrial work after the implementation of planning. Their labour was needed more and more to complement that of the commuters and of the newly arrived men in the city. Men's wages, which were barely enough to cover the basic needs of young individuals living in a dormitory, or even less to rent a room, were totally insufficient for starting a family. As we saw in the previous chapter, wages were kept so low in the first years of planning that most of the time women had no choice but to join the factories, and to add their income to that of their husbands or fathers. It is hard to tell if this was a coherent strategy to attract women into industry or simply an unintended consequence of the general tendency to keep wages as low as possible. Conscious or not, keeping men's wages low proved a good strategy to push women into the factories. Moreover, although in state socialism equal pay was guaranteed by law, because they were generally unskilled and they were not considered as the main breadwinners in their households, women were often pushed into lower paid jobs than men's, even within the same industrial unit.[61]

Female workers had not been such a rarity in the city's interwar industry, but they had generally been relegated to large industrial units and to those factories that needed almost exclusively unskilled workers.

Double-earner families tended to be rare, and in most households only the head of the family was employed in the factory. A small proportion of the households in Cluj (5–10 per cent) also sent their children to work in the factories.

In large industrial units, like János Herbák, factory work was common for the daughters and wives of skilled industrial workers, who worked side by side with their husbands or fathers, and sometimes were better skilled than them. They were also involved in structures of apprenticeship,

Table 3.3 Gender structure of industrial workforce in Cluj in 1938.

Industrial employment	Skilled (%)	Unskilled (%)
Head of the family only	82.90	75.22
Both husband and wife	17.10	24.78

Source: Bindea, 'Conditiunile', 12.

although it was generally expected that any woman would be 'skilled' anyway for certain tasks like cutting material or sewing. Given this structure of the leather and footwear factory workforce, it was not surprising that it was families that came to the fore of the struggle in the strike of 1946 at Dermata. It was also not surprising that they brought with them solidarity networks built around the old working-class neighbourhoods in the north-eastern part of the city.

Women from the outskirts of the city had also been an important resource for the factories in Cluj since the interwar period. Many of them were ethnic Romanians, and tended to join the factories to complement their husbands' precarious incomes as unskilled workers or day labourers. Like their male commuter counterparts, they also travelled long distances by foot to get to work, and combined subsistence agriculture with industrial employment.

The best account available for women's prewar employment in Cluj is a social inquiry – realized in 1936 by two students at the Superior School of Social Assistance 'Principesa Ileana' in Bucharest – at the Tobacco Factory, an industrial unit with a largely feminized labour force: 519 women to 174 men.[62] For their study, titled 'The Working Woman', the students sampled one hundred women and asked them about their income, their work conditions, and their family life.

The women's declared reasons for starting to work were poverty, the desire for financial independence, being an orphan, the desire to have a pension, their husband's unemployment and the need to support their many children. Many of them came from the Mănăştur area, and owned houses with gardens and sometimes a bit of land. The lack of cash to support agricultural production and to build, repair or improve their houses was one of the most important incentives for women to work before the Second World War, which suggests a quasi-similar logic of reproducing one's survival structure of possibility as in the case of the rural families.

Table 3.4 Income structure for the families of the Tobacco Factory women.

Main source of income	Number of households (%)
Woman's earnings	17
Husband's earnings	70
Inheritance	10
Pension	3
Total	100
+ Children work to supplement family income	10

Source: *Femeia muncitoare în fabrică*, 6. See note 62.

Women were brought into the factory by their parents when they retired, by their husbands or by other relatives. They started when they were 14–15 years old, and later brought their children to work temporarily in the factory. At the moment of employment, for most women at the Tobacco Factory it was not their first work experience outside their homes. Most of them had already worked temporarily or by the day, and had helped their husbands at their workplaces. Most their husbands were journeymen, and those who did have a stable income were employed mainly in the Romanian army or lived on state benefits. Their earnings were always insufficient for sustaining the family, so their wives and children took up the task of supplementing the family's money.

Women's dexterity was often praised at the Tobacco Factory but it was not enough for ensuring them better wages. They were *all* unskilled, whereas almost half of the men in the factory had benefited from a form of professional training. Almost one-third of the women were illiterate. Their work norms were extremely high as they were always set against the speed of the best worker on the shop floor. The social inquiry reported that most women could not even stop to drink water until noon because of the way the production targets had been set. They worked in very harsh conditions, constantly falling sick because of the dust, cold and nicotine. Women's loss of pregnancies was much higher than in other factories, and tuberculosis was also very frequent. In 1936, more than half of the workers at the Tobacco Factory had some sort of pulmonary problems. On average, workers got sick more than three times in a year. Although the factory had a nursery, grandmothers, neighbours and older brothers actually took care of the children, because the workers could never count on a regular schedule. On average, the women from the Tobacco Factory worked twelve hours a day in the factory and spent more than two hours walking to and from work. After hours, they continued to work at home – cooking, cleaning and working their gardens.

While industrial work was not uncommon in the interwar period, it was still not central in women's lives. Even late into the 1950s, many women in Cluj were still not employed in state factories or institutions, but continued to run their households. Many of them, especially the *hoștezeni*'s wives and mothers, contributed to their families' revenues by selling agricultural products on the local market. Unemployed women remained a category especially vulnerable to nationalist and religious rhetoric, and the party considered them a risk for the stability of the city's industrial neighbourhoods and semi-rural outskirts. This constituted an extra incentive for the agitprop to conduct active campaigns to attract them into the factories.

As women's industrial employment slowly became the norm, the meaning of what a 'good girl' was also began to change. At least for urban and newly urbanized workers, a woman's worth came to include a good factory or commercial job. According to former workers' own assessment of their colleagues' desire to start a family, young people who migrated to the city seemed to be quick in getting married, both for pooling resources and for coping with the sense of loss and loneliness when faced with the new world of the city. Commuters must have felt less pressured to get married after coming to town, as their money was needed by their parents and younger brothers. Moreover, with no land to inherit, they probably needed more time to save in order to be able to support a new family.

Not only women but also children continued to enter the factory gates. They were especially important for those periods when the ban on employing extra workers became paralysing. In the summer months, this interdiction was doubled by the obligation to allocate a certain period of the summer for workers' vacations. Although employing supplemental workers during the summer was not allowed, the factories by-passed the regulations by using a simple method. Since many industrial units were required to offer a space for the mandatory training of youngsters in production, they used children and students, the sons and daughters of their employees, as their last resort.[63] At János Herbák, employing children and students for the summer was only possible if a parent made an official request to the Light Industry Ministry or to the Leather and Footwear Central Department. Hence, the factory management circulated a collective announcement during lunchtime (the preferred communication channel of the party), requesting their employees to ask that their children be sent to their own factory, where their summer work was much needed.[64] The possibility of keeping their children under surveillance while they were earning extra money for the household was enthusiastically received by workers, who responded promptly to the director's request. Still, this was far from enough to solve the problem.

Replacing apprenticeship with professional schools constituted another source of cheap labour for the factories. In the 1950s, professional schools started to function under the patronage of the factories, who paid for students' accommodation, meals and education. Teenagers were hosted in dormitories, had their own cafeterias and learned a craft by working in the factory in the afternoon, for the duration of their schooling. Parents signed a contract through which they agreed to pay for their children's education if the youngsters did not stay in the same factory for three years after their graduation, which was the corresponding duration of their schooling. This way, professional schools had the double logic of producing skilled workers and ensuring continuity in production for at least six years. In time, moving the secondary socialization from the family to the factory proved to be fundamental not only for ensuring a pool of cheap and easily controlled labour, but also for forming loyalties and a sense of solidarity on the shop floor. Nonetheless, most professional schools were just in their infancy. Parents still needed their children in the countryside to work the land, and girls were still likely to stay at home, under their parents' control, until they got married. Those parents who decided to send their children to professional schools did so precisely because life in the countryside was dwindling and they could get rid of 'another mouth to feed'.

In the early 1950s, the youngsters received a fixed salary for their work in the factory. But at the end of the Five-Year Plan, when production was destabilized by shortages, unaccounted absences, lack of discipline and labour turnover, their hours in production increased from 24 to 36 hours weekly. Moreover, piecework also became part of the trainees' experience when they started to be paid according to the quantity and quality of the goods they produced. The measure was presented as advantageous for the youngsters, but the novices could not keep up with the pace of the older and more experienced workers, so they ended up working more but earning less than before. The disappointment made many of them leave the factory, never to return.

The army was also a source of cheap (sometimes free) labour for the factories, who needed not only more workers but also disciplined ones. Soldiers were easy to control and their fate was ultimately not the responsibility of the management. Prison inmates also came to be used more and more for the most physically challenging tasks in several factories in Cluj. János Herbák, for instance, used both soldiers and inmates in construction work and in the tanneries, where ordinary workers refused to enter because of the unbearable smell and because of the heavy lifting required. The inmates were brought in in the morning by truck, permanently guarded during the day, and sent back to their cells in the evening. This practice was common until the 1980s in the workshops where mechanization was not possible and the work conditions were dire.

The party also made an effort to integrate Roma people into the factories, mainly in the fields where they had also been seasonally employed before the war. In Cluj county, the first attempts to settle Roma population were related to the Agrarian Reform in 1945. Orchestrated by the Romanian Workers' Party, this complex endeavour hit the wall of the historical fractures between the structure of Roma livelihood and the more sedentary, regulated forms of life.

The struggles of the party activists in Cluj county were wonderfully described in a fragment of the memoirs of Egon Balas, a party activist himself:

> We created all kinds of incentives for the Gypsies to settle down. From being nomadic semi-beggars, they had now become landowners, and we told them that if they worked they could become respectable, well-to-do farmers. We set up courses to teach them how to work the land and gave them all kinds of financial advantages. Settling the Gypsies successfully was for us a matter of party prestige – one way of exposing the falsehood of the racial prejudice that held Gypsies to be inherently lazy, inclined to thievery and disinclined to work. But it was incredibly hard. We did not give up, of course – communists never give up, nor do they admit defeat. But in order to accomplish what the party wanted, the Gypsies had to be literally forced to stay on the land and forbidden to leave the village under threat of arrest. Of course, forced farming cannot be good farming, and the Gypsy village, poor at the start, remained poor.[65]

In the 1950s, Roma people in the city of Cluj still lived in semi-nomadic groups and slum areas. Almost all Roma workers were unskilled. Thus, they earned little, were placed in the heaviest jobs, and were even more tempted to leave the factories and find day-by-day solutions for survival.

In a City Committee meeting, the director of the brick factory was complaining that 250 unskilled Roma workers missed work in June 1954. They were recruited to work in the countryside in other Transylvanian regions, and preferred to leave the factory because 'we introduced piece rate but they did not work thoroughly so they could not earn enough. They were very upset and left the factory without having our permission'.[66] Years would pass until some of the Roma people employed in the factory could start seeing their workplace as more than a temporary life strategy.

Another category of new and inexperienced workers was that of the former civil servants, magistrates and clerks. Some of them were made redundant because of various administrative reforms, especially in 1949, when 97,000 governmental jobs were eliminated and 66,000 people were left without employment. Many of them were sent into production, together with former landlords, artisans and owners of small shops, as a path to redemption. Their 're-education' (*reeducare*) required first of all their transformation into productive citizens. The former 'well-offs' were offered a possibility to become 'useful'. Foremen, engineers and leaders in production were asked 'to give them comradely help in order to learn faster. They should show them patiently how to handle each tool, taking into account that these clerks are way beyond the age of apprenticeship. But if they are taught how to work, they can become productive elements.'[67] After the Office for the Reallocation of the Labour Force was created in March 1949, it started to direct these people to the economic sectors that were developing most rapidly. Heavy work was preferred as a pedagogic instrument for their self-transformation but, accidentally or not, they ended up simply where a labour force was most needed.

These categories of workers had fewer options to leave their factories if they were ill-treated. They needed special permits to work, and were less employable because their biographies were far from being 'healthy', even after they passed through a process of purification. These constraints often extended to their sons and daughters, who had to accept any kind of job although there were so many openings around.

The integration of the former 'better-offs' in the factories proved to be difficult, and opportunities to humiliate them abounded. In some factories, the foremen refused to find any other work for several former magistrates other than cleaning the floors. In others, the workers made obscene drawings with chalk on the back of their new colleague, or handed them very hot tools, which severely burned their skin. The easy explanation for workers' behaviour lay in the modalities in which the social category of 'the ex-' was constructed through political representation of the 'class enemy', which proliferated in every poster, newspaper article and theatrical representation. But it was probably more complicated than this. Workers' acting out might have been rooted in what some of them must have felt when allowed to believe (even for a moment) that they were finally in the now, in an empowering historical present.

The workers who were used to covering the productive needs of the factories in the 1950s – commuters, seasonal workers, women, inmates, soldiers and children – might have been part of a flexible workforce, but they were also unreliable, unruly, unskilled and politically uncomfortable. Their relationship with the factories, and thus to the socialist state as a manager of production, varied according to people's own strategies of survival. What all of them had in common was that they failed to fall under the total control of the factories. Thus, the making of the socialist economy and the exercise of state power heavily depended upon historically grounded systems of provisioning that the socialist state at once attacked and preserved.

From the state's perspective, the 'peasant' confronted the 'proletarian' as artificially made categories of rule. But in the city, the *vinituri* settling next to old Clujeni pushed forward a move that, in William Roseberry's words, was rather from 'peasant' to 'other' than from peasant to urbanite.[68] The encounter between peasants, women, former better-offs and old workers was also going to prove a complicated one. As a 'transition' to a specific process of industrialization, it was going to be painful – rather a passage 'from a disordered past to a disordered present',[69] always facing a universally bright and abstract future but always chasing it in a present that was ethnicized, gendered and classed.

Notes

1. Murgescu, *România și Europa*.
2. Konrád and Szelenyi, 'Social Conflicts of Underurbanization'; Harloe, Andrusz and Szelenyi, *Cities after Socialism*.
3. Szelenyi, 'East European Socialist Cities', 49.
4. Bodnar, *Fin de Millénaire Budapest*, 27.
5. This claim is more valid for cities like Cluj, placed at the margins of socialist accumulation, than for other cities in Romania, which were included differently in the developmental logic of the state, had a stronger industrial tradition, or benefited from dissimilar rural–urban migration patterns.
6. Turnock, *The Romanian Economy*. The same strategy was going to be used by multinationals in the 2000s when they placed their industrial units in the countryside, making use of a cheap labour force that could combine industrial work with subsistence agriculture. See Petrovici, 'Neoliberal Proletarization'.
7. N. Stern and M. Costache, 'În legatură cu repartizarea socialistă a forțelor de producție în industrie' [About the socialist distribution of productive forces in industry], *Probleme economice* (June 1956), 3–16. The figures are calculated on the basis of *Anuarul Statistic 1939–1940* and *Enciclopedia României*, vol. II, 3–16.
8. In her book, Manu Goswami offers a similar interpretation of the consequences of infrastructural growth in colonial India. Drawing on Anderson's *Imagined Communities*, she shows brilliantly how infrastructural development contributed to the consolidation of the capital flows within the British Empire, but it also produced a form of economic, social and territorial integration that made the notion of 'India' (as an entity distinct from the metropolis) possible. Goswami, *Producing India*.
9. Stern and Costache, 'În legatură cu repartizarea socialistă'.
10. S. Zeigher, 'Planul de stat al RPR', *Probleme economice* (January–March 1949), 42.
11. Petrovici, *Zona urbană*.
12. Stern and Costache, 'În legatură cu repartizarea socialistă'.
13. Durkheim, *The Division of Labor*, 85.
14. For a discussion of Durkheim's notion of organic solidarity as struggle, see Pearce, *The Radical Durkheim*.
15. Lux, 'Industrial Development'.
16. The contradictory character of territorial development that accompanied socialist industrialization is well captured in the literature on the Soviet Union and Eastern Europe. See, for example, Moshe Lewin's explanation of the bureacratic crisis of the 1920s–1930s in the Soviet Union as a consequence of the incapacity of the state to respond to the issues that appeared in the trail of rural–urban migration, dislocations, and the integration of peasants into the socialist cities, in Lewin, *The Soviet Century*. For Poland, the everyday implications at the level of community building and integration, see Kate Lebow's wonderful incursion into the building of Nowa Huta, in *Unfinished Utopia*. For Romania, the reader can consult Sampson, *National Integration*; and Mărginean, *Ferestre spre furnalul roșu*. These works, however, focus on cities that were central in the accumulation logic of the state, articulated around investments in heavy industry as foundation for primitive socialist accumulation. However, there is still a lot to be understood about the marginal spaces of industrialization and their place in a broader history of the region, and in the making of socialist economies.
17. Turnock, *The Romanian Economy*.
18. Ronnås, *Urbanization in Romania*.
19. The results of this failure to develop equally various regions of the socialist countries were obvious in the 1970s, when according to Gabor Lux, the industrial jobs as a share of the total in Eastern and Central Europe still varied from under 35% to over 61%.

20. These patterns were complemented by seasonal long-distance migration and by all the other strategies to keep factories alive. It seems that urban centres attracted the most temporary migrants but state farms and rural industry also absorbed seasonal work. Some occupations that traditionally involved movement across the country – like sheep grazing and forestry – also attracted an important number of seasonal workers (see Turnock, *Economic Geography of Romania*). Among industrial branches, constructions were notorious for the use of seasonal and temporary work.
21. Ronnås, *Urbanization in Romania*, note 26.
22. This is a classical case of what Eugen Weber called migration as 'an industry of the poor' in *Peasants into Frenchmen* (278).
23. Levy, *Ana Pauker*.
24. Verdery and Kligman, *Peasants under Siege*.
25. Hotărârea nr. 147/1952 cu privire la efectuarea reformei bănești și la reducerile de prețuri; see also Turnock, *Economic Geography of Romania*, 181.
26. 2 lei 80 bani for one rouble. The gold content of the new leu was established at 0,079346 grams of fine gold.
27. 1 new leu for 100 old lei – up to 1,000 old lei; 1 new leu for 200 old lei – between 1,000 and 3,000 old lei; and 1 new leu for 400 old lei – anything over 3,000 old lei. For bank deposits, 50=1; 100=1; 150=1; 200=1.
28. Gurley, 'Excess Liquidity'.
29. Ronnås, *Urbanization*, note 82.
30. Verdery and Kligman, *Peasants under Siege*; Iordachi and Dobrincu, *Transforming Peasants*. In the mountains, many villages were never collectivized and so peasants could keep their individual plots and some of their animals in exchange for animal products and wood cutting. However, the state's lack of interest in the mountain areas meant that investment also failed to come in many of these and other rural regions, and kept them more backward than their counterparts in the plains.
31. The CAP pensions proved to be a catastrophe in postsocialism, when an aged rural population was utterly shattered by the devastating effects of the collapsing economy in the countryside and their lack of cash.
32. Turnock, *Economic Geography of Romania*, 17.
33. The idea was that villages should be within ten kilometres of a town, so more than 300 new 'towns' were planned to be built in the 1970s to ensure that commuting was easy.
34. Later, the state aimed to control population movement through the introduction of a residence visa, Decree 53/1975. The visa was given by the local police of the town or village where the person wanted to relocate. It could be permanent or renewable (for three or six months). Residence visas in fourteen of the largest Romanian cities were severely restricted, with the exception of newly married couples if one of the spouses was already a resident. Dependent children and parents were also allowed to move to these cities if they were to live with their families. Work could be a reason to migrate to a large city, but only if the director of the institution could prove that there was nobody else who was already residing in that city who could perform that job. Cluj was one of the fourteen cities.
35. Turnock, *Economic Geography of Romania*, 17.
36. Ronnås, *Urbanization*, note 176.
37. Literally, 'those who came'.
38. Pieces of corn flour baked in the oven.
39. M., former clerk, Hungarian, female, born in 1922.
40. Țara Moților was an especially problematic region. A mountain region with a pastoral population, it was considered extremely backward by the party activists. After the war, an outburst of typhus and syphilis required complex and radical sanitary interventions in the area. However, with the people moving a lot and coming to town for work, the epidemy could not be controlled for years.

41. ANDC, CR P.M.R. Cluj, Fund 51, Materiale prezentate în ședințe de birou și plenare, Proces verbal, ședința de birou a Comitetului Raional Cluj, 22 February 1952.
42. Bindea, 'Conditiunile', 13.
43. ANDC, Fund 2, CJ P.C.R Cluj, Raport politic, October 1946.
44. ANDC CR P.C.R. Fund 13, 93/1955, 55–60.
45. Relying on HCM 1509 and 4299 and on the Decree 78.
46. ANDC CR P.C.R. Fund 13, 93/1955, 56.
47. Gordeeva, Drancă and Orăștean, *Cluj-Napoca 1939–1960*, 30; interview Reka K., Hungarian.
48. Interviews, J., Railways Workshops.
49. Interview, A., female worker, Armătura.
50. ANDC Fund 13, CR P.M.R. Cluj, 36/1951, Proces verbal 36, 29 May 1951.
51. ANDC Fund Clujana, 28/135/1950.
52. ANDC Fund 55, CO P.M.R. Cluj, 3/1953, 21, my emphasis.
53. ANDC Fund 55, CO P.M.R. Cluj, 3/1953.
54. Decree 51/ 10 February 1949 pentru vărsarea beneficiilor.
55. The director's fund represented a quota from the benefits of every factory – 4 per cent for the heavy industry ones and 2 per cent for the others.
56. Ronnås, *Urbanization*, 154.
57. HCM nr. 441 din 25 Aprilie 1950; and ANDC, Fund Clujana, 28/135/1950.
58. Lampland, *The Object of Labor*, 45.
59. Verdery and Kligman, *Peasants under Siege*.
60. Ronnås, *Urbanization in Romania*.
61. This was admitted by two factory directors in the 1950s, and coroborated in interviews with female workers who told me that the foremen, or sometimes one of the representatives of the party organization in the factory, tried to convince them to move to a different workshop because work was easier. I have no evidence of any negative consequences for their refusal.
62. Ministerul Muncii – Oficiul de studii sociale și relații internaționale, 333/1937, Școala superioară de asistență socială Principesa Ileana, *Femeia muncitoare in fabrică*. (The study was carried out using 100 working mothers at the Tobacco Factory in Cluj. I am grateful to Alexandra Ghiț for making this survey available to me.)
63. ANDC, Fund Clujana, 0/1949.
64. Ibid.
65. Balas, *Will to Freedom*, 171. Egon Balas was a fascinating figure of the party. As a young Jewish intellectual and a communist, he was deported from Transylvania but survived the war. He was an activist on the rise but soon suffered from the anti-intellectual stance of the party leaders in Bucharest. He was arrested by the Securitate and interogated. Later, he emigrated to the United States where he took a chair in mathematics at a prestigious university.
66. ANDC, Fund 55, CO P.M.R. Cluj, p. 196.
67. ANDC, Fund 3, CJ P.M.R. Cluj, 106/10.
68. Roseberry, *Anthropologies and Histories*.
69. Ibid., 58.

II

TIME AND ACCUMULATION ON THE SHOP FLOOR

CHAPTER 4

'HIDDEN RESERVES OF PRODUCTIVITY' AND THE QUEST FOR KNOWLEDGE

Knowledge for the Plan

In the broadest sense, the socialist projects in Eastern and Central Europe represented a specific way to fight backwardness and open the social world to progress through scientific rationality. Socialist regimes were discursively and pragmatically committed to the twentieth-century Western modernizing project: hierarchical work management, standardization and quantification of social life, secular boundaries to the workday, universalistic time frames and a welfare system built around a nationally bound division of labour. In the postwar era, this commitment unabatedly relied on the pillars of Soviet – and by extension Western – industrialization: the rationalization of production, scientific management and a wage system based on piece-rate and quantifiable work/time units.

As Martha Lampland teaches us, 'the stark numbers we will eventually see in the work unit value matrix are the product of thoroughly social processes, not the crystallization of isolated elements'.[1] The way in which the early socialist 'project of commensuration and quantification' was 'tethered to time and place' is the focus of Part II of this book, which analyses how the plan figures became part and parcel of the Stalinist rearticulation of the Romanian industrial relations in the 1950s, and how in turn they captured the frailty of these relations. While the plan has often been imagined as a bureaucratic instrument imbued with the power to materialize a hyper-rational social order and to propel an ever-increasing productivity in the socialist factories, in the following chapters I will focus on planning as a bottom-up process that was subjected to struggles and negotiations on the shop floor and strongly impacted by what happened in the sphere of social reproduction.

The next three chapters focus on the mechanisms of socialist accumulation on the shop floor and on the politics of productivity that accompanied the implementation of central economic planning between 1949 and 1955. I reconstruct the concerns of the new economic executives when dealing with the requirements of a multidimensional transformation of the shop floor into an object of knowledge, into a disciplinary space, and into an ethical realm. I further explore the impact of the daily struggles to reproduce a cheap and flexible labour force in between the city and the countryside on the possibility of controlling and mobilizing workers on the shop floor, as well as putting their tacit knowledge to use. I suggest that the practical everyday reality of the early socialist factories can be seen as the last breathing moment of a long-standing effort to shape industrial life along the lines of a combination between Taylorism and the Marxist conceptualization of time. These chapters will thus show how the daily operations of planning encapsulated the multivocal nature of socialist labour – as labour power, as living labour and as bearer of an advanced historical consciousness – and how they translated the encounter between contradictory temporal horizons into an ethical regime that was rooted directly in production. The chapters follow the tribulations of planners and factory managers when their attempts at hyper-rationalization of production confronted the reality of workers' livelihoods. On the shop floor, these attempts targeted both the necessity of making the labourers work more, faster and better, and the hopeful possibility of securing their enthusiastic consent.

Before anything else, converting the expanding productive potential of socialist labour into reality required the emergence of a complex knowledge production apparatus. This apparatus was articulated in three ways: by constructing legibility structures; by making labour into an object of scientific and managerial knowledge; and by transforming the state's agents into skilful ethnographers. This is precisely the conceptual sequence I follow in this chapter, which opens with an exploration of the knowledge infrastructure required by the implementation of planning, then investigates the ways in which knowledge became the cornerstone of an economic imaginary centred around the notion of 'hidden resources', and ends with an analysis of deep participant observation as a type of knowledge meant to make sense of the intersection between production and life.

From the very beginning, devising a plan as 'a mere sequence of figures and tasks' proved a daunting endeavour. Having a plan presupposed a rational determination of production and consumption needs, and a global view of the necessary input of raw materials, labour and fixed capital. Planning required an increasing power of aggregating data at higher levels of complexity and was reliant upon mathematical modelling, which evolved in time from simplified forms of input/output matrices to linear modelling of growth, and then to cybernetic integrative schemas towards the end of the regime.[2] The technical dimension of planning included mechanisms for harmonizing labour processes in different locations, for allocating labour force, for balancing supply and demand, for minimizing production costs, for shortening transportation routes and for easing access to resources. Consequently, planning can hardly be understood without a vocabulary of labour rationalization or outside a broader set of managerial practices, which dominated the world of production in the twentieth century.

This chapter will show that learning about the factory proved to be a continuous struggle during the first years of planning as this knowledge required the creation of specific legibility structures capable of functioning for nascent categories of rule. The emergence of these legibility structures was not only uneasy but also insufficient, as they could not capture the daily routines of the production process. The Soviet version of Taylorism was called upon to complement statistical knowledge, and stopwatches and flow charts soon became familiar to the Romanian workers as the material infrastructure of an attempt to constantly push their norms up and threaten their earnings. Consistent with Preobrazhensky's idea that surplus extraction under the conditions of primitive socialist accumulation relied on workers' willing self-restraint, the workers were supposed to step up from being objects of scientific management to becoming knowledge producers and innovators themselves. Relying solely on Taylorist-inspired tropes was still not enough, since shop-floor practices could never be separated from the social fabric on which the factories themselves were embroidered. Hence, the local party committees, the government's offices and the factory managers also relied on a type of knowledge of an ethnographic inspiration, for which observation and participation in the factory life were central.

During the first years of planning, these different types of knowledge became intrinsic to the logic of governmentality in which the factories were caught. The practical necessity of relying on various forms of knowledge was rooted in one fundamental characteristic of planning: the fact that it was always prospective. Although the parameters of production were by and large set in advance, they were also considered to be unknown, as the factories were always hiding reserves of productivity that could not be determined at the moment of planning. In the logic of planning, the shop floor was actually bearing a yet undiscovered potential for increasing quantity, speed, quality and efficiency through a better organization of the production process. Factory managers and workers alike were going to find out the *real* capacities of their industrial unit when trying to surpass the expectations of the planners. These 'hidden reserves' (or 'inner reserves') could never be exhausted because the act of work itself was self-regenerative. Thus, the increase in the plan figures had its roots in the idea that infinite growth was possible by endlessly expanding and improving workers' *current* practices.

This was crucial, since the postwar capital hunger, the pressures of war reparations, and the consequent low level of investment meant that the increase in labour productivity could depend solely on the rationalization of work methods, on workers' and managers' mobilization on the shop floor, and on the elimination of waste.[3] Consequently, revealing the 'hidden reserves' of the socialist factories became one of the most important missions of the technical stuff, from foremen to government officials.[4] The state dedicated the 1949 and 1950 one-year plans to learning about existing economic processes and to training personnel who could process newly acquired information about the nationalized factories. The activities of these formative years were mainly directed towards transforming the state itself into an extraordinary machine, which was able, in a relatively short time, to originate its vision in 'seeing'.

At least theoretically, early socialist economies functioned on the assumption of an infinitely expanding productive potential of socialist labour, and with an understanding of the producer not as a given unit of planning, but as an 'always-in-the-making' entity – someone who would go through a continuous process of self-transformation in order to produce more, better and faster.[5] Ideally, this self-transformation was not driven by financial incentives or by the whip of necessity, but by an ever-increasing political awareness. This 'labour for growth' impetus appeared as the outcome of a vision that had self-transformation at its core, with personal development, skilling and the formation of a new work mentality as its main dimensions.

Investigating the factory as the ground on which central planning was made possible opens a broad space for a critique of James Scott's argument that 'legibility as a central problem in statecraft' became the ultimate way of knowing in modernity.[6] According to Scott's celebrated book, the gaze of the state and its 'politics of measurement'[7] came to involve the simplification, the quantification, and the standardization of knowledge through the suppression of *mētis*, understood as local and informal knowledge, practices and spontaneous improvisations. Eliminating other forms of knowledge and replacing them with techniques of counting and mapping was necessary as an instrumental intervention in reality, which was supposed to be 'sliced', represented and remade.

The import of the Bolshevik socialist project in Romania had all the elements of a high-modernist project: an administrative ordering of nature and society; an authoritative state; an almost blind faith in scientific laws, technical progress and rational social engineering; and an absent civil society. Nonetheless, my findings will demonstrate that the Romanian socialist government relied not only on statistical, standardized and schematic information, but also on local knowledge, extracted from contextualized practices of the factory managers and from workers' 'ways of doing'. The state was predominantly interested in an efficient organization of work, and socialist planners regarded this efficiency as a task of governing concrete locations. Against James Scott's line of thinking, I argue that socialist planning could not function by suppressing practical, locally situated knowledge. Instead, many economic decisions were based on information coming from specific situations, described in the documents of the time with an attention to local practices very different from the universalizing knowledge predicated by Scott. Not only did the party know the limits of knowledge simplification beyond numerical production, but it also addressed these limitations by using other forms of learning about their object of governance. It is my claim that, alongside standardized observation coming from the scientific management tradition, the production of ethnographic knowledge was central to this project.

The factory documents of the time bear witness to a continuous effort of centralization, always emerging from the articulation of the plan figures. The necessities related to planning led to the emergence of specific legibility structures, which reflected shifting power hierarchies within the factories, and brought the plan to life by breaking it into millions of pieces and space/time fragments. However, the archives also reveal an everyday struggle to make production understandable beyond numbers, while the direct involvement of the state on the shop floor led to an increasing reliance on observation and interpretative work.

Ethnography, both as method and as a specific form of knowledge, has been vital to modern statecraft, and was often explicitly linked to administrative practices of domination and control. The Romanian ethnographic tradition itself was tied to the interwar societal project of rural emancipation, and served as a political tool for nation building and state formation.[8] Most of these efforts stopped after the war, as their relationship with nationalist politics was deemed dubious by the state officials. In the 1960s, when experts in development returned to ethnography, their efforts were tied once again to a re-emergence of a nationalistic turn in Romanian political life. Little is known, though, about the place of observation, description or interpretation in socialist factories.

This chapter shows how the state produced personal interpretative accounts of practices, routines and interactions, based on direct experience and limited time immersion in bounded locations. They were part of a 'grand-scale ethnographic work',[9] which involved not only the Secret Police but also institutions as diverse as schools, hospitals and universities. In the factories, this concern to document reality in situ was visible in the ordinary interactions between members of the party organization, managers and workers. It can be followed in their weekly and monthly reports, in their interventions in the production minutes, and in their daily interference with the production process. I will emphasize, though, the role of the activists trained in the party schools to take up work in the documentary sections of the regional party committees. They were taught to sample locations according to the most relevant criteria for the problem under study, to contact informants, to ground their findings on multiple sources, to analyse the ways in which their presence affected the behaviour of the workers and to write detailed reports comprising not only crude facts but also their interpretations. This distinctive set of methods and instruments involved a notion of 'being there', which can be easily compared to the classical anthropological one.

Focusing on planning and centralization as 'economy in the making' allowed me to uncover various forms of knowledge employed by the state in its attempt to make the world readable and manipulable. First, I will show how the state indeed produced quantified, simplified and standardized information about economy, territory and population, by using techniques similar to those covered by Scott's notion of 'legibility'. Although crucial, legibility structures were not enough to ensure production management or political control. Numbers could not link economic performance to work practices and daily routines, nor reveal the productive 'hidden reserves' upon which early industrial socialism as a labour-intensive regime depended. Most importantly, the numbers that were always filling the reports for the party county committees or the corresponding ministries were unable to capture the production process as movement. The state – as a manager-state this time – appealed to the Soviet transposition of Taylor's principles of scientific management in an attempt to extract workers' embodied knowledge and to understand production processes on the ground. The materialization of an image of the plan as a conveyor belt that would link the whole national economy in an uninterrupted chain of actions and knowledge ultimately depended on understanding every worker's practices at the workbenches.

Although notions of 'efficiency' and 'productivity' were articulated on an unprecedented scale, the party officials could not stop there. Their data, no matter how complex, did not yet render understandable the relationship between production and life, nor between the productivism of the manager-state and the moral regulation of a workers' state.

Neither statistics nor classical sciences of labour could help the state to understand how economy and society were entangled in the everyday functioning of the plan. Accordingly, the state needed a form of knowledge of an ethnographic inspiration that was able to capture the messy, contradictory and fragmentary character of everyday interactions and practices at the factory level, and their embeddedness in people's everyday lives.

The use of ethnography in the factory is a powerful case against Scott's impoverished notion of 'legibility', because it shows that, while the factories appeared as categories (reductions or simplifications) in the plan's figures, through the use of other forms of knowledge they preserved their position as cases in the accumulation logic of the state. More importantly, it shows that socialist accumulation itself was understood as more than a projection of plan figures. While Scott rightfully argued that totalizing projects are organically related to schematic knowledge, he failed to notice that socialist states – as manager-states – did not just administer populations and resources, but also ran and created social production processes. In addition, these social production processes were classified and acted upon not only according to their efficiency, but also according to their political relevance. For the socialist states – as workers' states this time – a particular interpretative endeavour was necessary to assess the evolution of the relationship between labour and the state. Ethnographic forms of knowledge provided a different, non-quantitative measure of the advancement of working-class consciousness. It was fundamental for supporting the main raison d'être of the socialist state: directing subjectivation processes towards a new form of rationality, loyalty and self-awareness, totally absent both from Scott's accounts of high modernist projects and from the classical Taylorist vision.

Understanding the place of various forms of knowledge in the socialist construction project enables us to understand differently the evolution of socialist modernization. Factories, as key spaces for state making in socialism, offer a unique opportunity to explore the complex ways in which knowledge is related to what states do and to what states are. Both the failures and the limited successes of the socialist projects in the twentieth century seem to have little to do with a poor mastery of knowledge. Different models and practices of knowledge production suggest another way to understand the 'socialist state-idea', as Abrams would have put it. 'Seeing like a state' appears to be intimately related to seeing the state itself as a multidimensional, unfinished project, in which certain categories are the object of its action, the mirror of its evolution and the active agents of its making. This exploration of planning as an activity of assembling information flows is in line with any anthropological tradition that considers state functioning as depending upon its capacity to make the world readable and understandable, further hinging on the ability of its local officials to transform any kind of political project into a situated reality.

Constructing Legibility Structures

Many forms of knowledge used in the process of planning after 1949 had their roots in the immediate postwar years. By the time central planning became an intrinsic part of Romanian industrial life, the factories had already possessed the experience of the war economy and of the six-month postwar reconstruction plan of 1947. Consequently, their administration was not going to appear that different in terms of everyday practices and routines.

Before the nationalization and the collectivization processes started, the government conducted national-level agricultural and industrial censuses, as well as local housing censuses.[10] In 1947, a census of all industrial and commercial units was conducted by the Central Statistical Institute at the request of the Governmental Commission for the Economy Recovery and Monetary Stabilization, allowing the state to produce an image of the most important constituents of the national economy.[11] It targeted the enterprises whose activity was going to be integrated in the postwar reconstruction plan, and it represented the most crucial dimension of infrastructural knowledge for preparing the nationalization.

The initial lists were built on the records of the Industry and Trade Chamber and on a 1941 war census, which took place everywhere in Romania except for Northern Transylvania. The state officials aimed to trace the following categories of industrial units: the producers and users of energy, regardless of size; all industrial and trade units employing more than five people; all transportation units; all units in the chemical industry and the ones producing instruments for precision measurement. Accordingly, the technical staff or the managers of the enterprises had to fill in the following information: an inventory sheet, the list of manufactured goods sold on the market during the last year, the number of employees, the year when the economic unit was founded, the names of the owners, the address, the productive capacities, the territorial branches, the stores, the former productive capacities, and the sources and level of electricity consumption.[12]

The unions were called on to support the government's efforts to produce accurate industrial records and to uncover the 'hidden reserves' of the shop floor.

> The unions consider that the census will lead to finding new possibilities for increasing production, which are not used at the moment because of the sabotage practised by industrialists. There is still equipment that can produce more than the documents of the industrial units show, as well as raw materials hidden at the back of storage rooms instead of entering the production process immediately. Bringing these resources out into the open means more products on the market, the strengthening of the stabilized leu and a higher purchasing power of workers' wages.[13]

Any technical representatives of the industrial units or managers who would not comply with the obligations of the census or who provided false information were legally prosecuted under the accusation of economic sabotage.

When handing the forms, the factories got a certificate attesting to their participation in the census. Without the certificate, industrial units could not extend their clearance for functioning, could not benefit from fuel allocation and subsidies, and could not purchase raw materials. One representative of the factory committee had to sign the forms, confirming that the information provided by the factory managers was accurate.

The two financial reforms analysed in the first part of the book also worked well as visibility instruments. They functioned as surveys of liquid asset distribution, with citizens being forced to bring their cash out in the open. This newly enhanced transparency allowed further levies, requisitions and calculation of product deliveries in the countryside (especially for the 1952 Reform), as well as an assessment of the banknotes within the country's borders (especially important in Northern Transylvania in 1947). When large sums of money were exchanged, the bank representatives could check the source of the funds, which made profiteering more transparent.[14] Based on the industrial census and the Monetary Reform of 1947, the state could calculate the profitability gap of the factories, which included the losses due to low levels of productivity, to lack of demand for their products and to the deficits produced by the monetary stabilization itself. The planners could then make recommendations regarding the concentration of investments into profitable production units, and the unification of smaller enterprises into larger ones.

After the nationalization of the means of production in June 1948, the Romanian state officials had only six months left to gather the information they needed before they implemented the first one-year plan. But the party lacked the experience, the cadres, and even the conceptual categories required to produce this knowledge.[15] Learning about the factory required first of all the creation of specific structures, capable of capturing emergent categories of people, objects and relations. In James Scott's terms, the state's need to map its object gave birth to legibility structures, which were built exactly on the information routes that connected the factories to the local party committees and to the government.[16] These structures were not simply bearers of the state's will; they were created because of the plan and for the plan.

Statistics was called for again to reveal the way in which the rapid expansion of industry and the corresponding wage policy were impacting workers' everyday lives. Immediately after the nationalization, the government conducted a survey of the Romanian employees' living standards.[17] The survey unfolded over fourteen months, with the first two months dedicated to accumulating methodological experience, 'both for the surveyed families and for the researching personnel'. More than 16,000 family booklets were distributed over two months. Around 7,500 were returned to the researchers in August and 6,700 in September with the required information filled in. Industrial workers were the obvious focus of the survey (almost 65 per cent of the sample, 30 per cent skilled workers). The research targeted the following areas: the composition of workers' families; food consumption; housing facilities and comfort; the number of people per room and bed; the distance between the home and the workplace; and the available means of transportation. The explicit aim of the study was to establish a basis for the calculation of living cost indices and for the setting of nutritional standards according to the duration and intensity of work. These nutritional standards were then going to be used for the calculation of prices for the rationed goods.

According to the study, the 'typical family' earned an average monthly income of 13,242 lei, which meant 3,391 lei per family member. The survey showed that only 50 per cent of this amount came from the main professional activity of the head of the family. More than 4 per cent came from extra activities; another 4 per cent form selling goods and personal belongings; almost 2 per cent from subsidies and other forms of unspecified support; more than 6 per cent from payments in kind; and a staggering 24 per cent from loans and credit, wages paid in advance and money previously lent to relatives and co-workers.

Based on other studies conducted in this period, the General Confederation of Labour calculated the cost of workers' lives for the period October 1948 – October 1949 at 12,480 lei for a working-class family, with an average wage of 5,381 lei. The purchasing power for the same period was 43 per cent of the living costs, when the minimal daily nutrition standard of 7,000 calories per family was taken as the basis for calculation. The normal daily calorie consumption was established at 11,600 calories per family, in which case the purchasing power dropped to 26 per cent of the living costs. The survey completed this meagre picture by showing that the gross income covered only 47 per cent of the living costs of the typical working-class family. Almost 60 per cent of the family income went on food, while the average wage could not even cover the basic caloric needs of the workers. The ration cards were supposed to compensate for this situation, but the survey showed that they covered less than 15 per cent of the family consumption, while the goods purchased on the market made up around 85 per cent. The reports compared these figures to the purchasing power of the average income in 1938, which was around 58 per cent, with 18 per cent of the family income going on food. Except for the prices for housing, water and fuels, all others had basically doubled by 1948. The purchasing power of the average income in 1948 dropped to less than 68 per cent of its 1938 level.

The researchers pointed out further methods of data collection and analysis. In line with the highly individualized wage policy and the logic of planning, they included recommendations to use the individual, not the family, as the basis for future investigations, and to break the data down to the county level in order to establish the purchasing power of every region, and thus orient the activity of the Trade Ministry towards a more rational distribution of goods in the territory. The most important issue, though, was the capacity of the state apparatuses to analyse the data in due time, so governmental policy could make use of up-to-date information. The reports drew attention to the fact that the reduced workforce of the Central Statistical Institute was going to produce further delays in the investigation of workers' living conditions.

Although presented as the first attempt to research the family life of the Romanian employees, the study had actually been preceded by surveys of living standards in the interwar industry, including the one that took place in Cluj in 1938, as mentioned in earlier chapters. While recognizing the rich research tradition of village and peasant life in the interwar period, the 1938 investigation also claimed to be the first one of its kind for Romanian industry. Under the title 'The Life of the Worker in Cluj', the prewar survey represented an exploratory moment on which future studies of work, life, family budgets and time budgets were going to build. The survey established that 'the salary represented almost exclusively the only income of workers' and clerks' families. Given this, the well-being or misery of these families depended mostly on its level'.[18] This was in stark contrast with the findings of the 1948–1950 survey, which found that salary only made up half of the average worker's family income.

Industry-related legibility structures in the 1950s explicitly relied on the expertise of the institutions and people involved in the first attempts to implement industrial standardization during the interwar period and on the institutional routines established during the war. Some of these institutions were direct continuations of war economy structures, like the Undersecretariat of State Industry, a simple renaming of the State Undersecretariat of War Industry.[19] The cornerstone of this institutional configuration was the establishment of the State Planning Commission,[20] with six departments: planning, plan coordination, plan execution, studies and documentation, personnel and administration, and publications. To deal with the centralization of prices and the setting of wages, the State Planning Commission was going to rely on the experience of a wartime institution, the General Commissariat for Prices. The National Standardization Commission created by the Romanian Workers' Party government in 1949 was going to make use of the experience of the old Commission of Norms for the Romanian Industry, founded in 1928 – the organization that elaborated the project for the first industrial standardization methodology.

The uniformization of the statistical reports and the creation of the most appropriate frames for this numerical production represented very early priorities for the State Planning Commission. The 'Standardization Bulletin', a register containing the official standards for all the products manufactured in Romania, appeared in May 1949. In June 1949 (one year after nationalization) the commission had the first set of minimal technical and economic indices ready for use by the planning services in the factories. The same logic of making the world readable and manageable also encompassed other dimensions of economic activity, such as the elimination of barter, the uniformization of prices and, as we saw in Chapter 2, the employment and circulation of labour force. One of the main activities of these offices was the establishment of industrial standards for all aspects of the production process: quality, quantity, raw materials and necessary labour time. But the fixity of standards was illusory. They were going to change multiple times in the years to come at the National Standardization Commission level, and were going to be challenged in the planning offices of every factory for the whole socialist period.

These continuous changes made life extremely difficult for the new economic executives. In 1950, an exasperated representative of the Economic Division from the Regional Party Committee in Cluj distributed to the factories a detailed list containing the items required for a correct mode of reporting on industrial production.[21] All industrial units had to send to the Regional Party Committee multiple tables containing a complete list of their products, the number of employees, the names and the qualifications of the employees (from director to unskilled worker), the necessary security measures, various observations regarding the loyalty and obedience of the people in the factory, descriptive and quantitative assessments of their fixed capital, as well as production graphs for every month of 1950.[22] The process did not go smoothly, and the party leaders at all levels constantly complained that the factory administrative personnel was simply unable to fill in the forms correctly and on time. The factory managers responded bitterly that the requirements of the upper echelons were impossible because the factories did not have the necessary personnel, time or experience needed for these tasks. Moreover, the formats of the reports were changing monthly, and 'if in April the factories finally learned how to fill in the IPL form, this was replaced with the ETL form in May, and the problems started all over again'.[23]

Although the interwar experts were crucial to the new regime, the totalizing character of socialist planning required a dramatic increase in the production of standardized knowledge (especially the introduction of standardized accounting at all levels) and a quick professionalization of accountants and statisticians. This process started in November 1948 with the census of the industrial units, and continued with the founding of the Institute for Planning and Economic Administration, which in the following years produced new generations of planners to take their places in every factory, department and public institution.

They were going to act upon the received wisdom concerning the information prerequisites of the planning process, which was a specific type of 'knowledge of the socio-economic realities in movement and in their totality'.[24] While in the first stage of the planning process statistics had to function as an assessment of the foundation on which the plan figures were about to emerge, in the second stage it became the mirror of the plan's fulfilment and, as we will see in the last chapter, of workers' political consciousness. Following Stalin's words, the official discourse of the new Romanian executives required that statistics was 'a faithful mirror to reality, dialectical and not metaphysical'.[25]

In an essay titled 'The Role of Statistics in Planning', the author clearly stated that 'serious knowledge of the economic situation without statistics cannot be conceived', but he referred to a very particular understanding of the matter.

> An essential condition for statistics is that it is not 'pure statistics'. Nobody can imagine that statistics can exist and develop independently from the political and economic realities. Such speculative statistics, making itself busy with complicated calculations and all sorts of curves with no connection to reality, was criticized by Stalin, who called it a 'playing game with figures' [*joc de cifre*]. This kind of statistician is very surprised when social phenomena do not conform to the curves they draw, so they conclude that social phenomena tend to 'deviate from the statistical laws' ... The development of statistics outside or above the tasks set for our economy is inconceivable.[26]

The politics of calculation underlying the mechanisms of planning were explicitly recognized as 'class statistics', in opposition to 'bourgeois statistics', which was denounced as 'a means to prove the eternal nature of the capitalist regime, to represent the capitalist regime as the best possible, to hide the contradictions that eat its insides, and ultimately, to hide reality itself'.[27] The methods through which reality behind the figures were obscured by bourgeois statistics were mercilessly exposed: hiding important variation behind averages, the problematic political choice of categories for nominal variables, and relying on absolute numbers for interpreting social trends, while ignoring the eventful nature of the real. The bourgeois politicization of statistics was made explicit in several telling examples: noting the average consumption of sugar to obscure the fact that the owner of a factory used to consume nine kilos of sugar and the worker only one; separating the child mortality of out-of-wedlock children in order to hide class inequality in children's survival chances; or showing a decrease in the number of workers participating in the strikes of 1933 without mentioning the biggest strikes of the railway workers during that year.

In Cluj, planning and accounting departments were created at the factory level, with the explicit mission to reproduce the logic of the plan and to convey it to its final destination point: the worker/machine unit. These offices needed to be staffed by people who were going to embody this rationality. As we have seen in Chapter 1, in 1948 all factory directors were replaced by the party with workers who were considered loyal to the regime at the time of nationalization. Many of the second-rank economic executives were also removed due to their prewar far-right allegiances, and as a way to prevent resistance to new economic policies. The situation was further complicated by the need to find Romanian-speaking specialists in an area where, historically, industry had been dominated by Hungarian capital, management and labour. Of course, the official discourse maintained the Bolshevik revolutionary assumption that the vanguard party had the unique capacity to see the political and economic situation as a whole. However, the Romanian Workers' Party officials knew from the very beginning that in the process of building a new society they had to rely on the knowledge of the old one's members. Thus, many interwar experts were kept in factories and demoted (rarely retaining their status), simply to keep production going. Some of them had been directly involved in the forms of economic centralization characteristic of the war economy, and their expertise in management and planning was invaluable. They remained under the supervision of the party organizations and of the Soviet consultants who watched over the USSR's interests in the factories until the end of the 1950s, when the Red Army left Romania.

This was only a temporary solution, and soon the production of new competent cadres was at the top of the party's agenda. The activity of producing good norm-setters, accountants and administrators was systematically checked, and the Economic Section of the County Party Committee kept track of all good students from the first cohorts of the Institute for Planning and Economic Administration.[28] This emergent socialist bureaucracy was linked to the production of numerical information of all sorts and to the quantitative logic that was soon to become the frame for how people thought about their daily work. The production of numbers and statistics quickly transformed the factories into 'calculation centres',[29] which were directly or indirectly linked with *one* centre. Thus, centralization primarily depended upon being central in the flows of information, which were explicitly meant both to represent the social and to produce its future.

Even the language of planning had to be defined and disseminated before it could become the language of the economy. The most important programmatic journals of the time, *Economic Problems* and *Class Struggle*, introduced a recurrent section with the title: 'Helping the Planner: Basic Terms for Planning Activity', which was used to define fundamental terms like 'industrial unit' or 'synthetic indices of production'. The journals were often read during production meetings in order to help the new economic executives, lacking both experience and formal training in economics, to better understand the proceedings.

The subsequent stabilization of these categories was furthered by the adoption of this language by the factory directors themselves, for justifying the impossibility of fulfilling the tasks set by the plan. Not only were the first plans part of the struggle to make the existing world calculable, but they also helped to (re)create it in a new form through numerical inscription and the reification of categories used in everyday practice by accountants, statisticians and, above all, planners. The first economic plan in postwar Romania seemed designed as a perfect illustration of Corrigan and Sayer's idea that 'state formation, because it is cultural revolution, donates the terms through which "the State" may be worshipped, criticized, grasped, reformed, reconstructed, denied, held together, affirmed and carried onwards'.[30]

Immediately after the nationalization, it was not even accumulation itself that concerned the state officials, but rather the possibility to assess the capacity of the factories and to clearly understand the hierarchical chains through which any decision had to flow.[31] Detailed instructions about how to calculate labour productivity, about how to assess the number of hours actually worked by the factory employees or about how to set the work norms were sent to the factories and represented the top preoccupation of the state officials from then on.[32]

Although overfulfilling the plan represented the core of socialist accumulation, discovering the sources of this accumulation was more important for the state officials than surplus itself. Attempts to 'freeze action' in order to get a fixed image of the resources and the capacities of the socialist units resulted in temporary interdictions against overfulfilling the plan. In 1950, at János Herbák, the direct Instructions from the corresponding government office set the following prohibitions:

> We ask the comrade directors together with the chief engineers, the technicians, the workers, the party organization and the union to analyse and to disseminate the plan figures, and to assess the possibility that these figures could be accomplished before the deadline. Until 28 February, the industrial units will communicate to our Planning Service if the plan can be accomplished before the deadline – and if it can, by what date. These Instructions do not give the right to the factories to overfulfil the plan or to shorten the time needed for its fulfilment without a written approval from the Director of the Office. We draw attention to the fact that, until now, the office did not approve any overfulfilment of the plan or its realization in less than twelve months.[33]

In the following months, the factory managers who overfulfilled their production plans were always scolded by the local party leaders who were present at the factory meetings. A general assembly quickly transformed into a public teaching moment when comrade Rado was admonished by comrade Ungar: 'Who gave you the order to overfulfil the plan, even if you had to use overtime? For this year, the ministry demanded a fulfilment of 100 per cent of the plan. No slogan for the overfulfilment of the plan could have been heard by comrade Rado in our factory, because all the industrial plants had been programmed at their maximum capacity'.[34]

These freezing moments indicate the fact that although standardization was supposed to lead to the crystallization and stabilization of economic structures, the flow of the production process was puzzling to the planners, who tried to fix its image in artificial ways. The Romanian party officials quickly came to realize that statistics were inadequate in situations that required mastery of how things were actually done on the shop floor. Contextual knowledge about the labour process as movement proved hard to grasp. It was also extremely difficult to exploit, as production figures could be easily manipulated if the gaze of the state did not penetrate the walls of the factories. The use of scientific management came as a first solution for this partial blindness of the state.

The Manager-State: Seeing the Movement

Like in Taylor's original proposition, employing the principles of scientific management in the socialist factories was supposed to increase productivity, pacify labourers and lead, in time, to an organic cooperation between workers and management. Scientific management was born as a family of ideologies and techniques designed to maximize productivity through analysing and reorganizing the shop floor. It relied on the fragmentation of the labour process into discrete tasks, which were then timed and analysed by the managers in order to reveal wasteful movements and to prevent systematic soldiering. At the level of practices, the everyday managerial anxieties of the Romanian economic executives of the 1950s appeared to be hardly different from those faced by patronate and industrial leaders in postwar capitalist enterprises, from Sweden to France, from the United States to Japan, and from Germany to Spain. From this perspective, factories in Cluj appear as a variation on the polyphonic theme that counterposed the logic of productivity to the logic of workers' everyday life in the second part of the twentieth century.

Scientific management was initiated by Frederick Taylor in the United States and widely adopted in large-scale manufacturing in French, Soviet and Japanese factories.[35] Through Western experts and local elites educated in New York, London or Berlin, its ethos also travelled to capitalist peripheries.[36] Wherever adopted, Taylorism led to a rearticulation of shop floor hierarchies by separating conception from execution, and by transferring authority from foremen to managers and technical staff. It played a crucial role in the historical process through which workers' individual performance became linked to a wage system based on piecework, and it marked the transformation of work as a moral concern into labour as a category of political economy.

In interwar Romania, dependency on foreign capital entailed a channelling of Western managerial ideologies and practices through the multinational corporations operating on Romanian territory.[37] The nascent Romanian industry in the interwar period was also tributary to the need to safeguard industrial peace and to depoliticize the shop floor, which went hand in hand with a top-down industrialization process and with the state's efforts to 'Romanianize' the factories. Scientific management became part of the new higher education courses in industrial organization just before the First World War, and it got strengthened in the aftermath of the conflagration by the activity of the Romanian Institute for the Scientific Organization of Labour. The institute was led by a team of economists, sociologists and psychologists, who published a *Bulletin* and offered consultancy to the multinational corporations in heavy industry and mining.

Worldwide, Taylorism was by definition highly interdisciplinary and regimented teams of experts coming from industrial psychology, physiology, ergonomics and engineering. In the intellectual field of the early and mid twentieth century, it complemented and sometimes confronted other traditions of thinking that attempted to make workers' bodies, skills and resistance to effort into objects of scientific inquiry in order to solve the generalized 'crisis of factory discipline' around the First World War.[38] Together with its main competitor, the science of labour, scientific management promised to offer a purely technical solution to industrial conflict writ large, to the antagonism of shop-floor relations and to the instability of the production process itself as embodied in the technological system of the assembly line.[39]

Scientific management was designed as an anti-politics machine that was going to translate the language of class into the sanitized vocabulary of 'efficiency', leading to a depoliticization of the shop floor and of the 'economy'. Its spread was accompanied by intense resistance from the unions, as well as from various leftist and Christian humanist circles, for leading to the dehumanization of the workers' bodies, to de-skilling, to an imbalanced power relation between labourers and managers, and crucially, because the sometimes spectacular increase in productivity was destined to expand capital's share in the profits and not labour's. Braverman's classical critique became the golden reference for several generations of sociologists and historians who revealed the impact of scientific management on the factory organization and showed how technical vocabularies and practices became ideological engines that drove capitalist relations in the twentieth century.[40] They explored how the transformation of labour into a commodity went through a transformation of the work process, which involved the reification of people, of their minds, and of their bodies.

While revered everywhere in the capitalist core, scientific management became a religion in the Soviet Union. In Moscow, the Central Institute of Labour [*Tsentralnyi Institut Truda*] came to be known colloquially as the 'citadel of socialist Taylorism'. Under the leadership of Aleksei Gastev, a cult of the machine developed at the institute, around a position that advocated chronometry and the complete standardization of workers' movements as the foundation of all work norms.[41] The commitment of the Soviet technical intelligentsia to a narrative of modernization through technological advancement and hyper-rationalization was no less fundamental for the evolution of Soviet labour relations than their belief in an equal world. This generation of Soviet experts would impregnate the shop-floor culture with an ethos of self-made personhood in the context of the war economy, scarcity and militarization of industry.

Unlike the USSR in the first decades after the Bolshevik revolution, when the Soviet fascination with scientific management was made explicit,[42] in Romania Taylor was seldom if ever mentioned in the official discourse. In addition, despite a promising start in the interwar period, the scientific organization of production was in its infancy during the first years of planning.[43] Instead, factory managers became familiar with the 'Soviet methods of organizing production' in the meetings with the representatives of ARLUS – The Romanian Association for the Strengthening of the Relationship with the Soviet Union. However, Taylor's notions of 'efficiency', 'control' and 'rationality' lived a full life in the Romanian enterprises. The plan itself came to be imagined as the possibility to bring Taylor's fundamental principles to scale: standardization of products and tasks; the fragmentation of the labour process in discrete sequences and its simplification; the generalization of piecework; and the implementation of differential wage schemes.

Starting from the classical Taylorist assumption that workers together possess a kind of traditional 'embedded' and 'embodied' knowledge,[44] which was hardly accessible to the management, the manager-state tried to extract this knowledge and translate it into forms that allowed for its governance. Thus, from the start, the instruments for accumulating knowledge had also been established as instruments of party control over the factory management and over the workers.

The technological chart was one of these instruments that was meant to enhance discipline, to follow the manufacturing of each item and to help the planners to decide how much raw material or fuel was needed in a specific production cycle. At the time, the new economic executives hoped that the generalization of the technological chart would enable them to introduce 'a scientific plan for an optimal usage of all the capacities of the industrial unit, from industrial equipment to a differently skilled labour force'.[45] The individual charts of production were another privileged instrument of control. They were meant to teach the workers to evaluate themselves, by checking when they slowed down, how often they stopped and what stood in the way of achieving their work targets. Things like the layout of the workbench, the worker's bodily position, the sequence of the operations and the cleanliness of the machine were supposed to be noted by the labourers, then analysed with their foremen in order to optimize the labour process. Organizing this system was the task of the Socialist Competition Bureau, a body that mainly included members of the union but also Stakhanovites and some of the best workers, whose main responsibility was to mobilize the others to reach their best in production.

Not only the economy as a whole but also workers' practices had to be observed as movement, which involved a deep understanding of the production process. The effort of establishing the right workload for the workers in each industrial branch involved, first of all, the need to explore the capacity of these workers, not through abstract figures and indicators, but through a profound analysis of what they actually did when manufacturing a shoe, a nail, a chair or a faucet. The factory directors were constantly complaining that they lacked precise instructions for the establishment of work norms, which resulted in work norms that 'were not scientifically set, because they were *mainly based on statistical data*' (my emphasis).[46]

The factories struggled to infuse the production process with the ethos of scientific discovery that was a marker of Taylorist techniques of observation. Managers, engineers and university professors were involved in the design of the time-and-motion studies that stood at the foundation of the endless attempts to introduce fully scientific work norms in Romanian industry.[47] In the case of rate-setting, observation was, by far, the preferred method. Some methodological decisions had to be made about who should be observed, when and in what conditions. Another question was whether or not the workers should be made aware that they were being observed. The rate-setters knew that the workers were slowing their motion when they saw the chronometer, clearly resisting a rise in their norms and the corresponding cut in their wages. While slide rules, drawing canvas and stopwatches motivated highly skilled workers and Stakhanovites to work faster and learn how to use their bodies in a more effective manner, it made most workers slow down their work in order to keep norms low and earnings decent.

The methods of gathering information about workers' practices became more sophisticated as scientists and university professors became involved in the process. In 1955, at the end of the First Five-Year Plan, a study was conducted at Armătura. The team was led by university professors, engineers, economists and the members of the technical club of the factory. Their central goal was to 'photograph' the workday of 175 of the factory's productive personnel by registering the different time costs per operation in a chronological order. The end result was going to be a report accompanied by detailed diagrams showing as precisely as possible how workers moved and what abilities they used in the process. Although the notion of 'photographing' was used as a metaphor and no photographic material (in the visual sense) was produced during these sessions, the metaphor in itself is telling because it speaks back to the obsessive need of the party officials and economic executives to transform social production processes into representations they could analyse, aggregate and use as bases for intervention.

While seventy-five workers were observed by their team members, the daily routines of the other one hundred had to be recorded by the workers themselves, in what the team called 'self photographing'. The method was of Soviet-Taylorist inspiration, and the study was meant to 'reveal the losses in the use of working time, the causes of these losses and the possibilities to improve the use of the working time'.[48] The methodology of the study was explained in detail:

> Photographing and self-photographing need thorough preparation, which includes choosing the workplaces where the analysis will be carried out, elaborating an action plan, and convincing the workers, especially those whose activity will be investigated, to participate. ... Selecting and preparing workers for photographing differ according to the purpose of the action – rate-setting or uncovering working time reserves. The workplaces of the good workers will be chosen for observation in order to elaborate the progressive technical norms, and optimal conditions will be created on the day when they are observed. If the purpose of the observation is the discovery of internal reserves of working time, typical workplaces from all categories will be selected, in such a way that among them we will find leaders in production, mediocre workers and the weakest ones. In this case, no change should be made to the working conditions of these workers on the day of photographing. In any case, for every workplace many observations will be carried on. For identifying internal reserves of working time, the observations will be conducted in different periods of the month to control for diverse working conditions and for changes in the production rhythm. For discovering the causes behind the lack of uniformity in the production rhythm, for the delays at the beginning of the month and the 'assault' at the end of the month, at least three observations will be conducted: at the beginning of the month, at the middle of the month and at the end. If there is more than one shift, it is better to take photographs of the labour process for each one of them.

The aim of reorganizing production was better supervision and control, as well as profit increase through lowering the production costs (and above all the share of labour in the production costs), like in any enterprise that uses scientific management. But in the socialist factories, this ideal had to be permanently confronted with the expectation that workers would 'manage' themselves and the labour process in such a way that they would ease the task of the factory management. They would willingly increase work norms, be more productive and 'rationalize' their work within a system of scientific self-management. Instead of struggling with workers' resistance on the shop floor, the state expected workers to extract the best working methods from themselves willingly. Apart from Taylor's old idea that scientific management was in the workers' best interest because their earnings would increase, workers' rationality would assume an expanded form in socialism as an explicit dimension of the ethical and pedagogic project aimed at achieving the transformation of society through the transformation of each individual.

Some forms of producing knowledge about workers' routines were founded precisely on this assumption, but the methodological worries that accompanied the idea of 'self-photographing' showed that resistance was expected along the way.

> The party organization and the union were instrumental in convincing the workers to respond to this initiative by self-photographing their workday and to participate voluntarily in 'the struggle for a better use of the working time'. The self-photographs are prepared daily; the workers describe their time losses for each day and the causes for these losses. They also suggest methods to eliminate these problems. This way, this action transforms into a mass action of the workers in their struggle to improve the factory activity. In addition, it will be possible to assess the permanent or the variable character of the deficiencies revealed by this method.[49]

Ideally, no worker should have been forced to participate in this kind of research. Workers had to realize that at a non-tangible level, as accumulation rates looked more promising, they were actively building a future for all of them. They would have benefited from an unprecedented level of redistribution of goods and services, even if workers had little control over this redistribution. Working more efficiently meant producing more. And producing more was required from them not only as workers but also as political subjects.

Thus, there was explicit pressure on workers themselves to rationalize and innovate in the production process, together with the foremen and the engineers. Workers' practical knowledge came to be highly valued by state planners, no matter if it referred to the possibility of fixing broken or outdated industrial equipment, improvise its replacement with cheaper and local solutions, or save raw materials and labour. By 1950, the workers who were proposing innovations became highly appreciated as exemplars of a new attitude towards work. They were distinguishing themselves from the masses who were labouring 'just for wages', and came to embody the party ideal of workers' involvement, mobilization and loyalty. Their efforts were financially rewarded and symbolically recognized through popularization on the factory billboards. The 'creative initiative of the working people' was considered decisive for bringing out 'those possibilities that could not have been known when the plan was conceived but that exist within the heart of the socialist factories', and which 'can be unveiled only when the plan is executed through perfecting the organization of work and production, through enhancing labour discipline'.[50]

The logic of socialist accumulation and the role played by the workers' knowledge in this logic come close to the surface in these examples. Knowledge was always prospective; it was always oriented towards the future and towards discovering what society was veiling. There was always an assumption that there was more than met the eye of the planner in each factory, in each workshop and in each worker. Although the capacities of the factories were planned, they were also always considered to be unknown, as they bore an uncovered potential for increased quantity, quality and mobilization. The continuous increase in the planning figures was grounded in the belief that people could do more every year due to their involvement in a permanent learning process. Supposedly, society held reserves of creativity, productivity and labour which could not be exhausted because they were perpetually regenerated within the labour process itself. Uncovering these hidden resources became one of the central tasks of government and, according to official discourse, one of its major achievements.

The Ethnographer-State: Governing beyond Numbers

As the party leaders knew very well, labour control was as much a production problem as it was a political one. Within the space of the factory, the workers encountered the state not only as employees to be managed but also as political subjects. In a workers' state, they were also supposed to become active agents of state making. This productive/political metamorphosis was a central dimension of the specific relation the Bolsheviks (and the Romanian Workers' Party implicitly) had with history, especially with regard to their belief in the political capacity of the socialist state to compress what was seen as the necessary stages of a civilizing process. Since '[t]he Bolsheviks ... set out to accelerate the historical process by acting on the economic base, social forms and culture all at the same time',[51] they needed to rely on a form of knowledge that could intimately relate representation and action, particular and universal, backwardness and an ideal image of the future. Socialist construction required forms of knowledge that linked production politics to state politics at least as much as the Sociological Department in Ford's company needed to link them to corporate interests.[52]

In-depth, contextual knowledge was crucial precisely because it was able to capture this dual nature of the state as a manager-state and as a workers' state, with the dual nature of its subjects and the problematic boundaries of the factory as the institutional setting of their encounter. For the socialist states, productivity was never separated from workers' political loyalties or from their everyday concerns. Producing more pairs of shoes or more fittings could not be understood outside a complex relational field whose elements were at once specific for every factory and common to many of them. Thus, thick descriptions about one factory shed plausible light on the problems of all factories.

Party officials came to a very strong anti-positivist stance, refusing to consider statistical facts as scientific facts and choosing observation instead of other methods when they needed to understand the problematic of production. Although the Economic Section of the Party County Committee received statistical reports from the most important factories in the region, sometimes even daily, the party officials complained that they did not get sufficiently rich and detailed information documenting the problems of the production process. In the reports, positive and negative examples, concrete results, locations and names were heavily underlined in pen or pencil, while the statistical and general information seemed to go almost unnoticed.

There was an almost universal awareness that if the government wanted to read what was happening on the ground, they required the stories behind the numbers and needed to separate discourse from facts. The local party officials insisted on concrete information as often as they could, and the most successful reports were always the ones offering detailed descriptions of the most trivial aspects of workshop activity. The reports were supposed to offer a special kind of knowledge, an ethnographic inspiration, which was meant to enable the party officials to understand the practices beyond numbers. In this way, the state was trying to separate discourse and 'quantifacts'[53] from very mundane practices, as a veritable ethnographer-state, demonstrating full awareness of the weaknesses of the processes of knowledge production presupposed by the (socialist) modernization project. Simply put, socialist planners knew that real limitations in their capacity to see represented drawbacks in their capacity to act.

In 1951, a member of the Agitation and Propaganda Section of the City Committee of the Romanian Workers' Party took the floor in a plenary meeting. He presented the results of an ethnographic inquiry titled 'Report on our findings from the field about the unhealthy atmosphere now prevailing at Armătura, and which prevents the implementation of the plan for 1951'.[54] The report showed that 'a complete disorder dominated Armătura', as 'comrade director Rakoczi Ladislau [wa]s not capable of keeping things under control'. The audience was reminded of his lack of popularity among the workers, his lack of authority and his incapacity to find good methods to lead.

Reports following this investigation confirmed the chaos in the industrial unit:

> Because there is no strict control, the workers are allowed by their foremen to leave their workplace or even the factory. Even worse, they are considered

'present' although they are not there. The task cards are distributed only after a task has been executed and not before, as directives, so the workers get to choose their preferred tasks and not take the plan into account. The production costs were exceeded because of the high percentage of components rejected by clients.[55]

Another 'field note' from János Herbák reveals the most important issue the foremen were confronted with in the 1950s, when trying to organize socialist competitions: the formal character of the more than 5,200 contracts for socialist competitions, although the 'enthusiasm' of the workers when signing these contracts had been proudly reported by the managers only a few days before.[56] The interviewed foremen underlined repeatedly that socialist competitions 'are not for everyone', and showed that actually the factory had never produced more than 430 leaders in production (compared to the almost 1,000 officially reported). Moreover, even key workers lacked socialist discipline, skipping workdays whenever they wanted, 'like the rest of the workers'. They tried to report those who were late or were missing work to the party organization and to the upper echelons of the factory management, but nothing happened except for the noisy inauguration of a noticeboard in some sections, where the names of those who were late were displayed, with the respective delay under their name. Some workers even broke the equipment intentionally, especially after new norms had been implemented and their income had dropped. The walls of the factory were full of inscriptions – political, religious and chauvinistic – but 'nobody ever found out who the authors were'.

Following the Soviet model of party organization at local level, documentary sections were founded at the regional level.[57] Their employees were specifically responsible for documenting in an ethnographic manner the processes at play within the factories, offices and villages. As governmental instructions show, the activists were especially trained for these actions by people who were acquainted with similar practices in the Soviet Union, either through training or, more frequently, through lectures at the party schools. The party leaders considered that 'the importance of documenting production processes comes from the idea that there cannot be fair government without knowing the state of affairs on the ground. Life confirms at every step that not knowing the pulse in the field makes leadership formal, without foundation and disconnected from real life.'[58]

Between May and November of 1954, the Documentary Section of the Cluj Region produced no less than twenty-four informative notes about factories and villages in the region. They were called 'field notes' and were written as ethnographic accounts in the first person. The field notes documented the problems of the factories and of the collective farms, with an emphasis on how people worked and lived. The factory was reconstituted as an object of inquiry within a broad set of relevant relations. The instructions that accompanied the party documentarists in their investigations stated that the final reports should contain information about workers' home conditions, their health problems and their expressions of discontent during production meetings. Accounts about people's reactions and opinions related to any new governmental measure were especially valued. If problematic interactions were observed between the Hungarians and the Romanians, or between the foremen, the technical staff and the workers, they had to be described accurately, in as much detail as possible. An interpretation of the factory situation as a whole was requested from all activists, alongside comparisons with other industrial units, and an account of the explanations offered by the actors themselves for certain sensitive issues.

A special methodological report complemented these impressive small monographs. It extensively shows how the state not only produced ethnographic knowledge but also surrounded this process with some of the worries that any anthropologist carries in the field.

> I will show concretely how I proceeded to prepare the informative notes. Before I left for the field I *studied* in detail the Decisions of the Central Committee of the Romanian Communist Party about the repartition of individual plots and ... about the creation of the zones destined for the cultivation of vegetables around the cities and industrial centres for an improved supply of fruits and vegetables for the city. Following their lead, I prepared my *work plan* and decided to ask the factories with individual plots and annex farms to provide informative notes on their functioning ... After I got the notes from the factories, I *analysed* them in detail. I contacted the Agricultural Division from the city committee and asked them to come with me in the field to *study* the annex farms and the allotments ourselves ... To write the notes I constantly consulted *informers* from the party committees, although they ultimately gave me little help. They did not have the data required by the Regional Committee, which provided a full list of orientation points ... Because it was impossible to *generalize* for all the industrial units, as the Documentary Sections had asked me to, I took in my work plan two factories, where I *studied in depth* the activity of the party organization and of the enterprises themselves.[59]

Although the party documentarists accompanied their endeavours with obvious methodological worries related to sampling, generalization power and good reporting on data, their presence in the factories was regarded in a purely interventionist way. There was a general awareness that factory managers correctly perceived the presence of these activists as a form of control. Many of the new economic executives took immediate measures to solve the problems of their factories before the party ethnographers went back to write their 'field notes'. The fact that those who documented factory life acted as a form of pressure on factory employees was never considered a problem. Moreover, there was no dream of neutrality or detached observation from the party activists who were observing factory life. On the contrary, their ideological commitment as well as their potential for action were the mandatory lenses through which reality was filtered.

There were many actors involved in this type of knowledge production at the factory level: party activists, external observers and party documentarists. This reconstruction of the factory as a research object from various accounts coming from multiple perspectives is indicative of the way the party understood the positionality of these accounts and the necessity that they be cross-referenced. The external observers were generally university professors or lower officials from the County Party Committee who had long-term involvement with certain factories. The party documentarist replicated the same studies, sometimes year after year, being essential for monitoring subtle changes in the production process and in the people's mood. The party activists who were also employees of the factory were actually doing 'ethnography at home'. Only they had the privilege of intimately knowing their colleagues and developing the long-term, deep and sometimes mutually advantageous relationships with their informants, as described by anthropologists who spend years in the same community.

Following the social life of a plan, one can easily argue that the suppression of indispensable local knowledge, informal processes, improvisation and practices was not accomplished or even intended in socialist Romania. Not only were state officials highly conscious of the role of local knowledge (in this case workers' knowledge about the best way to get things done), but they also did all they could to harvest it and to use it. The awareness that 'any production process depends on a host of informal practices and improvisations that could never be codified'[60] competed with and ultimately surpassed both the fascination for numbers and the admiration of Taylorist-inspired management.

My findings also go against the classical liberal critique of centrally planned economies. Hayek's argument in the socialist calculation debate was that central planning was based on statistical information, which could not capture specific 'circumstances of time and place', and made accurate prediction impossible.[61] This chapter shows that the Romanian state officials did perceive the limitations of the statistics they produced. Therefore, making the world readable involved not only simplification and standardization, but also many different types of knowledge: managerial, statistical and ethnographic.

At least in its initial phase, the reliance of socialist planning on people's knowledge was not merely a problem of translating universal scientific ideas into practice, but rather a fundamental resource the state was prepared to extract and use. There was, of course, an ideological drive for one centre to control everything, including information and its standardization. However, there was also a full awareness of what Hayek called 'the economic problem of society', as 'a problem of the utilization of knowledge not given to anyone in its totality'.[62] The state had to rely a great deal on 'knowledge of the kind which by its nature cannot enter into statistics and therefore cannot be conveyed to any central authority in statistical form'.[63] The image of how knowledge emerged in centrally planned economies appears to depend more upon the scale used in the analysis than on anything else, and its liberal critique seems to be less sensitive to an anthropological perspective on production than the socialist state ever was.

Observational and interpretative accounts of what was happening on the ground allowed the state to act locally, upon concrete situations. At this stage, the role of unions and of local party organizations was crucial for linking knowledge with mobilization, control and the reorganization of production. They were explicitly asked to see what was happening within factories, to discover what was going wrong in any given situation and to understand why things were not as they should be. Knowledge was produced through first-hand experience, or, as Geertz would have put it, by being there.[64] Placing 'a heavy emphasis on the present',[65] but always relating this present to a dark past and to an ideal future, the state constructed the factory as an ethnographic object by producing descriptions and narratives about routines, practices, work-related rituals, and ways of breaking the rules. Even feelings or emotions (taken as proxy for political loyalty) were the purpose of its inquiry. The lives of 'informants' and 'subjects' were reconstructed not only through observation, but also through gathering texts of all sorts: declarations, interviews and institutional records.

Furthermore, the use of ethnographic knowledge enabled the state to produce a kaleidoscopic image of the social world it intended to govern. Knowledge about local 'ways of doing' also allowed for rescaling and centralization. It was articulated in political tropes like 'problems in production' or 'work improvement', and further surfaced in the formulation of laws, governmental instructions and political priorities. As the methodological reports of the party activists reveal, worries about case choices and about the possibility of generalization explicitly accompanied any study of factory life. The state officials used ethnography both to understand what was happening in every factory, and to shed light on what was happening in other factories of the same kind.

Socialist planning opened the shop floor to a complex programme of revealing and actualizing its potential. The use of ethnographic knowledge was essential for unveiling those fields of local relations that made numbers and productivity reports meaningful. These findings transform our understanding of how factories were represented by the socialist state. We learn that they were operationalized not only as bearers of planning rationality but also as nodes of politics and everyday life. Following Gibson-Graham here, we can say that the socialist factory was more than a space of production. It was regarded more as a 'mystery', 'an open, rather than given, complexity – a site continually transformed both by "internal" forces such as historically changing technological patterns and administrative models, and by more general processes shaping the society within which it exists'.[66] In this context, ethnography had to function as a knowledge fix for the almost impossible task of making the factory life visible. This necessity of seeing behind numbers and behind the norm-setters' chronometer was rooted in the fundamental belief that economic growth was *already there*, hidden in current practices and routines, which ranged from modes of calculating and reporting to the labour process itself.

Notes

This chapter is derived, in part, from an article previously published as Cucu, A. 'Producing Knowledge in Productive Spaces: Ethnography and Planning in Early Socialist Romania' *Economy and Society* 43(2) (2014), 211–32.

1. Lampland, *The Value of Labor*.
2. Mathematical modelling in early socialist planning rested on the use of input–output tables (static Leontieff models); see Kornai and Liptak, 'Two-Level Planning'.
3. Wise, 'Work and Waste'.
4. Pittaway, *From the Vanguard to the Margins*.
5. It also started from very specific forms of calculating and anticipating what the consumer wanted, but this is beyond the purpose of this book. The interested reader can consult Neuburger and Bren, *Communism Unwrapped*.
6. Scott, *Seeing Like a State*, 2.
7. Ibid., 27.
8. Rostás, *O Istorie Orală*.
9. Poenaru, 'Methodological State Apparatuses'.
10. Șerban, 'Surviving Property'.
11. Law 41/1947 for the census of industrial units. M.O. no. 70, 25 March 1947; Decision no. 4889, M.O. no. 228, 3 October 1947.
12. The collectivization was preceded by an agricultural census, organized in 1948 as a public event, with villagers declaring their ownership of land, inventory and livestock in front of several witnesses: neighbours, the census representative, and another resident, who was required to verify the information.
13. ANIC, Fund Comitetul de stat al planificarii (henceforth CSP), 91/1948, 484.
14. Gurley, 'Excess Liquidity'.

15. In 1947, a census of all industrial and commercial units was conducted, allowing the state to produce an image of the most important constituents of national economy. Law 41, Recensământul întreprinderilor comerciale și industriale, M.O. no. 70, 25 March 1947.
16. This was especially visible in extractive branches, like mining and the oil industry, where the reorganization of the Ministry of the Economy allowed the subordinate ministeries the possibility to create production plans, establish quota and distribute means of production; Glonț, 'Nihil Sine Carbo'.
17. ANIC, Fund CSP, 1948–1951, 90/1948.
18. Bindea, 'Conditiunile', 11.
19. The establishment of the State Planning Commission, B.O. 45 / 46, M.O. 171 / 1949.
20. 'Regulament pentru organizarea și funcționarea Comisiunii de Stat a Planificării', [Statute for the organization and functioning of the State Planning Committee] M.O. 171, 27 July 1949, 6172–75.
21. ANDC, Fund 55, CO P.M.R., 1/1950, 26.
22. ANDC, Fund 13, CR P.M.R., 25/1950.
23. ANDC, Fund Clujana, 33/41/1949.
24. ANIC, Fund CSP, 93/1948, p. 173.
25. ANIC, Fund CSP, 93/1948, p. 175.
26. ANIC, Fund CSP, 93/1948.
27. ANIC, Fund CSP, 93/1948, p. 174.
28. ANDC, Fund 55, P.M.R., 1/1951.
29. Rose, 'Governing by Numbers'.
30. Corrigan and Sayer, *The Great Arch*, 164–65.
31. ANDC, Fund Clujana, 33/41/1949, 64.
32. ANDC, Fund Clujana, Dosar 33/105/1949, 2.
33. ANDC, Fund Clujana, 33/41/1949, 64.
34. ANDC, Fund Clujana, 24/23/1950, 117.
35. The Bedaux System in Britain, Fayol's system in France, and industrial rationalization in Germany.
36. Akgöz, 'The German Way to Scientific Management'.
37. The technocratic approach to industrialization reached its peak at end of the 1930s, with the proposal of a Romanian 'University of Labour'; see Cîrjan, 'Reimagining the State'.
38. Perrot, 'The Three Ages'.
39. The science of labour (*Science du travail* in France and in Belgium, *Arbeitwissenschaft* in Germany, *scienze del lavoro* in Italy, and *ciencia de trabajo* in Spain). For an in-depth exploration of the relationship between the European science of work, scientific management, and the evolution of labour relations in Europe, see Rabinbach, *The Human Motor*.
40. Braverman, *Labour and Monopoly Capital*.
41. Guillén, *Models of Management*; Hanson, *Time and Revolution*.
42. For the evolution of Taylorism in the Soviet Union, see Bedeian and Phillips, 'Scientific Management'; Beissinger, *Scientific Management*; Filtzer, *Soviet Workers*; Sochor, 'Soviet Taylorism Revisited'.
43. Cucu, 'Why Hegemony Was Not Born in the Factory'.
44. Van den Daele, 'Traditional Knowledge'.
45. ANDC, Fund Clujana, 24/23/1950, p. 43.
46. ANDC, Fund Clujana, 16/30/1951, p. 22–24.
47. Lampland, *The Value of Labor*.
48. Kecskes and Kerekes. 'O metodă'.
49. Ibid.
50. Ibid.
51. Hirsch, *Empire of Nations*, 6.
52. Clarke, 'What in the Ford's Name is Fordism?'

53. Comaroff and Comaroff, 'Figuring Crime'.
54. ANDC, Fund 55, CO P.M.R. Cluj, 1/1951, 266.
55. ANDC, Fund 13, CR P.M.R. Cluj, 9/87, 203–8.
56. ANDC, Fund 13, CR P.M.R. Cluj, 37/1951, 181.
57. I suspect the emergence of documentary sections followed in the trail of the Soviet 'controllers'. Having even older roots in the tsarist times, the controllers had been closely related to the idea of state/plan/labour discipline in Stalin's Soviet Union. They were instrumental in fighting local allegiances and bureaucratic ossified traditions. In Johanna Bockmann's words, '[f]or controllers, economic problems resulted from a lack of work discipline, inattention to the economic use of materials, self-serving attitudes, illegal activities, sabotage, corruption, and underestimation of resources. Controllers examined state institutions, punished those responsible, and 'educated' employees about problems that were discovered. Controllers formed a relatively direct link between policy makers and the objects of policy. For controllers, there was no separation of economics and politics; they monitored all state institutions.' Bockman, *Markets in the Name of Socialism*, 37.
58. ANDC, Fund 55, CO P.M.R., 2/1954, 151–53.
59. ANDC, Fund 13, CR P.M.R. Cluj, 37/1951, my emphasis.
60. Scott, *Seeing Like a State*, 6.
61. Hayek, 'The Use of Knowledge in Society'.
62. Ibid., 520.
63. Ibid., 524.
64. Geertz, *Works and Lives*.
65. Asad, 'Ethnographic Representation', 57.
66. Gibson-Graham et al., *Re/presenting Class*, 39.

CHAPTER 5

PRODUCTIVE FLOWS AND FACTORY DISCIPLINE

> For there is no such thing as economic growth which is not, at the same time, growth or change of a culture; and the growth of social consciousness, like the growth of a poet's mind, can never, in the last analysis, be planned.
> —E.P. Thompson, 'Time, Work-Discipline, and Industrial Capitalism'

State/Labour/Plan Discipline

The implementation of the first one-year plan in 1949 confronted the economic executives with a new trope: the connection between the discipline of the state, the discipline of labour and the discipline of the plan. In the words of János Herbák's director in a factory committee meeting:

> The concern for the plan must be deeply imprinted in our comrades from those services and sectors that are directly related to production ... The discipline of the state ... must be expressed in the way we strictly fulfil the hierarchical orders we get ... The enterprise must respect work discipline, the iron proletarian discipline. We must imprint in every person the need to respect our given directives. State discipline is the discipline of the working class, the discipline of the proletariat, which will strengthen the spirit of the individual responsibility ... We must have an iron discipline, based on democratic centralism.[1]

As evidenced in production minutes, party meetings and political speeches, 'discipline' became a political project that explicitly linked work, life and individual responsibility with the plan figures.

The assumption behind economic centralization was that the plan itself would function as a scaled analogy of the Fordist enterprise: hierarchical style of management, processes of production guided by the materiality of the assembly line, and increased productivity linked through wages and benefits to workers' consumption. Historically, all features of Fordism were predicated on the possibility of keeping the lines of production going continuously. The socialist plan made no exception to this logic. But on the ground, socialist planners were confronted with a different reality: stoppages, slow-downs and sudden accelerations made up the actual rhythms of the shop floor, and they were rather breathing together with the rhythms of the workers' lives than with the tasks of the plan.

As Part I of the book showed, the implementation of central planning was accompanied by two important developments: the generalization of piece-rate work and the fall in workers' real wages. With wages functioning as a rather poor incentive, the debilitating lack of housing in the cities and the slower pace of collectivization in the countryside, many workers regarded industrial work as a supplemental source of income and proved impossible to 'fix' in the factory. Early socialist factories emerged as fluid spaces, marked by labour shortages and instability, while managers struggled to contain a workforce that was cheap and flexible, but at the same time unruly.

Labour shortages and instability combined with a severe penury of raw materials, equipment and fuel to produce what János Kornai theorized as an 'economy of shortage'.[2] Like elsewhere in East Central Europe, Romania's First Five-Year Plan was centred around the rapid development of heavy industry in already industrialized regions, while consistently starving other sectors like light industry and agriculture, and sacrificing workers' and peasants' living standards. Cluj fell behind the investment priorities of the state in the first years of planning, and the consequences of the shortage circle were even harsher than for other regions. Factory managers could witness in rapid motion how underfulfilment of the plan in one factory led to further shortages down the line of the supply chain, and to new underfulfilments.

In his excellent analysis of the Stalinist factory regime in Hungary between 1948 and 1953, Mark Pittaway extended the analysis of informal practices to the relationship between labour and the state to reveal how the establishment of a remuneration system based on piece-rate and individualized work targets collided with the discipline of the plan.[3] As Pittaway argues:

> At the heart of the failure of the regime to subordinate workers to the goals of the plan through remuneration attached to their 'politics of time' was a wage system that rested on the assumption of continuous production. In reality, the interaction of the plan and the shortage generated by the plan created its own peculiar rhythm of production, with serious effects on the shop floor and the earning potential of industrial workers.[4]

Not only the managers but also the workers counteracted the state's disciplinary ethos through a heightened level of informality and through a complex rearrangement of shop floor solidarities that set the 'social limits of state control'. Thus, in the early 1950s, bargaining became not only an issue of political economy but also an all-pervasive everyday reality of the shop floor, which was further connected to the emergence of a new working-class identity.

Having Kornai's analysis of managerial practices and Pittaway's investigation of the Hungarian shop floor as a starting point, this chapter focuses on the consequences of the systematic breaks in production that plagued industry in Cluj. My findings substantiate an already commonplace in scholarship on socialism: continuity in production was under constant threat, and so was the stability of the supply chains. The consequences of these disruptions went beyond the realm of production. I follow here an old conceptual line opened by the French sociology of labour in the 1950s to analyse the political implications of the fact that the plan itself could not function as an uninterrupted, coherent sequence of knowledge, decisions and actions. I argue that while the plan had to function as a formidable machine to produce modernity, the impossibility of following its tasks rhythmically set material limits to the type of authority that could be established in production.

In Chapter 15 of *Das Kapital*, Marx described the emerging factory system as 'technical oneness', simultaneous 'pulsations of the common prime mover',[5] and stressed the fact that objects and bodies should ensure a continuous flow of the production process, which was essential for capital accumulation. As technology advanced, the shop floor was going to become '[a]n organized system of machines, to which motion is communicated by the transmitting mechanism from a central automaton, ... a mechanical monster whose body fills whole factories, and whose demon power, at first veiled under the slow and measured motions of his giant limbs, at length breaks out into the fast and furious whirl of his countless working organs'.[6]

Walking in Marx's footsteps, the French tradition of sociology of labour linked the materialities of production to the possibility of instituting authority in the factory. Alongside hierarchical orders, 'installations' that maintain the productive flow were also considered part of any institutional network of instructions. Georges Friedmann extended the category of *auctoritates* not only to written texts but also to material objects like tools, industrial equipment and buildings. In the Fordist factories, the conveyor belt was the most important among these *auctoritates*, having the role of an 'artificial leader' of the production process.[7]

In the Romanian factories, the ideal of a conveyor belt was inscribed in the very act of planning. Theoretically, hopes for a rapid and dramatic increase in productivity, the decomposition and recomposition of tasks, the standardization and the interchangeability of parts, the separation of production from conception, technological dynamism, and the easy discovery of bottlenecks were all part of the idea of socialist management. All these were possible solely if the plan ensured the continuous movement of raw materials, goods and instructions. Nonetheless, the failure to produce a stable labour force and the frequent discontinuities in production due to shortages and local negotiations of the plan figures made the worker–machine units dysfunctional for long periods of time, and prevented socialist factories from becoming coherent wholes, capable of always producing 'faster, better and cheaper'.

Discontinuities in production were disruptive because if people did not assume a fixed place, the timing of production could be neither calculated nor anticipated. Not controlling the unfolding of the labour process also meant hours, days or even weeks when the state could not control the workers. When workers left the factory, they followed their own aims and routines, which led to 'alternative deployments of bodies in time' and in space.[8] As other authors show, labour control became essential 'to make up for the nonoptimal distribution of the other productive resources',[9] by seizing time from workers once needed. But as this book has already demonstrated, the workers found ways to reappropriate their time in unexpected ways. Since this form of reappropriation could not be anticipated, it could also not be planned. Planning required bodies to carry it on, and those bodies had to be in place, to be trained, routinized, and to continue the activity of other bodies. In these conditions, 'not only was materiality incapable of guiding action, it was expressly deprived of any authority – all of this, of course, was rather paradoxical in a country that was officially led by a materialist ideology'.[10]

Thus, continuity in production was regarded as an important managerial achievement. It depended on the capacity of the factory managers to articulate a field of disciplinary practices around what the party propaganda apparatus was obsessively referring to as 'the rhythmic accomplishment of the plan' and 'the 480-minute workday'. As exemplaries for a failed attempt to discipline labour in socialism, 'the rhythmic accomplishment' and 'the 480 minutes' shed light on the lack of effectiveness in controlling the factories. Both the complete usage of the working time and the constant pace of the labour process were always measured against a notion of 'normal conditions of production', which remained rather ambiguous for a long time, despite the socialist planners' efforts to specify it.

The impossibility of maintaining a continuous productive flow produced its own field of practices within which the ethics of 'individual responsibility' had to be articulated, and effected a feeble form of authority in the Romanian socialist factories. This generalized incapacity of the factories to become nodes of the state/labour/plan discipline logic was the main source of the fragility of the socialist state. Since factories functioned as productive state apparatuses, how power relations were played out on the shop floor produced specific state effects, which were directly rooted in production. Unlike in capitalism, where the illusion of the separation between economy, society and the state has generally obscured their mutual constitution, production in socialism was directly and openly connected to state functioning. In Yves Cohen's words, 'the regime of industrial efficiency was a part of the political regime of state efficiency. In particular, managing industry meant managing the public sphere, as well as manufacturing goods.'[11] Thus, in the last instance, the rhythms of the plan and the control of the working day stood as witness to the fragility of the state as a social relation of production.

The Rhythms of the Plan

In 1950, the state shifted back decisively from the learning mode explored in Chapter 4 to a productivist one, and the new economic executives launched a fierce assault on indiscipline. The call to conform to the 'discipline of the plan' became a central one in the discourse of the party and in the concrete instructions received by the factories from the ministries.[12] Two threats to the fulfilment of the plan figures stood out in this period: the fragmentation of the production process into chaotic rhythms that could not be coordinated; and working-time wastefulness.

Stagnation was considered dangerous for the fragile economic equilibrium achieved after the war. Hence, factory managers and workers alike were flooded daily with indications for 'the rhythmic accomplishment of the plan'. Raw materials and products had to circulate perpetually, and immobility was fought on all levels. Having items that 'have been manufactured but are still in the storage'[13] was as scary as not producing enough of them. Any break in production had to be immediately communicated to the County Planning Centres, to the party committees and to the corresponding governmental offices.[14]

Shortages and postponements in supply made the factory live by specific rhythms. While the beginning of the month was idle and the production often stopped, in the second part of the month workers were constantly using overtime and the factory managers were obsessively chasing the achievement levels set by the government, as a factory report from János Herbák shows:

> If we analyse our activity, we ascertain that in the first two quarters of the year the production plan was overfulfilled but in the third quarter our tasks were not realized. In the fourth trimester, the figures of the plan were massively exceeded, partly because we needed to clear up our obligations, and partly because we had to meet our commitment to fulfil the plan before the deadline; the same applies to producing commodities in excess of the plan. The unwanted consequences of our supply problems prevented us from following the legal provisions with regard to a uniform rhythm of production.[15]

The fact that factories and departments set up different rhythms of production made the articulation of the plan difficult, within and between the industrial units. 'Chaos' and 'long unproductive time' forced the workshops to wait one after the other and not take account of the needs of other sectors when deciding what components to manufacture next. Stocks of semi-fabricated commodities were finished quickly at the end of the month, without regard for their quality. The same 'end of the month' pressure was responsible for the rapid solution of replacing lighter products with heavier ones, so that the quantitative targets of the plan could be fulfilled. Since the ratio between small components and the larger pieces was not respected, every factory created further shortages in other economic sectors.

During the second one-year plan of 1950, the problem of articulating the productive tempos of various divisions of the factory became central to the reorganization of the nationalized enterprises according to the new governmental regulations for the functioning of the state factories, which were specifically designed to smooth the coordination between the industrial units. However, in practice things went very differently. One report from János Herbák shows how the production of the tanneries could not maintain the pace of the shoe factory, forcing the management to supply the industrial unit with imported raw material.[16] Another document reveals how the management of the industrial unit used the months of August and September to exemplify, ironically, 'the wonders' of one of its departments, where 'on the 25th of the respective month only 40–50 per cent of the plan was fulfilled' and yet, by the end of the month, the plan was 100 per cent realized.

Even worse, the planning process itself became a source of fragmentation in production, making life difficult both for the factory managers and for the workers. Although the need for constancy was preached as crucial for the functioning of the plan, interruptions in production were often imposed by the ministries themselves, and complaints from factory managers about how sudden changes in governmental instructions were breaking the pace of production abounded.[17] The fabrication cycle was also regularly disrupted by innumerable requests from other commercial enterprises and factories. Since many beneficiaries had not been properly scheduled at the moment of planning, the distribution orders often bore mentions like 'urgent', 'extra urgent' or 'immediate', interrupting the normal flow of fabrication and delaying the fabrication of other items.[18]

Factory managers were often complaining that there was never enough time to work out all the details before the plan was put into motion. 'The deadline for putting together the plan figures was short', a chief engineer from János Herbák said in a production meeting to a party activist who was visiting the leather and footwear factory:

> Several days are necessary for the plan figures, the forms and the instructions to arrive. Then they have to be communicated further to all our main and secondary factories. Then all the links between these have to be discussed. Putting together and harmonizing the entire apparatus necessary to elaborate the plan requires several days dedicated only to clarifications, deliberations and calculations. Especially for the secondary factories, it is impossible to elaborate their plans before the main units crystallize theirs. All these considerations imperatively require a longer execution time in the future. The more time we have at our disposal, the better our deed.[19]

A rhythmic flow of production was prevented by delays in the communication of the plan tasks, which were frequently sent long after the beginning of the year.[20] In these conditions, factory managers had to decide by themselves on the sorts and quantities of goods to be produced. However, once they arrived, the figures in the plan rarely matched their initial decisions. Endless exchanges of messages between factory managers and government officials followed these 'mistakes'. Although industrial units could not actually wait for the plan figures to arrive from the ministries, factory managers were always the ones admonished for their 'lack of awareness'. Their incapacity to divine the plan figures was equated with being wasteful – more concretely, with wasting important sources of accumulation on the shop floor.[21]

State/labour/plan discipline became the expression of a practical field of attempts to tighten governmental control over the factories. The first thing the socialist planners tried was to enforce a stricter frame around the plan figures themselves, and to undercut the possibility of their constant renegotiation between factories and the governmental offices. Ideally, figures of production could not be modified by any means during the year. Almost no requirements for extra raw material, industrial equipment, labour force or working time were accepted by the governmental offices, even when the factories received supplemental tasks six or seven months after the plan targets had been set.[22] A note of the Planning and

Statistics Service of the Central Office of Leather and Footwear (CIP) to the director of János Herbák, Mauriciu Devenyi, reads:

> Through this note we let you know that in the future, complying with the discipline of the plan will be required in the most rigorous way. By this statement, the director of the Central Office of Leather and Footwear understands that the plan tasks have to be accomplished not only as a whole but also for every type of commodity individually. Any deficiency can be the object of an official inquiry by the official competent bodies.[23]

The 'official inquiries' carried the risk of dismissal, fines or (rarely) imprisonment, and the capacity to go through the year without asking for 'extras' and without trying to renegotiate the plan targets was always read in a political key. Hence, plan figures came to be important not only as global images of economic success but also as sociological indicators for the political obedience of workers and factory managers.

These efforts to undermine the renegotiation of the plan figures were complemented by trial and error transformations in the way of reporting and communicating between different bureaucratic layers. In order to keep the productive flow going, operative sessions and daily reports at the factory level were accompanied by individual charts to monitor people's work progress. They were centralized by the Planning Service of the factory. Both the achievements and the problems in production had to be reported every morning before 8.30, and any delay in the execution of the plan was analysed in detail on the spot. A complex hierarchical chain was put in motion for solving any situation threatening the fluidity of production for more than a few hours.[24] Information circulated daily on two channels: a technical one – from foremen to engineers, to factory directors, and then up the governmental offices that were organized for every industrial branch; and a political one – going from the party organization of the factory to the City Party Committee, then to the Regional Committee, and, depending on the seriousness of the problem, to the Central Committee of the party in Bucharest. Still, since factories were generally planned at their maximal capacity with the hope that they would find their 'hidden reserves' in the future, this mobilization of the technical and political hierarchies around the plan figures was of little help. Most industrial units in Cluj actually had to reorganize the production process several times every year to meet their obligations, but the repeated restructurings further produced stoppages and disharmonious rhythms.

While the new economic executives did indeed search for the 'hidden reserves' of the factories, they also became active in the process of hiding resources themselves.[25] We have already seen how hoarding labour and employing temporary workers was made possible by diverting enterprise funds towards paying workers. Chapter 2 showed that labour shortages were partly driven by the drop in workers' real wages, so any additional loss of income due to production stoppages pushed people out of the factory gates. With the generalization of piece-rate work in the Romanian factories, shortages and discontinuities of production had a direct effect on people's earnings. As shown, the possibility to fulfil the norm was unequally distributed, so the unskilled employees coming from the countryside were the first to leave. Shifting workers into higher wage categories was also a common occurrence, especially for light industry factories, where the management readily assigned labourers better earning possibilities in order to level the field with heavy industry and keep people in the factory.

Other ingenious management strategies also came into play. Simply lying about the capacity of the factory and about the assortments that the factory can produce when the plan figures for the next year had to be estimated was common. Government officials vehemently argued against generalized practices like exaggerating the supply plan or hoarding materials and labour. Government officials also complained about how factory directors picked certain indices of the plan while failing to comply with others. Although quantity and production costs were by far the most important indicators of success or failure when the achievements of an industrial unit were reported, factory managers interpreted both 'in very creative ways'.[26] They did not respect the assortments set by the plan, and chose to manufacture those items that were heavier or easier to produce, as they required less skilled work and less expensive raw materials. The same imaginative way to read plan figures and the instructions from the ministry applied to the financial indicators. The new economic executives chose the most expensive products and failed to produce cheaper goods, which were nonetheless crucial for the functioning of other factories or for the consumption needs of the population. In other cases, unfinished products were included in the final reports and calculated as 'fulfilment' of the plan but they never came to be delivered to the beneficiaries.[27]

Economic executives were regularly admonished for their failure to find more rational solutions, to expand the use of Soviet technological solutions, to replace certain raw materials whose supply was deficient, to employ a smaller labour force, not to use overtime and not to increase the wage funds of their industrial units. In certain factories or industrial branches, the government even tried to limit the overfulfilment of plan figures to 2–3 per cent for each commodity,[28] in an almost desperate effort to undermine the strategies used by the factory managers to bypass the rules of the game.[29]

Economic executives had to apply a disjunctive logic and decide which plan figures would be the most important. They also had to sense the quasi-hidden priorities in the momentary logic of accumulation, which was not always fully transparent to them. This capacity to 'see' the state from within and to act according to fluid and not explicit parameters was crucial for (political) survival and for getting by at all levels. Since indices were arbitrarily chosen by the managers and equally disregarded by workers themselves, the plan as an articulation of supply chains became problematic. The quantitative indices of the plan were easier to meet, easier to follow, easier to be controlled by the higher echelons of economic executives, and harder to be ignored by the workers. However, even these plan figures were read and interpreted in imaginative ways.

Quality in production was a field of battle that functioned differently from the battle for quantity. Already at the end of 1949, a director from the Central Office of Leather and Footwear was complaining that the factories were exaggerating a lot their successes, reporting as much as 45 per cent improvement in the products' quality.[30] The reason was simple: numbers related to quality improvement were the easiest to manipulate in reports and the most difficult to be checked by the hierarchically superior cadres. Reporting quality improvement was the easiest way to ensure bonuses for the workers and the technical staff, thus a tacit alliance at the workshop level between the local party activists, the management, the union and the workers themselves emerged very early after the implementation of planning. So, the factories reported quality improvement all the time, although the Factory Party Committee and the union theoretically supervised quality control closely. However, neither the party nor the union had any reason to contradict a factory's official reports, and it was soon going to be obvious that everybody gave up the fight for quality improvement. At the end of 1950, the quality of the products could still not be compared to its 1938 level. At János Herbák, the poor quality of the footwear led to a series of reclamations from the consumers. Even more seriously, several lots of military boots were returned to the factory by the Red Army, and the whole lot needed to be manufactured again at a higher quality. The best workers were assigned to this emergency task, which destabilized production everywhere else in the factory.[31]

Poor quality work was often listed as a 'bad habit', which had to be exposed in the pages of *Viața uzinei noastre* [The life of our factory],[32] the newspaper of János Herbák. Comrade Biji, a quality controller in the boots section, was publicly scolded for a presumed alliance with the irresponsible workers who did not respect quality standards. As the newspaper's story went, comrade Biji 'bought some boots for his son and they broke very soon. With much shame he observed that they had been produced by our own factory.' Comrade Biji realized that his failure to return the products to the workbench, even when he observed their poor quality, reverberated in the everyday lives of his fellow workers. He represented 'a telling example' of what happened when the quality controllers did not realize the importance of the fact that 'those who were going to buy the products of their factory were also working people'. It seemed comrade Biji learned his lesson because '[s]ince then, he has been very thorough in his work and he understood the essential: 'We work for ourselves!'[33]

The writers at the factory newspaper used comrade Biji's example for complaining that quality controllers were not 'ideologically well prepared' and failed to understand the necessity of building a larger solidarity between the working people instead of prioritizing local interests and friendships. His case was made part of a much broader discourse against 'familialism' in the factory, a term covering the old shop-floor hierarchies and alliances, which the party had tried in vain to dismantle because they generally affected the state's control over workers' wages, bonuses and social benefits, as well as over their possibilities of earning an extra income. On the other hand, factory managers and planners alike knew well that in the last instance, these informal networks around kinship, geographical origin and friendship were precisely the ones making the shop floor activity possible.

Keeping workers happy was one of the most important tasks of the newly appointed directors, so the ability to foresee and negotiate among the contradictory logics of the manager-state and of the workers' state was fundamental. Early socialist managers always had to calculate how much pressure they could put on people and how to save their financial incentives, regardless of the problems that prevented the factory from meeting the production figures. As a result, workers did not get penalized for not meeting quality standards, certain levels of productivity or the cost-reduction benchmarks set by the plan; they did, however, get a special bonus if they met these indicators.

> In order to get the special financial bonus for the fulfilment of the plan, all three conditions must be met: production, quality and cost; there will be no bonuses if the fulfilment or the overfulfilment of the plan are chosen against quality or cost. The cost of *any* product should be at least equal to the one in the official publications, minus the benefit of the enterprise ... For those cases when the plan is quantitatively overfulfilled, each extra percentage will be awarded a fixed bonus. For reductions in the costs of production, people will get a fixed bonus multiplied by the reduction percentage. For quality improvement, the bonus will be calculated according to the instructions from the brochure 'Quality Control for Establishing the Right to Financial Bonuses'.[34]

It is easy to see how the quality controllers became important nodes in the factory 'familial' system, as they were linked both to people's chances of earning more and to the managerial strategies of getting through the maze of the first years of planning.

Financial incentives did not produce the desired outcome simply because meeting the quality standards was impossible.[35] At János Herbák, although the instructions from the Central Office for Leather and Footwear or from the Light Industry Ministry always emphasized the obligation of fulfilling the plan exactly as it was imagined, the factory managers could not comply with these rules. They were required to use as little raw material as possible but without decreasing the quality of the products. Or, as the factory director in one of the production minutes at János Herbák said: '[T]he government and the party ask from us cheap footwear for the working people, but in large quantity and of good quality'.[36]

Every time production stopped and the flow of manufactured goods became so unreliable that it compromised production elsewhere, somebody needed to take the blame for the small mistakes and decisions that had led to the endangering of the plan. Proceedings of the production meetings and reports to the corresponding ministries reveal the question that had haunted managers, foremen, engineers and workers alike since the early 1950s: *Who is responsible for the failure of the plan?*

The answer to this question always entailed a mixture of at least three elements: workers' indiscipline, the poor organization of the production process, and the contingent alliances between various actors in the factories. Things as different as the strategies used by the workers for stalling or the fluctuation of the labour force were conflated with problems related to deficient supply, outdated machinery, and the difficulty of generalizing the practice of working in three shifts, or to familialism, lack of loyalty and intentional lying to the party.

As people quickly adopted strategies to counter the possibility of being found *responsible* for any concrete task, maintaining a fearful atmosphere on the shop floor had the side effect of paralysing interactions that were crucial for the functioning of the factories. Workers and managers alike generalized these strategies to all spheres of activity, including the most mundane concerns. The piles of documents from the factory archives in Cluj stand witness to the 1950s compulsion for ensuring a paper trail for all things related to production. Every small detail had to be written down and signed by someone, explicit directives were required for every step, and no one accepted any task without official approval.[37] In the factory, if something wrong happened, the party and the union were the first to know.[38] This was especially important when industrial equipment broke, workers had accidents, or production stopped for any reason. Responsibility was replaced by fear of retaliation as, when needed, any production process could easily be transformed into a political one, and any economic failure could be read as 'sabotage' or as 'undermining the national economy' – both were punishable by imprisonment or death.

Avoiding responsibility was more complicated given the insecurity and disorientation that resulted from the impetus for changing things at a very rapid pace. The chief of the mechanical workshop at János Herbák complained in a production meeting that the pressure to change things was sometimes chaotic and irrational: 'There are too many transformations every day. As you can see, we have made 260 changes, but I am not able to determine if we were right to make all these changes.'[39] Effecting these changes in a mechanical way, not questioning them, and then not being accountable for them was not only *his* way to deal with pressure but also that of his colleagues. 'There is a kind of hysteria in the mechanical sector', the chief of the mechanics stated in the same meeting. 'When something is broken, everybody says they would not be held responsible if the plan is not fulfilled for this reason.'[40]

Discursively, everybody was encouraged to use 'the weapons of critique and self-critique', but the high level of exposure presupposed by the meetings where individual blame was produced and articulated was often followed by conflicts in the workshops. Hierarchically, party leaders and economic executives hardly accepted the critiques of the ordinary workers.[41] Workers were also upset when publicly shamed, and sometimes their hurt feelings made them raise their fists in angry encounters with those responsible for such exposure. Self-critique – a form of public self-acknowledgement of one's mistakes that was supposed to produce further effects in the conduit of the worker – usually followed critique, or it functioned as a means to anticipate it. But sometimes the workers simply refused to comply with this requirement and failed to assume responsibility for their mistakes or bad practices.

For instance, the response of comrade Papp Irma, criticized on 28 March in *The Life of Our Factory* for 'disheartening' the young workers and not offering them enough support, was analysed in the pages of the newspaper:

> Comrade Papp totally rejects our critique and blames comrade Racz Ileana by presenting any situation in such a way that comrade Racz Ileana, who just came out of school, appears as negligent, coarse, distant and arrogant. But we ask comrade Papp: who is called to help comrade Racz Ileana to eliminate her mistakes if not precisely comrade Papp, who has both life experience and professional knowledge?[42]

Thus, the weapons of critique and self-critique as dimensions of the struggle for self-improvement met with resistance in the factories, while people found ways to escape individual responsibility by placing themselves in a diffuse network of collective accountability in which workers were rarely to be blamed for anything.

The ideological difficulty of blaming the workers as a collective subject for problems in production also made the placement of responsibility on the shoulders of *one* worker very problematic. Since fines and firing were on the line for more serious mistakes, establishing individual responsibility was equated with attacking one's income and playing against the local solidarities formed on the shop floor. Both the party and the factory managers considered it a dangerous game and avoided it when possible. 'Not to be held responsible' became one of the most important sources of subjectification for a large proportion of the population, and it was entangled both with managerial strategies and with everyday routines at the workshop level.

The responsibility game further produced a convoluted relationship with materiality itself. In January 1950, when the factory managers from János Herbák invoked the poor quality of leather received from another enterprise for the failure of their export plan, the government executives were not impressed. They promptly reacted to the attempt by these factory managers from János Herbák to pass the responsibility for not fulfilling their export plan onto the shoulders of the employees from the Light Industry Ministry. One part of their response letter was especially telling; it read:

> We must state clearly that our planning activity cannot take into account this reason. If the production of your leather sides had gone normally – which is what our Planning Office assumed, *because it could not have anticipated otherwise* – you would have been able to fulfil your export plan. The quality of the leather sides manufactured by your factory is *your* fault.[43]

As the only concern of the government was to make clear that the failure of the factory in their jurisdiction was due to factors that were external to the conception stage of planning, one can easily see that the strategies used by the mechanics or by the lathe operators when explaining their failures were not much different from those employed by the new economic executives at all bureaucratic levels.

Except for the cases when a witch-hunt started and purges were on their way, individual responsibility was hard to isolate from the failures of the production process itself. The quote above assembles practices and materiality into a notion of 'normality', which functions here as precondition for planning itself. Responsibility was a standard, always related to a specific set of practices which constituted what the documents called 'normal conditions of production'. 'Normal conditions of production' in an emerging planned economy presupposed temporal regularity in terms of sequential structure, duration, temporal location and rate of recurrence of practices and actions.[44] These 'normal conditions of production' were taken as standard when plan figures were calculated. This meant that since during the calculation of the plan figures the production parameters were considered to be constant and uniform, factors like bad quality of the raw materials, truancies, and thousands of daily delays could not be taken into account because they could not be truly anticipated. However, as this chapter has made clear, the 'normal conditions of production' against which any concrete situation had to be measured were most of the time ambiguous and arbitrary, and to a great extent out of the state's reach.

A 1954 report of the Economic Section of the Regional Party Committee is a good synthesis of the problems that had led to discontinuities in production in the enterprises in Cluj during the First Five-Year Plan:

> Failing to accomplish several plan indices at the industrial units in Cluj is the result of poor organization. The technological flux is not well integrated, there is a constant gap between the forges, the foundries, and the processing sectors. The industrial equipment is not used completely, and many machines just lie there unused for half the month. At the end of the month, the assault on production starts and the quality of the products falls below the line. In several factories, the indices for the use of the machines is very low: 45 per cent at Armătura, 57 per cent at János Herbák, and 41 per cent at Menajul. Production costs are very high as the amortization is spread over many more years than was initially calculated. We are behind time with the planned costs of technological advancement, and the situation is getting worse.[45]

Added to that, the outdated industrial equipment made the 'rhythmic accomplishment of the plan' impossible. It needed permanent fixing, and demanded a continuous development in the capacity of the repair workshops, which came to have 'the appearance and the proportions of an industrial plant'.[46]

Factory managers endlessly complained that the repair plan was not being fulfilled and that many pieces of equipment were lying unused on the floor. At János Herbák, the 'lack of enthusiasm' of the mechanic-in-chief was first to be blamed for this situation. The head of the repair workshop responded that some of the machines were so old that fixing them was a total waste of time. He bitterly countered the personal accusations against him, showing that their department hardly lacked 'enthusiasm', but rather lacked workers, especially skilled ones. He grumbled about the uselessness of working in shifts when workers were nowhere to be found, showing how during the afternoon shift twelve of the eighteen available lathes generally remained unused. After recounting many other problems in his division, his conclusion was simple: 'You can be sure that when our work is planned for 16 hours, we can actually do it in 160'.[47] This cynical conclusion synthesized the almost impossible situation created by labour instability in the late 1940s and the 1950s, which had important consequences for the functioning of the factories, both as planned productive apparatuses and as disciplinary spaces. And this is where we turn now.

A 480-Minute Workday

Another fierce battle was unfolding in the factories around the use of the working time itself. The 480 minutes of a workday became the most precious resource for growth, the resource the communists were counting on, but continuously escaped them nonetheless. These 480 minutes were a permanent measure of the transformative power of the state, which had to prove able to transmute them into living time and to eliminate any idle time – any time whose content was not ennobled by work. The obsession with using the whole working time was a synthetic expression of productivity as compressed time, which was from the start a fundamental dimension of industrial socialism and capitalism alike. But using the whole productive time was not imagined as just another political trope. It was supposed to produce material effects in workshop relations and in the production process. In short, it was supposed to produce disciplinary effects.

The techniques of measurement and control associated with time discipline reached the Romanian factories in the interwar period, together with ideas of scientific management accompanying the presence of the American companies in the region. They were supposed to gain full momentum in socialism. However, this modernizing ethos had limited success in the industrialization process. The structure of the labour force, its rural roots, the fluidity between production and life, and the perpetual attempts to keep wages as low as possible made the appeal to Taylorist principles a form of mockery rather than a systematic improvement to the labour process.

The documents from the factories and from the Regional Party Committee in Cluj are full of endless complaints about workers' absenteeism and lateness.[48] The number of complaints increased predictably around every round of governmental regulations trying to limit the conjugated effect of workers' indiscipline. During the second one-year plan in 1950, the calculations of the State Planning Commission showed that the planned production costs could not be met if the workers did not use at least 83 per cent of their working time every month.

> For the second trimester, you have to take action to use at least 83 per cent of the working time, to reduce the justified and unjustified absences from work, to eliminate the stagnations in the production process, to decrease the percentage of sick leave through preventive and curative measures, and to spread the vacation leaves throughout the year in such a way that they will not hamper the production. You will also extend the piece work within the factory, so at least 77 per cent of the labourers will work according to the piece-rate system.[49]

Factory managers were theoretically made directly responsible for enforcing a more disciplined way of working and for integrating the rationality of modern industrial development on the shop floor. They were to take the blame for the workers' continuous movement between the productive logic of the factory and an 'outside' life.

Party leaders, the youth mass organizations and the unions were also held accountable for their incapacity to show 'comradely warmth' to the newcomers and for their inability to communicate the advantages of constancy to their colleagues. As the reports showed, when tens of workers were missing for several days or when others were late for almost an hour every morning, it was not the workers but the party organization that was made liable for these situations:

> Regarding the attitude towards work, because the local party organizations have not shown sufficient dedication to their activity, many problems persist, especially those relating to the workers not fully using their working time but skipping work whenever they want. Counting only the days they skipped in October at Industria Sârmei, we find out that these amount to 2,356 working days, which represents eight man-years of work. And this happens because neither the party organizations nor the unions have taken this problem into their hands. They have failed to educate the workers politically and they have not managed to eliminate this problem until today.[50]

The party organizations immediately acknowledged 'their mistake', and promised to 'enrich and intensify' their agitprop activity.[51]

In the official discourse, missing work was immediately transformed into 'hundreds of tons of fabric' or 'tens of thousands of pairs of shoes' that did not enter the economic circuit.[52] Most often, though, absences and truancies were not calculated in days off, but as an ideal working time for an abstract worker.

The official account over the activity of the City Committee of the Romanian Communist Party in 1954 reproduced the same logic of calculation, stating that the incapacity of some industrial units to fulfil their plan and to keep production costs low had its roots in workers' lack of discipline.[53] The party officials reported that more than 170,000 workdays were lost in Cluj in one year because of workers' truancies, equating them to the one-year production of a factory with 620 workers. The expression condensed the main concerns of the party in the 1950s: the disastrous effects of rowdiness over production. It was a way to underline the gravity of the lack of discipline among the workers and an expression that intimately connected ideal work to an ideal time flow and to an ideal labourer. But to its dismay, the state had to work with actual workers, thus truancies, delays, stalling and wasting time became the object of a political struggle. As the managers would recollect in their interviews, this was going to be a task for generations, never fully accomplished and contingent upon future transformations of the regime.

The logic of the 480-minute workday was turned on its head by the workers themselves when they refused extra tasks or when asked to organize their work differently. A foreman at János Herbák was complaining to the factory managers that he could not 'imprint a sense of cleanliness' in his people, and that 'a young comrade, when asked to deposit his trash in a different part of the workshop, refused bluntly. He said that he wanted to earn money, not carry garbage from one place to another and waste time.'[54]

The alliance between the foremen and the workers was under attack immediately after the first one-year plan was implemented. In 1949, an official notice from the director of János Herbák, read as usual during the workers' lunch break, announced that any leave permit from the foreman had to be countersigned by staff from the Personnel Office:

> Working time is shortened by many comrades who leave the precinct of the factory under various pretexts. They have their permits signed by their foremen. Taking into account the fact that fulfilling the State plan depends upon fulfilling the tasks in time and the fact that the control at the factory gate is made difficult by the increased traffic, we are introducing a new system for checking the personnel who leave their job during working hours.
>
> In future, all those who want to leave their job during working hours, after getting the consent of their foremen, have to come to the Personnel Office where they will get the final approval or rejection of their request.[55]

Letting the bureaucrats have the last say on workers' possibility of moving around and solving their problems during their working hours was received with hostility, and people started to boo the announcement and to throw bread towards the loudspeakers. It was not long until undercutting the authority of the foremen had consequences in the disciplinary regime of the factories, and a new legislation for 'repairing' the authority of the foremen and motivating them financially was needed. This was going to be partially achieved by the wage-system reform in 1957.

A continuous effort was made to replace archaic rhythms of the seasonal passing, religious holidays or personal celebrations with a uniform and homogenous use of time throughout the year. The whole notion of 'break' or 'vacation' received a new meaning and was made fully dependent upon the necessities of production. Theoretically, workers' vacations were spread according to the rhythm of production, the flows of raw materials and the rapidly changing requirements of the ministries.[56] They were to be distributed throughout the year, as an alternative to the prevalent choice for a summer break, when people used to work their land plots outside the city.[57] However, every summer of the First Five-Year Plan was painful proof of the contradiction between the need for continuity in production and the need to keep a rural-urban workforce in the factory. Because their labour was so badly needed, on the rare occasions when the peasant-workers were threatened with firing, they simply stayed home for the summer and looked for employment in a different factory in the winter. As we have seen, things only got worse when not only the commuters but also some of the urban workers left the factories to work in the countryside for several months a year.

Asking people to work during a religious holiday was another source of discontent. For the state, dismissing religious holidays had a double function: it kept the production going and it marked a passage to a 'modern', secular time. Nonetheless, people found ways to undercut the strategies of the factory management during religious holidays. For instance, a 1951 production report from János Herbák showed that during the week when the Hungarians celebrated Easter, the production figures dramatically fell. The production of a workshop with a predominantly female workforce basically stopped when women announced en masse that they were sick. A quick check at their homes found them cleaning their houses and baking for Easter. Some of them were found cleaning other people's houses for extra money. Women were summoned to come back to work immediately, but they simply refused and promised to make up for their absence the following week. They did, so no sanctions were issued.[58]

At the same factory, religious celebrations became an issue of ethnic conflict. Rumours appeared that the government would only allow the workers to take free days during the Orthodox Easter. As the Romanians were Orthodox and the Hungarians were Catholics, Unitarians and Calvinists, the Hungarian workers cornered the director (Hungarian himself) on the corridors and threatened that they would all leave if they were not allowed to celebrate Easter 'in peace'. The Hungarian workers did indeed miss work the day after the Easter Sunday. No sanctions were issued but 'the bad situation at János Herbák' became the topic of some very heated debates between members of the Regional Party Committee and the factory managers themselves. The proposed solution for 'the Easter problem' was to find a unique date for its celebration, both for the Catholic and for the Orthodox believers. The solution proved to be unrealistic for the ethnically contested factory space of the 1950s. When announced to the Hungarian workers, they were immediately sure that unifying the two celebrations actually meant that the 'Hungarian Easter would be cancelled'.[59] The leaders of the factory party organization panicked and advised their superiors to let people have their religious holidays celebrated 'in the way they have always done'. They expressively showed that workers could not be convinced that 'celebrating Easter meant not accomplishing the Plan'. The problem quickly ceased to be 'a planning issue' and became a political one, which was immediately translated into an ethnic key. The Securitate reports on the workers' mood warned the higher party officials that the situation in the factory could escalate if they tried to stop people celebrating 'their' Easter.

The complementary requirement for the full usage of the working-time was to cut overtime completely, or at least to reduce it as much as possible. Forcing the factory managers to drop overtime as a strategy for fulfilling the plan became the subject of some of the first post-nationalization instructions sent by the communist government to the newly appointed factory managers, who were asked to 'pay attention to the overtime regime and to use it only if it was mandatory to fulfil the production programme', because 'overtime was not profitable'.[60]

Since for the newly nationalized factories the necessary overtime was generally a question of guessing and approximating based on experience, the government tended to reduce it by continuously pushing the workers and the managers to reorganize production. For instance, in June 1948, a factory got the authorization to use 15 per cent overtime every month. In December, the factory used only 12 per cent of the authorized overtime. In January 1949, the new target was immediately changed to 12 per cent, although theoretically its 15 per cent overtime was authorized for the whole year, until June 1949.[61] During the first one-year plan, in 1949, overtime was set to a maximum of 3 per cent of the baseline wage.

The decision to employ overtime in specific situations had to respect a hierarchical chain, which went up to the Ministers Council. It was presented in this form to the factory managers:

> You are not allowed to exceed 5 per cent overtime. Up to 3 per cent, overtime must be approved by the Director of the Central Office of Leather and Footwear. Overtime between 3–5 per cent will be approved by the Adjunct Minister. Anything above 5 per cent must be agreed upon with the Ministers Council. Necessary productive time will be calculated taking the total number of the employees as the base, and then multiplying that by 8. No exceptions are possible.[62]

The 'no exceptions' rule seemed to be fictional. In 1949, the first year of planning, the amount of overtime approved by the government in the leather and footwear industry was 5 per cent of the wage fund at factory level, and a maximum of 25 per cent of a worker's salary. However, some workers at János Herbák earned an extra of 60–70 per cent of their wage by adding working hours to their daily activity.[63] The only 'sanction' for the management was an ironic note from the Light Industry Ministry, offering some loose guidance for the future.

Lack of direct consequences was neither universal, nor permanent. Officially, labour shortage was rarely accepted as a reason for overtime by the higher echelons of the party. Poor organization of production and unconvincing persuasion work among the labourers were generally considered the main problems underlying the necessity to use overtime in the factory. The party organizations, the unions, and the factory management were, as usual, made culpable for not being successful enough in demonstrating to their fellow workers that employing overtime led to a chronic lack of efficiency at the shop-floor level.

Detailed instructions for the rationalization of the production process, and for how the factories could do 'everything possible to eliminate overtime'[64] were issued by the Central Office of Leather and Footwear as part of the 1949 effort to regulate the space of the factory. An example reads as follows:

> We indicate the following means to eliminate the overtime:
> a. The revision of the machines and of the installations has to be done necessarily after work or on Sundays. For this type of operation, you can institute a different work schedule and another rest day than for the ones who work in the productive workshops.
> b. The overtime needed for unpredicted work, like accident repairing, unloading wagons which come too late and others, must be compensated in such a way that the total number of hours worked in a month equals eight hours multiplied by the number of the working days and by the number of workers.
> c. For every piece of work that needs continuity in the production process ... the factory is allowed to employ one extra worker for every six others. He

will replace the other six on their rest days, which will be spread over the week.
d. To prevent the necessity to use overtime because of the inherent moments when the workers miss work for health reasons or for rare accidental reasons, the factory will hire 2–3 per cent extra workers, over the necessities of the plan. You will use them for maintenance when there are no missing productive workers.
e. To compensate for the lack of skilled workers, you will pay attention to the professional schools in your industrial units. This way, you will create your own skilled workers.

Nevertheless, the need for overtime was growing.

In January 1950, the Footwear Factory reported a 0.03 per cent overfulfilment of the plan. The small achievement suggested that the factory was reaching its limits; the fact that it was possible only with the help of many overtime hours showed that the figures of the plan could not have been met at that point without more workers. In the factory committee meetings, the chief engineer, comrade Rado, underlined some problems in production: many sick workers, many leaves of absence and a huge labour turnout and discontinuities in production made overtime a daily necessity. In fact, he declared firmly that the fulfilment of the plan was impossible without asking people to work more, sometimes even without paying them.

Since hiring new workers, buying new industrial equipment, and finding raw materials on the market were strictly prohibited, the factory managers tried to use unpaid overtime to compensate for the lack of productive resources. From a report on the activity of János Herbák for the third trimester of 1950, we learn that in February the workers executed 30,000 hours overtime, compared to a monthly average of 23,000 hours.[65] The factory management could not make any decision with regard to the payment of these hours and had to wait for a solutioning of the case by the Light Industry Ministry, whose executives considered that 'the plan must be executed without overtime, because it makes workmanship expensive and it reduces the outturn of labour'.[66] After one month, the executives were only allowed to pay for 34 per cent of the overtime while the rest of the money was imputed to the director and to the chief accountant.

Meanwhile, the workers grew impatient about their money, and manifested their discontent in a noisy fashion, loudly complaining to the union and to the party organization of the factory, who reacted instantaneously by asking management to cover overtime as a whole, and pay the workers immediately. In their report, presented at a meeting for analysing the activity of the factory in November, the representative of the party organization furiously attacked the management: 'Not paying the overtime created a bad political atmosphere within the enterprise. In a word, it reversed all the work done by the party until now. These practices were normal habits for capitalists, not for us.'[67] They reproached the economic executives for executing the instructions of the ministry 'in a mechanical way', and not taking account of the discontent of the workers created by such a measure.[68] Comrade Turos, the leader of the party organization in the factory, put things in order:

> According to the party organization, our superiors executed the instructions in a mechanical manner. Overtime must be paid. Unpaid overtime created a bad political atmosphere within the factory and it overturned the whole political work of the party. These types of procedure were characteristic of the capitalist times. The comrades from the factory management must present the real situation to the Leather and Footwear Direction, and they must insist on a favourable solution without fearing for their jobs.[69]

Besides the political mistake of making the workers angry, the factory managers committed the error of not informing the Central Office of Leather and Footwear that the plan had been realized by using overtime. The factory managers were authorized to use the director's fund for covering the extra hours, but were threatened that next time they would have to pay them from their own pockets. However, the plan for the following months was increased, and even more overtime was needed for its fulfilment.[70] This was going to become a common occurrence in the negotiation of overtime and, as my interviews with factory directors in the 1970s show, the use of overtime was also going to become a chronic feature of the late socialist factories.

The accusation of mechanical application of orders was also quite widespread in the factory meetings when a problem remained unsolved for a long time. 'Formalism' and 'mechanicism' were opposed to a creative style of management and an intuitive interpretation of the hierarchical directives. But the ambiguity created was used not only by the local party activists and by the government officials but also by the factory managers themselves, who invoked both 'creativity' and 'following orders' to justify concrete actions.

The quick and firm political response in the situation created at János Herbák, described above, proved that ultimately the party was determined to protect its workers. Making people use their entire working day was the direct responsibility of the factory but it made sense only if the factory could be understood as a political space par excellence – as an important space where moral regulation was accomplished. Ruling over productive time was central for the state, both in its pursuit of accumulation and in its political project.

The appropriation of people's time was part of the global 'transition' to 'industrialism', an experience historically specific to nascent capitalist industry, which was also presupposed in the stage of primitive socialist accumulation. As E.P. Thompson shows in his celebrated 1967 article 'Time, Work-Discipline, and Industrial Capitalism', the path from 'natural' rhythms to modern capitalist time needed first of all a divorce from task-oriented time. The danger of task-oriented time for industrial discipline was that it was 'more humanly comprehensible than timed labour', more social, less clearly separated from 'life', and had a 'wasteful and lacking in urgency' appearance 'to men accustomed to labour timed by the clock'.[71] Most importantly, time in the factory made people experience 'a distinction between their employer's time and their "own" time', while 'the employer must *use* the time of his labour, and see that it is not wasted: not the tasks but the value of time when reduced to money is dominant. Time is now currency: it is not passed but spent.'[72]

To this day, workers have resisted the capitalist model of time-discipline wherever it was exported together with 'modernization' and 'development'. The capitalist time-discipline model was used against the Mexican peons transformed into miners at the beginning of the twentieth century, who were described as lacking initiative, being unable to save time and money, having too many holidays, indolent, infantile and subsuming industrial work to agriculture-based subsistence.[73] The model was linked to complex accounting systems in the Spanish royal monopoly on tobacco production.[74] It was employed to moralize workers in colonial Nigeria and Cameroon, to help the colonizers prove the 'natural inferiority' of the natives in Latin America, to calculate the distance from standard expectations of modernity in Zambia,[75] and to silence workers in the Bombay cotton mills. Industrial time-discipline has travelled across centuries in the feminized Malaysian factories of late capitalism, where 'spirits' resisted it by taking control over women who were undertaking their own transition from peasant life to factory constraints.[76] Time-discipline was also central to the Bolshevik vision, as it was supposed to mark the passage to a New World and to a New Man on the post-revolutionary shop floors of the NEP, and in the Stalinist industrial plants of East Central Europe.[77] The struggle around time-discipline on the shop floor seems simply inevitable wherever industrial accumulation regimes emerge, and where 'the insistent energies of industrial man' need to be released.[78]

Notes

1. ANDC, Fund Clujana 24/23/1950, 7.
2. Kornai, *Economics of Shortage*; Kornai, *The Socialist System*.
3. Pittaway, 'Social Limits of State Control'.
4. Ibid., 108.
5. Marx, *Capital*, 260.
6. Ibid., 262.
7. Friedmann, 'Esquisse d'une psycho-sociologie'.
8. Verdery, *What Was Socialism*, 40.
9. Ibid., 43.
10. Cohen, 'Matter Matters to Authority', 12. Cohen, *Le siècle des chefs*.
11. Cohen, 'Matter Matters to Authority', 21.
12. ANDC, Fund Clujana 24-76/1950.
13. ANDC, Fund Clujana 16/1950, 4.
14. ANDC, Fund Clujana 33/105/1949.
15. ANDC, Fund Clujana 18-4/1952, 16–17.
16. ANDC, Fund Clujana 16/1950, 3.
17. ANDC, Fund Clujana 16/1950, 4.
18. ANDC, Fund Clujana 16/1950, 4.
19. ANDC, Fund Clujana 16/1950, 10.
20. ANDC, Fund Clujana 18-4/1952, 31.
21. ANDC, Fund Clujana 29-23/1952.
22. ANDC, Fund Clujana 24-76/1950, 26, 44, 84.
23. ANDC, Fund Clujana 24-76/1950, 56.
24. ANDC, Fund Clujana 24-76/1950.
25. As Kornai's corpus of work shows, Romania was far from being a singular case among the socialist countries, where planning offered more a picture of perpetual bargaining than the idealized image of a top-down decisional flow. His work had a long-lasting influence on the scholarship of the region, for socialist economies became simply the equivalent of 'shortage economies'.
26. ANDC, RC PMR Cluj, Fund 13, 9/87.
27. 'De ce productivitatea muncii trebuie să crească mai repede decât salariul mediu?' [Why labour productivity must grow faster than the average wage?'], *Lupta de clasă* V/XXV (10) (October 1955), 105–10.
28. ANDC, Fund Clujana 24-76/1950, 59.
29. ANDC, Fund Clujana 24/23/1950, 13.
30. ANDC, Fund Clujana 33/41/1949, 307.
31. ANDC, Fund Clujana 24/23/1950, 13.
32. *Viața uzinei noastre*, 29 November 1951.
33. Ibid.
34. ANDC, Fund Clujana 33/41/1949, 252.
35. ANDC, Fund Clujana, 33/41/1949.
36. ANDC, Fund Clujana 33/41/1949, 273.
37. ANDC, Fund Clujana, 31-18/1953, 30.
38. ANDC, Fund Clujana 24/23/1950, 3.
39. ANDC, Fund Clujana, 24/23/1950, 6.
40. ANDC, Fund Clujana, 24/23/1950, 3.
41. *Viața uzinei noastre*, 15 August 1953.
42. *Viața uzinei noastre*, 15 May 1953.
43. ANDC, Fund Clujana, 24-76/1950, 34.
44. Zerubavel, *Hidden Rhythms*.

45. ANDC, RC PMR Cluj, Fund 13, 9/87.
46. ANDC, Fund Clujana, 16/1950, 2.
47. ANDC, Fund 3, CC PMR Cluj, 103/7/1949, 3.
48. ANDC, Fund 13, CR PMR Cluj 6/1950.
49. ANDC Fund Clujana, 24-76/1950, 108.
50. ANDC Fund 13, CR PMR Cluj, 34/1951, 93.
51. Ibid., 96. At another factory, the foremen reported around 30–50 truancies daily. An extra 800 minutes were lost daily because of workers being tardy. They equated to two days of work or 700 lost days in one year, or with the yearly workload of two workers.
52. ANDC, Fund 3, CC PMR Cluj, 253/64, 3.
53. ANDC, Fund 55, CO P.M.R. Cluj, 2/1955, 236.
54. ANDC Fund Clujana 24/23/1950, 8.
55. ANDC Fund Clujana 0/1949.
56. ANDC Fund Clujana 28/135/1950.
57. ANDC Fund Clujana 33/41/1949.
58. ANDC, Fund 3, CC P.M.R. Cluj, 65.
59. ANDC, Fund 3, CC P.M.R. Cluj, 248/73, 65.
60. ANDC Fund Clujana 33/105/1949, 2.
61. ANDC Fund Clujana 33/41/1949, 74.
62. ANDC Fund Clujana, 33/41/1949, 47.
63. ANDC Fund Clujana, 0/1949.
64. ANDC Fund Clujana, 33/41/1949, 74.
65. ANDC, Fund 3, CC P.M.R. Cluj, 253/64.
66. ANDC, Fund Clujana 24-76/1950, 76.
67. ANDC, Fund Clujana 24/23/1950, 80.
68. ANDC, Fund Clujana 24-76/1950, 76.
69. ANDC, Fund Clujana 24-76/1950, 80.
70. ANDC, Fund Clujana 24-76/1950, 77.
71. Thompson, 'Time', 60.
72. Ibid., 61.
73. Thompson, 'Time'.
74. Carmona, Ezzamel and Gutierrez, 'Control and Cost Accounting Practices'.
75. Ferguson, *Expectations of Modernity*.
76. Ong, *Spirits of Resistance*.
77. The classical reference for the use of working time within the broader discussion about factory discipline in the Soviet Union is Filtzer, 'Labor Discipline'.
78. Thompson, 'Time', 93.

CHAPTER 6

PLANNED HEROISM AND NONSYNCHRONICITY ON THE SHOP FLOOR

Faces in the Factory Newspaper

On 12 October 1951, the workers from János Herbák received the first issue of their factory newspaper for free. The party organization from the leather and footwear factory in Cluj had decided a while ago that the time was ripe for the industrial unit to have its own publication. When reading *The Life of Our Factory* [*Viața Uzinei Noastre*], the workers could find new encouragements for their efforts to overfulfil the plan, they could understand the importance of fighting for quality in production, and they could learn a thing or two about carrying the international struggle for peace 'with the help of the Soviet Union's nuclear weapon'.

But the workers heading to the workshops in the autumn morning quickly realized that most pages of the factory newspaper were covered with the familiar faces of their colleagues. On the first page, the full names of three leaders in production were given, and a detailed account of their accomplishments. On the next page, the round face of a young woman stood next to a column titled 'Work discipline'. The picture was accompanied by a letter addressed to 'comrade Hegyi Luiza from sewing workshop no. 1' by one of her colleagues, Sárkádi Ludovic:

> Comrade,
> You committed to strengthen your work discipline for honouring the 7th of November. You did not carry out this commitment and you have been late repeatedly.
> Comrade, did you think what a delay of a few minutes means for the workshop, for the factory, and for our country? Did you think that being a bad example can induce others to be late, and the minutes can become hours?

Did you think that an extra pair of boots could come out our factory's doors during those minutes? So, the natural consequence of your being late is that we give our country one pair of boots less.

Think how much the class enemy rejoices in seeing your behaviour! And not without reason, because he knows what you too should know: that giving more pairs of shoes means we are stronger. Each missing pair of shoes weakens us and strengthens the class enemy!

Comrade, I am convinced you consider yourself among those who struggle for peace. Prove this by deeds, strengthen the commitment you made to honour the 7th of November by working wholeheartedly. Don't be late anymore, so others cannot say: 'If Hégyi Luiza may be late, so may I'.

We trust you, comrade![1]

The letter articulated much of the propaganda around the problem of factory discipline and its relationship with socialist accumulation. Through the factory newspaper, the party organization tried to convey concretely how failing to generate surplus weakened not only the factory but also the polity.

Since any worker could become a bad example for the others in an environment dominated by the idea of 'socialist emulation', larger consequences for individual misconduct in the factory were foretold, while a very specific notion of 'loyalty' discursively related the worker to the pedagogic concerns of the state. Because honour was considered an important dimension of any act of work, discipline was summoned for glorifying a historical event – the October Revolution. The lesson was clear: work had to be understood as a political act, with worldwide consequences. Workers' daily practices mattered, while production appeared to be simultaneously a source of material accumulation, a form of creating a global Other and a promise of political subjecthood.

A December issue of the same newspaper contrasted the bright present of the young Vasile Gădălean with his past as 'the son of poor peasants, a youngster who could not learn and who could not get on in the world':

> He is now free and uses every second to the full for personal development. He is never discouraged but always cheerful and waggish. He has already finished the qualification course, but now, after his daily shift, he learns how to work on a special machine from the leather gallantry department. He is a member of the factory choir. He livens us with his youthful impetuosity. Our work goes better like this: singing, joking and learning.[2]

The December portrait emphasized the embodied qualities of the ideal worker: young, skilled, passionate, enthusiastic, with 'healthy social origins', aware of his newly gained freedom, willing to stay in the factory after his strenuous working hours, continuously learning and investing in his personal development. Most importantly, the bright image focused on how the young man was mastering time by making 'every second' useful, and on how he was also able to mobilize others with the help of his cheerfulness and artistic nature.

Vasile Gădălean and Hegyi Luiza were both supposed to embark on a journey of self-transformation, closely followed by the eye of the party organization in the factory. Only Vasile seemed to be successful in his endeavour to become a true socialist worker, through a metamorphosis that allowed him to transcend his poor peasant roots and gain a new life, a factory life, that would bear no real resemblance to his past.

Taken together, the two portraits draw attention to the fact that the productivist and managerial core of early socialism were brought together in a pedagogic project, which was directed rather towards the individual labourer than towards workers as a class. By capturing the two most important sides of workers' self-transformation in the socialist period – becoming and participating – the two portraits reveal the 'dos and don'ts' of the early socialist factory, and the drive behind the state's exercise in pedagogy, ethics and legitimation. They also delineate the boundaries of the conceptual space in which the worker had to emerge in the 1950s, both as a producer and as a political subject.

Nothing else is known about Hegyi Luiza. We do not know if she stopped being late, if she gave the country 'one pair of shoes more' or if she became aware of the dangers carried by those minutes that were not saturated with usefulness. Probably not, otherwise her face would have appeared again in the factory newspaper, accompanying another successful story about increasing awareness and emerging working-class consciousness. After all, stories about slackers who remained slackers did not make for the best reading.

Only a few months later though, Vasile Gădălean's name appeared on a list of Stakhanovites from the leather gallantry department, the same place where his learning process had been captured in December. His evolution from a young villager into a Stakhanovite seemed a straightforward one: hard work, enthusiasm and the capacity to master his daily tasks better than anyone else would have accounted for his achievements. However, there was more than met the eye behind the celebratory discourse of the party. Stakhanovites like Vasile did not appear from nothing, simply due to their personal qualities and their unabated belief in the socialist project. They had to be made.

Based on documents from the local committees of the Romanian Communist Party in Cluj/Kolozsvár, factory records and interviews with workers and executives employed in the city's industry, I show how on the shop floor the process of making Stakhanovites was complicated and expensive, and never led to the heights of productivity expected by the state officials.[3] Moreover, creating a 'privileged caste of industrial workers' created animosity between workers, fracturing their solidarity and endangering their daily collaboration in the production process.

These findings are by no means surprising. Starting with the emblematic case of the Stakhanovite movement (Alexey Grigoryevich Stakhanov was the Donbass miner on which Stakhanovite mobilization was moulded), the heavy reliance on exceptional individuals who worked in assault to exceed their work norms proved to be problematic. These 'individual' records needed to be supported by other workers, who performed the additional tasks required by this type of performance, and by the extra efforts of the new economic executives, who needed to ensure that no shortages of raw materials or breakdowns of equipment would hinder these incredible achievements. Working in assault furthered the usual disruptions to production and placed stress on the machinery. Since these labourers pushed the limits of productivity for everyone else and contributed to the efforts of the party to raise work norms and diminish wages, the Stakhanovites came to be resented by other workers, and the fact that labour heroism was lavishly rewarded by the state officials did not make things any easier on the shop floor.[4]

In postwar Eastern and Central Europe, the Stakhanovite movement took a less heroic form and carried less financial advantage than in the Soviet Union. The movement quickly lost its momentum in the mid-1950s, together with other instruments for enhancing productivity coming through Soviet channels. In Romania, fewer and fewer mentions about the 'Soviet methods' were encountered in the newspapers and factory records of the 1960s and 1970s. Increasingly confronted with the pressures of world markets, dependent on technological advancement and subjected to the requirements of international financial institutions, the Second and the Third Wave of the Romanian socialist industrialization were bound to rely more on managerial ideologies directly imported from the West than on the heroic mobilization of labour. Socialist competitions survived, but in most cases remained on paper, sometimes accompanying celebratory moments, as part of what Burawoy and Lukács called 'painting socialism'.[5]

Any discussion about slackers and Stakhanovites in postwar Eastern and Central Europe could stop here. We could easily reduce it to just another inconsequential transfer of a propagandistic trope, self-serving to the politics of productivity promoted by the state in early socialism, and we would probably not be very far from the truth. However, there are questions that remain unanswered. If Stakhanovism (and labour heroism more generally) proved to be not sustainable in the long run in Stalin's Soviet Union, why was it so ubiquitously maintained in the blueprint of socialist construction in postwar Eastern and Central Europe? Why was it so central in the state's discourse associated to the implementation of planning? Since Stakhanovism did not directly increase factory productivity in the 1950s, was the movement useful in other ways in the effort to transform the factory space? In short, is there something more fundamental we can understand about the politics of productivity of early socialism by looking at how the state tried to separate the factory world into heroes and villains of labour?

I argue that during the First Five-Year Plan in Eastern and Central Europe, Stakhanovism represented the last breath for the specific temporal conception entailed by the Bolshevik project: the possibility of transcending historical time through an elevation of ordinary work practices. As 'socialist exemplaries', Stakhanovites epitomized the real possibility that time could be transcended altogether through the same practices that Taylorism and a rational management of time-discipline entailed, only boosted to a new level. Stakhanovites were workers – in some cases starting as ordinary achievers or slackers – who were able to deny the constraints of linear time and bring the future into the now. They were the symbolic carriers of the struggle against a long history of marginalization and dispossession, as produced at the intersection between backwardness, uneven development and their corresponding forms of exploitation in the region. Labour heroism was expressive of this struggle because it was supposed to connect mundane issues like productivity and factory discipline to the broader historical stakes of the communist project.

Boosting labour productivity was considered the main resource for accumulation in postwar Eastern and Central Europe. Alongside the nationalization of the means of production and the collectivization of land, price scissors and strategic investments in heavy industry and fixed capital, early socialist regimes were actively built on 'workers' self-restraint' in everyday life, and 'planned heroism' on the shop floor. These were also the pillars of primitive socialist accumulation as defined by Preobrazhensky in the 1920s, and trying to impose the former had a major impact on the capacity to achieve the latter.

In purely ideological terms, increasing productivity on the shop floor had to count on workers' progressive historical consciousness and self-transformation. Heroic acts of labour actualized the world of what was possible directly on the shop floor, thus making Marx's intuition that work was the only human activity able to transcend historical time more real than ever.[6] Stakhanovites and heroes of labour embodied the historical possibility of socialist accumulation as 'planned heroism', 'the simultaneous combination of revolutionary and time-disciplined orientations in everyday work habits',[7] and the hope that it would become the core of socialist political economy.

At a more pragmatic level, the practical ways in which the Stakhanovites were able to bring the future into the now in the act of work contributed to making the shop floor's reserves of productivity visible to the new economic executives and to the party organization in the factory. After several years of planning, the real nature of the factory's internal reserves was not 'hidden' anymore. For managers and labour alike, it was all about making workers squeeze more work into less time. As the pinnacle of labour heroism, Stakhanovism was there to demonstrate the fact that the inner reserves of the industrial units indeed resided in workers' muscles and in their own desire to improve.

Nevertheless, as factory managers and socialist planners knew only too well, workers' willingness to work more, faster and better was much more connected to seeing their wages increase than to any growth in their historical consciousness. While their assigned role on the shop floor was to reveal what workers could do if they only wanted to and learned how, what the Stakhanovites actually made visible on the shop floor was the contradiction between the collectivist horizon of 'socialist construction' and the fact that in the last instance, plan figures were addressing not the enterprise, nor the brigade, nor the working-class, but the individual worker.

Commodified labour, and thus workers' individual performance, were postulated as the basis of command economies. As Mark Pittaway shows, 'the individual became the unit on which the wage was established',[8] as well as the unit on which the new scientific production norms, the work targets and the labour cost of commodities were calculated.

> The state attempted to use systems of remuneration on the shop floor to bind workers to the goals of the plan. These systems of remuneration were individual rather than collective, suggesting that at the heart of classical central planning lay an apparent paradox between institutional centralisation and a high degree of individualisation at the point of production. Embodied in wage systems was a specific attempt to discipline the individual worker through using a specific 'politics of time'. This aimed to force workers to use every minute of working time to produce goods as laid out in the plan, to accelerate their work, improve their productivity and constantly surpass the goals of the plan.[9]

The pedagogic project conveyed in the newspapers and at the 'red corners' of the factories must be read as an expression of the simple reality of planning, which was predicated from the start on making labour power quantifiable, measurable and thus visible.

During the few months necessary each year for debating the plan figures, some initial numbers emerged from the government offices as 'promises', which were then confronted with other numbers that appeared to be expressions of local realities in the factories. Throughout the year, at each level, people were promising and justifying numbers. Among these, plan figures had a special status: they were never simply numbers that reflected the potential for socialist accumulation and its realization, but expressions of personal responsibility. They served as criteria for classifying people as trustworthy or not, according to how well they performed within this quantitative logic. The way a factory manager could meet the plan figures, or the way a worker could accomplish her work norm were read by the party officials as proof of compliance with the regime. In this way, knowledge about the economy met the mix of ethics and pedagogy on which socialist construction was founded, and the emergence of standards as 'forms of compression and representations of actions'[10] introduced from the beginning large inequalities in the way different categories of rule were acted upon by the state.

But several questions still remain. Why was socialist accumulation expressed directly in time-related tropes instead of being coined around quantitative or financial terms? Why was the political imaginary of the 1950s wrapped obsessively and explicitly around direct expressions of time–time compression rather than around quantity and quality? More concretely, what choice was made when people were requested to accomplish the Five-Year Plan in four years rather than being asked to produce a certain number of shoes, chairs or screwdrivers? Was this idiom a simple translation of its capitalist counterpart 'time is money' with a propagandistic twist? Or did it say something more, maybe even something different, about the relationship between accumulation, exploitation, and historical backwardness?

Slackers, Stakhanovites and the Time of Politics

The pre-nationalization Constitution of the Popular Republic of Romania established work as 'the fundamental factor of the state's economic life' and as 'a duty for every citizen', while the state was bound to support the working people 'in order to defend them against exploitation and to elevate their living standard'.[11] Work was stipulated as a basic right, which was to be gradually ensured 'through the organization and planned development of the national economy'. Only four years later, in the Constitution of 1952, the state's earlier promise of support mutated into an explicit productivist frame that connected work to the possibility of survival. The new fundamental law stipulated work as 'a duty and an issue of honour for every citizen who is able to toil, according to the principle that "who doesn't work, doesn't eat"', and directly connecting it with the 'socialist' principle: 'From each according to his ability, to each according to his work'.[12] Not by chance, the idea of 'planned heroism' appeared in this context, which linked survival to work and thus to a process of commodification of labour. In this configuration, slackers and Stakhanovites became the end of a continuum in which a productivist notion of citizenship was negotiated in early socialism. For workers like Hegyi Luiza and Vasile Gădălean, who saw their faces in the factory newspapers, the difference between slacking and what we can call 'ordinary heroic deeds' was one between being simply exploited as a workforce or becoming comrades, and it had profound implications for their everyday lives.

Soviet-style socialism started from the assumption that hyperrationalization of production could be extricated from its Western capitalist rationales and used to carve the realities of the new times. In postwar Romania, planning was driven by an even stronger commitment to time compression than capitalist manufacturing. It was going to bring together an individual remuneration system, the scientific organization of production and a plethora of measures to keep labour cheap. But ideally, socialist planning operated with a different model of personhood from Taylorism. Socialist workers could hardly be imagined as disembedded from their social worlds, and their rationality on the shop floor was supposed to come with a sense of history, a recognition of class struggle (as framed by the party), and an enthusiastic consent to pushing their limits in work and to practising a form of asceticism in consumption. This was, anyway, the justification behind keeping workers' wages low and constantly pushing their work norms up.

Not only were workers' rationality, historical consciousness and capacity to work entangled in early socialism, but they were also infinitely elastic. In the labour process, higher speed and accuracy could be learned and improved. Thus, planning was always concerned with future levels of productivity, taking the present as a base line that simply needed to be overcome. The ideological underpinning of socialist planning appealed to what Stephen Hanson called 'planned heroism' – the possibility that rational linear time can be transcended altogether within productive undertakings. The workers themselves would have become the authors of this historical leap, as they would have elevated the practices that Taylorism brought forward to unprecedented levels.[13]

Stakhanovites as leaders in production and norm busters were the materialized images of what was possible for the New Socialist Man to achieve. They were supposed to emerge as embodiments of good practices and moral standards for the young, inexperienced and hard-to-control labourers who worked next to them. Collectively, they were an 'imagined working class',[14] a space where the socialist state in its formative years could act *as if* these icons were representative for labour as a whole. Stakhanovites brought the future into the present through triumphant self-transformations, which could be pointed to as the solution for a necessary 'temporal leap from deficient modernity to modernity consummated', from the backwardness of the semi-proletarian to the advanced historical consciousness of the Stakhanovite.[15] This individual embodiment in the present of a collective future had to be made visible and celebrated.

And the celebrations indeed started, accompanying the launching and the unfolding of the First Five-Year Plan in 1951. The party members responsible for agitation and propaganda in collaboration with the unions started to organize artistic programmes for glorifying Stackhanovites and leaders in production, which were presented in the factory or at workers' homes. At the Railways Workshops in Cluj, the first brigades to fulfil their June 1952 monthly plan were greeted with flowers and congratulations at the end of the day.[16] One evening caught two Stakhanovites – Irina Erdös and Iuliana Deák from János Herbák – visiting each other. They did not expect the factory choir entering the door and starting to sing. The president of the factory committee addressed the warm salute of the workers to the two women, and encouraged them to keep up their work and 'raise more Stakhanovites' by teaching the youngsters 'what good work means'.[17] In 1953, these activities gained momentum as part of the state effort to improve productivity and prevent dissent in the factory through the use of moral and financial incentives rather than through disciplinary practices that had proved useless over the years. An informative note from the Light Industry Ministry suggested that the organization of small entertaining programmes in which a cultural group sang or danced for the best workers should be extended in every factory.[18]

Shaming slackers with music was briefly adopted as a practice in 1952, as a mirror of the celebration of Stakhanovites, but workers' reaction was far from what the party wished for, with gender playing a pivotal role in how they felt about the public humiliation of their colleagues. As former workers at the factories in Cluj told me in the interviews, for women, seeing their face and their name on the notice board under the 'bad examples' rubric was one of their most dreadful fears. When one of their colleagues ended up in this situation, women were ashamed for her and hardly discussed the matter, except for manifesting their sympathy. This level of exposure seemed completely inappropriate for a 'good girl', whose diligence was one of her most valued and appreciated traits.

Embarrassing the slackers did become a reason for gossip among the male workers, who seemed rather happy to make fun of one another. Nevertheless, their gossip and laughter can hardly be read as a success for the factory party organization in creating a current of public opinion against the slackers. Making fun of a bad worker did not mean that he was going to be reported by his colleagues for missing work, for being late or for executing poor quality work. One male worker from a younger generation – who was later employed at the Railways Workshops – was still angry when he thought about 'all those snitches' who 'were quickly running to tell everything to the foreman'. In his opinion, they were 'nothing. To tell something about your colleagues to your foreman ... you were nothing.' Thus, shaming practices were rapidly dropped as they only created anger among the workers, including among the leaders in production, who thought this manifestation of public opprobrium was 'just too much'.[19]

Laughter and jokes can be read more as a form of stratifying male sociality within a group than an expression of internalizing the aims and values of the socialist project. Good work did matter for workers. Being a good worker meant being a respected worker, especially if not 'one of them' – a 'fake' Stakhanovite, a snitch or a party leader. Being a bad worker or being less dependable may have been a source of amusement for some, but it did not mean that the worker was marginalized or that the other workers acted in any way as disciplinary agents. In interactionist language, as order-takers, the workers were alienated from the symbols and values promulgated within the factory space, and backstage they manifested cynically about them.[20] Jokes and laughter addressed values that the workers shared themselves – like respect for good work – but did not reflect the same logic as the party-led public exposure. In other words, colleagues' irony and laughter sanctioned bad workers, but in a markedly parallel universe, one that was theirs, not the state's, and in which the workers refused to take part in the appropriation of their own hierarchies.

Even the state's agents in the factory – the new executives, the party organization and the union's leaders – held contradictory visions regarding what shop-floor politics should be about. On the one hand, they continuously aimed to weaken the ties that kept some of the workers together by infusing the shop floor with a work ethics that was surprisingly utilitarianist in terms of incentives, and highly individualist in terms of achievements. On the other hand, their call for more, faster and better work was based on class solidarity and loyalty to the socialist project. Although it is hard to support this claim here, it is very probable that the organization of production according to the combination between Soviet

Taylorism and labour heroism indeed debilitated old solidarities, especially of the experienced, urban workers, by fragmenting and individualizing their interests. Nevertheless, although utilitarianist and individualist attitudes can easily be found in the abundant complaints about unfair payments, wrong placements in a certain wage category, or an uninspired distribution of bonuses, the workers did not unite against slackers. On the contrary, as the previous chapter revealed, 'minding one's business' and 'not being responsible' became dominant strategies in the socialist factories, endangering the formation of socialism as a disciplinary regime.

Since discipline was understood not only as an administrative problem but also as a political one, 'proletarian ethics' and 'proletarian morals' had to spring from the 'patriotic education of the youth, entangled with a certain intellectual attitude towards the collective'.[21] The workers became the bearers of certain 'definitions and pronouncements about morality', which ideally had to be acquired within the factory.[22] But the difficulty of transforming a 'moralizing discourse' as 'an explicit set of instructions about how human choices and practices should be organized'[23] into a material 'ethical regime' depended more on existing shop-floor solidarities than on the tropes of socialist personhood promoted by the party officials in their plenary meetings.

As 'socialist exemplary', the Stakhanovite not only produced more but also improved the process of production and helped others to achieve higher standards in their own work. She or he innovated, introduced new methods of production, learned continuously, saved raw material, improved quality, produced no waste and left their work station clean and tidy. Their enthusiasm was supposed to radiate around and to inspire their co-workers. They were also the first to introduce 'Soviet methods' of production in the factory. Organizing work according to the famous Soviet methods had the declared purpose of enhancing socialist accumulation through various techniques designed to save time and to shorten the production process. Many of them were used (or at least reported to be used) in the factories from Cluj: 'Ciutchin' for increasing quality; 'Corabelnicova' for saving raw material; 'Cotlear' for skilling the workers at their own workplace; 'Nazarova' for handing over the industrial equipment from the previous shift without stopping production; and 'Silaier', 'Balasov' and 'Klewsky' for shortening the manufacturing cycle.[24]

In a mobilizing piece of propaganda published in the factory newspaper under the motto 'Go ahead for the development of the Stakhanovite movement in our factory!', the young Stakhanovite Lörincz Ilona described how her work and life dramatically changed after implementing one of the most popular Soviet methods in the Leather and Footwear Factory:

> For the last two years I have been working according to the method of Lidia Korabelnicova, the Soviet Stakhanovite. In the afternoon, I prepare my tools in such a way that the next morning I can begin work exactly at 7 o'clock, thus using all the 480 minutes of the working day. When I follow the stencil, I use all the pieces of leather, even the small ones. This way, I can overfulfil my plan by 35 per cent, my work norm by 80 per cent, and my products have a quality of 95 per cent. Today [28 October 1951], I give the country products for April 1952. Since I have been using the method of the Stakhanovite Lidia Korabelnicova, my earnings have increased. Before that, I barely managed my work norm and I was earning an average of 6,000 lei per month. Today, using her approach, I earn more than 10,000 lei each month.[25]

The letter was meant to show how good money was supposed to flow from higher production, and how a better management of the self, according to methods already implemented in the Soviet factories, would help the workers to achieve them both. However, reality was quite different.

Although the party propaganda declared that Soviet methods were generalized in the Romanian factories around 1953, my interviews with factory managers and workers reveal that they were actually rarely carried through. Many times, both the workers and the factory management resisted the implementation of these Soviet translations of Taylorist scientific organization of production. For management, the Soviet methods were expensive, required new technology, destabilized production in other sectors, needed a long time to be mastered, and were ultimately 'not that useful'. Adopting Soviet methods meant costs they could not afford and industrial equipment they did not possess. Workers recognized them as just another attempt by the state to squeeze as much as possible from their work. As figures of the plan were constantly renegotiated, workers knew well that any overfulfilment of the plan would lead to higher requirements for the next year, and any personal achievement in production would make their work norms raise and their incomes fall.

Having the best labourers pushing the limits of the production process by doing everything more efficiently was supposed to be a major step in controlling ordinary workers. The exceptional productivity of certain individuals became an important asset in the renegotiation of work norms and wages, as it could function as a standard against which other workers' performance could be assessed.[26] This was crucial, especially when the Stakhanovites were not skilled urban male workers but young peasants who had just entered the factory gates and were showing the potential to improve every day. Since the lines that divided the best workers from 'the rest' were often the same ones that separated the skilled Hungarian labourers from the rural Romanian youth who entered the factory gates, Stakhanovism could only contribute to a further fragmentation of working-class identification processes. Peasant-workers or youngsters coming to Cluj from rural areas became the ones whose capacities needed to be continuously assessed and whose rowdiness had to be tamed. Stakhanovism and slacking turned into the ends of a continuum on which the transformation of this numerous category could find an objective measure: the relationship of every individual worker with the plan figures.

Samuel, an ethnically Hungarian worker now in his nineties, who had worked as a skilled sewer at János Herbák for forty-five years, described to me how Stakhanovites always required more than ordinary managerial measures to make sure they would work under 'normal conditions of production'.[27] The Stakhanovites needed to work with the best available material, tools and industrial equipment. Shortages and bottlenecks were out of the question when it came to assessing someone's work as a socialist exemplary. Other workers were often placed around, just to help the future heroes of labour with supplemental operations, like moving piles of raw material, cleaning their work stations and supplying their workplace with everything necessary for achieving their production targets. While the productivity of the Stakhanovites skyrocketed and their incomes increased correspondingly, many others around them produced nothing or very little. This was less than a happy outcome for the factory plan, and it was especially true when the party organization in the factory needed to prove that young communists without work experience or a high level of skilling could become Stakhanovites, or when a significant number of resources were used to push slackers to improve until their faces could appear in the factory newspaper among other leaders of production.

In many cases, work norms were raised immediately after such an 'achievement'. The new norms were generally announced in a public meeting, where the workers would be told by a party official that the slacker transformed into a Stakhanovite was living proof that anybody can become a 'true' socialist worker. Sometimes, skilled workers ended these meetings abruptly, storming out and shouting against the practices used to produce 'unworthy Stakhanovites' and against the inevitable drop in the other workers' incomes that would follow in the wake of such a 'success'.

Since Samuel was a Stakhanovite himself and held a low position in the party hierarchy, his story was full of moral judgements of other workers who had become leaders in production but who were actually 'good for nothing'. His experience was quite different. He had entered the factory as a 19-year-old youngster, holding a high level of education for a Hungarian worker at that time – eight years of school. Because his dexterity proved to be quite exceptional, he was quickly assigned to the sewing department, where he became the first man to work together with several dozen women, generally older and more experienced than him. He remained the only man around for decades, benefiting from a generalized maternal feeling from his women colleagues. As he got older, the nurturing emotions surrounding him faded away but were replaced by a respect for his seniority and for his seemingly extraordinary qualitative work.

While in the beginning he disliked the idea of working in a feminized job, Samuel – a highly intelligent and reflexive man – quickly realized that his position was a fortunate one. Being a young man, his colleagues offered him care, protection, and professional advice, and never contested his phenomenal results. 'We were like a family', he said to me,

> I respected them like they were all my mothers, they cared for me like I was their son. They never envied me for my savings. I built this house from bonuses I received for saving raw material. I built it with my wife. [He pauses and looks at the walls and at the ceiling for a long time; when he continues talking, he has tears in his eyes and a trembling voice] My friends [male workers from different workshops] were envious and even threatened me. They [his friends' colleagues] didn't like it when somebody had better results, because then the foreman always came to say: 'If Gergö can do this work in one day, why can't you?'

Other interviews confirmed the fact that the 'real' Stakhanovites also faced their colleagues' dislike when their example endangered the fragile shop-floor order and the bitter negotiation of the work norms.

Another worker recounted the story of a young friend from the same village, who had moved to Cluj, got employed at Tehnofrig and soon became a celebrated Stakhanovite. He got skilled as a lathe operator and proved to be so good that directors from other factories wanted to 'steal' him from Tehnofrig by offering him better working conditions and a house in Cluj. He fiercely negotiated to stay at Tehnofrig and got a housing lot, credit and the promise that his co-workers would help him with 'voluntary work', while the factory would provide him with building materials for his house. He was also persuaded to join the party. His achievements on the shop floor were unbeatable. However, later in the year, when he bragged that he could execute 40 per cent more pieces daily, his co-workers told him to slow down if he did not want to have his arms broken one day. When the norm-setters were around, he actually did so, afraid that his colleagues might transform their warnings into reality. However, his new pace brought him negative attention from the party secretary, who threatened him that he would be purged from the party and fired if he continued on the same line. When complaining to the foreman, he was drily told to carefully listen to what his comrades had to say. The help of his co-workers and the building materials for his house never came.

Various ways of participating in socialist construction metamorphosed in as many categories of rule with a social life of their own. All these categories bore benefits and limitations advanced through processes of inclusion, exclusion and subject transformation. Most of these benefits were further connected to the celebration of manual labour in industry as a 'gateway to full citizenship'.[28] Being a Stakhanovite did not matter only or mainly because of the questionable prestige attached to it, but because of the advantages it brought: tax exemptions, bonuses, free subscriptions to books and magazines, discounts of 15–75 per cent for workers' vacations, priority for factory housing and credits, as well as scholarships for their children, free and discounted tickets for theatres, sporting events, cinema and the opera.[29] Most of these expenses were supported by the Director's Fund. Since this money was one of the few resources the managers had at their disposal and which allowed them some flexibility to employ temporary labour or to pay overtime, the Stakhanovites' advantages were a serious inconvenience.

As we have seen, Stakhanovism was not unambiguously productive for the early socialist factories in Cluj. It was expensive for the management and it endangered the free use of the Director's Fund, which was one the few financial resources the factory managers had at their disposal to compensate for the severe labour shortages of the 1950s. Most probably, the peasant-workers, the commuters and the unskilled workers did not care about the Stakhanovite movement at all, as many of the advantages held by the heroes of labour did not concern them. It was simply resented by other skilled workers, who failed to see the leaders in production as embodiments of a certain work ethics, and perceived them as a menace to maintaining the fragile balance on the shop floor. Due to its inefficacy, the movement would be aborted in the mid-1950s, together with other instruments coming from the Soviet school of management. Together with the Stakhanovite movement, the temporal and the ethical regimes embodied in the idea of 'planned heroism' would also reach an end. And this is where we turn to now.

Starting with the First Five-Year Plan, 'being ahead of time' became the cornerstone of economic growth, the key feature of the party's political vision and the underpinning of a new ethical regime. In a historical configuration that had few resources at its disposal except for labour, the 'Five-Year Plan realized in four years' represented exactly this: a form of time–time compression, or the vision of time swallowed in the process of production. This vision carried with it the possibility of arriving in advance at a specific point in history. Although quality and quantity were important indices of the plan, when figures needed to be a direct expression of accumulation they were always articulated around the idea of time. When production was scheduled for the next year, the indication was not to manufacture 10,000 extra pairs of shoes against the requested 100,000, but to execute the initially planned 100,000 pairs of shoes in eleven months. Thus, the language of planning was not mainly articulated around quantity. When factory managers reported the overfulfilling of the plan, they reported that the plan was fulfilled *earlier*. For instance, in 1951, the János Herbák factory documents were already reporting not only figures of production but also the following 'socialist realities': the plan for 1950 was fulfilled before the deadline at the Rubber Factory (28 September), the Soles Factory (9 November), and the Footwear Factory (15 December).

Of course, these happy outcomes were possible only if the leap in time was also realized at the individual level. The wage policy of the Romanian Workers' Party in its first years of governance can be summed up as an attempt to establish the individual worker as the foundation for economic calculation. In the last instance, the unit of planning was not the enterprise but the worker.[30] More precisely, it was the abstract, standardized work unit that the manager-state envisioned as a basis for computing costs of production and for setting prices at the national level. The work unit was also crucial to the process of planning labour in the employment offices. Against the factory managers' strategies of hoarding labour and informally employing temporary workers, socialist planners employed a rather straightforward calculation device: once the quantity of a certain type of commodity had been decided at the ministerial level, the labour power necessary for production was calculated based on the existing norms. Then, the total quantity that had to be produced was broken down to the enterprise level, taking into account their current number of employees. Only on rare occasions could they supplement this number.

As shown in Chapter 2, the wage system of the First Five-Year Plan brought the productivist logic of the manager-state to the forefront. Both base wages and work norms were generally kept low, so a form of progressive piece-rate work constituted the most important part of workers' salaries. This system forced workers to push themselves towards norm breaking, while bonuses for meeting quality standards and for saving raw materials were added as supplemental incentives for the individual worker to work more, faster and better.

The wage system, implemented in 1947 and modified in 1949, was replaced in 1957, precisely for correcting its excesses. The discussions surrounding the implementation of the new wage system in 1957 showed that during the First Five-Year Plan the tariff wage had ceased to represent the most important part of workers' earnings.[31] Although labour productivity grew continually, piece-rate-based norm accomplishment represented more than half of people's earnings. Thus, the reform of 1957 redefined the ratio between the tariff wage and piece-rate work. Hourly rates came to cover more than three-quarters of most workers' incomes, while norms went up in almost all industries. In an effort to simplify the wage system and make it more transparent for workers, skill categories were reduced from over two hundred to just twenty. The small degree of differentiation between wages, the lack of incentives for workers' qualification (especially for the transition from unskilled to skilled categories of wages), workers' poor motivation for committing to a workplace, and the 'uninspiring' work norms were all brought up as problems whose only solution was the cointerest of the workers in the rationalization of the production process through appropriate incentives (read 'higher base wages'). One of the most important reasons for this late recognition was that, as became clear in the previous chapter, the strategy of keeping base wages down and generalizing the pay-by-result system proved disastrous for the possibility of maintaining the continuity of the production process in early socialist factories, even if initially it enjoyed a lot of support, not least from the workers themselves.

Historically, against the background of discontinuities, shortages and conflicting rhythms of production, the generalization of piecework during the First Five-Year Plan was essential for the commodification of labour and for binding the worker to the plan figures. As the young and enthusiastic Lörincz Ilona described in the pages of the factory newspaper, more products 'given to the country', breaking the norm and the labourer's individual earnings were all brought together in the act of working ahead of time. Sometimes, this happened in spectacular ways. At the same leather and footwear factory, on 7 November 1951, the Stakhanovite Vasa Axente, representative at the Party Regional Conference, was already working for 1953, while Ciupea Ion had been working for 1952 since 16 June 1951.[32] In October 1951, twenty-one people were already working for 1953, eleven of them being communists.[33]

Nonetheless, the possibility to conquer time was not equally distributed. Stakhanovism (and slacking as its mirror) made visible the tensions of a historical configuration in which the hopes and vision of the socialist civilizing process brought together scientific management practices with the expectation that the workers would enthusiastically embrace self-exploitation for the common good. This tension was transparent in the unequal relation between individual workers and the plan figures. While Stakhanovites and good communists were always supposed to be ahead of their time, slackers in production, semi-proletarians, rural and seasonal workers were not working at the same pace or with the same capacity to manage themselves while manufacturing a shoe or a nail. This way, production directly constituted categories of rule and legitimated claims, and was immediately translated into the language of class.

The incomplete transformation of peasants into workers was considered to be the underlying cause of acts of indiscipline like truancies, delays, leaving the workplace without permission, stalling and time wasting. Socialist construction as a pedagogic project was discursively built against 'backwardness', understood both as rural habitus and as dubious morality in general. Thus, on the shop floor, the politics of time that socialist accumulation entailed were rooted in the tense but mutually feeding relationship between disciplinary procedures and the ontological fracture presupposed by the emerging new world. Making 'new' workers could not be separated from managing the 'actually existing' ones, and the creation of the New Man could not be separated from the mundane concerns related to labour control. Production management in early socialism was placed in a disciplinary realm that had to be simultaneously created and transcended.

In practice though, rural workers – although spending more time outside the state's gaze – became easier to manage. As one of the factory directors told me in an interview, the difference between a worker from Cluj and one from the village was ultimately the fact that the urban labourer 'went home, got drunk, played cards and talked politics with his friends', while 'the peasant' went home and worked some more until the evening, then went to bed, slept for a few hours and came back to work. From the management's perspective, when they could be stabilized in the factory, the rural-urban workers were doing what they were supposed to do. Working the land was definitely less dangerous than constructing male sociability around the city pubs.

Counting on workers' participation in production did not mean that the state could actually control the forms taken by this participation. The moral fibre required for workers' willingness to enrol in a process of self-transformation generally came from sources the Romanian Workers' Party wanted to dismantle. In Cluj, the entanglement between class, religion and nationalism was one of the first fields of battle for the new state officials. More importantly, as we have seen in Part I of the book, the peasant-worker, with his attachment to land and his working rhythms related to household economy, was a central figure of early socialist accumulation. For the party, while the peasant-worker represented an essential category of labour for the functioning of the factories, he was also an image of the East and Central European semi-proletarianization as a 'failed' civilizing process. While peasants staying on the land during the First Five-Year Plan partly kept the costs of labour's reproduction outside their wages, revolutionary change required the worker to be freed from its rural and capitalist roots. Thus, the socialist worker embodied a tension between his objectification as the raw material of policies and management – as labour power, and his subjectification as the responsible, proactive and enthusiastic person, who can smile while producing more every day – as transformed living labour.

Working in the Future? Socialist *Ungleichzeitigkeit*

In this chapter, labour heroism and the Stakhanovist movement were employed as windows into one of the most challenging aspects of socialist construction in conditions of backwardness: the battle with time. The reader could see what stood behind the idea of 'planned heroism' in terms of shop-floor practices and relations, and how these practices revealed socialism – both as project, and as historical unfolding – as a conflicting temporal regime. But the struggle around time was not simply adding to the contradictions analysed in the previous chapters of this book – it was a generative one. First, because in conditions of backwardness, labour productivity was most of the time the only resource the state had at its disposal for the accumulation of capital. And second, because labour productivity itself had to spring from workers' progressive historical consciousness, which emerged at best as problematic in the early years of socialism. So, what remains to be done in this section is to understand more clearly the encounter between the temporal horizons which collided in the socialist civilizing process and in production itself; in other words, to anatomize socialist construction as nonsynchronicity.

Ernst Bloch's concept of 'nonsynchronicity' [*Ungleichzeitigkeit*] was coined as a tool to open the puzzle behind the right-leaning sympathies and loyalties of different social categories in 1930s Germany. Bloch reads this confusion as a temporal one, and argues that the existence of pre-capitalist economic structures and their accompanying irrational expressions, together with the economic and political backwardness of the German bourgeoisie, constituted the 'moist hummus' on which the Right radicalism of the middle-classes in Germany grew. The return to the past became appealing as an expression of 'homesickness', an idealization of 'home' as an undefined place in the past – security, peace, quietness, freshness.[34]

The revolutionary chronology of the Bolsheviks was also founded on the 'objectively nonsynchronous', not only as the after-effect of some 'declining remnants' of previous eras, but also on an 'uncompleted past, which has not yet been "sublated" by capitalism'.³⁵ The belief in the 'objective' necessities of development was based on a particular and narrow reading of Marx, especially regarding the determination of superstructure by the base and the abstract chronology of the revolution.³⁶ The Bolsheviks uncritically surrendered to a metanarrative of 'modernization' requiring first the development of the 'economic' infrastructure, with a radical change in property relations. 'State capture' was the unique strategy meant to materialize the new world.³⁷ As a political project, Bolshevism was more than anything a living radical negation of the past, but it also referred to a 'home'. The idealized 'home' of early socialist construction was always in the future.

When adopted by or forced upon East and Central European governments after the Second World War, this project was centred around the same conceptual lines and around the same ideal sequence. Crucially, early socialism operated both with an impoverished notion of production as technique, and with a crude notion of class, which tended to reduce social relations to ownership. However, although the development of productive forces must (chrono)logically precede social and political progress, this precedence had to be permanently negotiated, which made the Now a time of 'concessions' and 'delays' – in short, a disappointing time.

The fulfilment of the Five-Year Plan in four years, the fulfilment of the 1952 plan in November, the Stakhanovist Marian Vasile working in June 1953 for October 1954, and Tehnofrig working in August 1954 in the account of April 1955 were all expressions that linked accumulation directly to historical advancement. But slackers (as moral embodiments of backwardness) and non-proletarians (as its class incarnations) worked not in the future, but in the past. Since not all workers were capable of working in the future, the calculation of the precise point in time for which a specific worker produced was a painful mirror of all the different temporal horizons people brought with them into the factory. At the limit, within this space, planning as the bearer of labour-intensive accumulation and as a path out of backwardness became a hopeless vision. At the extreme, it became impossible.

Thus, instead of being simply a coordinating mechanism and a foundation for calculating needs and means, planning in socialism was the first means to assess the successes and the failures in producing a new ethical and political subject. But projects dwelling in the future put no less pressure on the present than those lingering in the past. They also devoid the present of substance and reality, by making it into a mere vehicle for a future instantiation of a bright vision. At the limit, not only the past but also the present is dismissed as a second-hand historical time.

Nonetheless, since the battle for the 480-minute workday was fought in the present, the Now always came back with a vengeance.

In planning, 'different years resound[ed] in the one that had just been recorded and prevail[ed]'.[38] These temporal horizons belonged not only to the skilled, experienced workers, but also to the not-fully-proletarian labourers entering the factory gates in the 1950s. Socialism needed workers, but the practices and mentality of the 'actually existing' ones had to be relegated to an 'absolute past'.[39] Thus, the unskilled, rowdy and truant peasant-worker synthesized the nonsynchronicity of the plan, both at a personal and at a class level. In Ernst Bloch's words again, 'a person who is simply awkward and who for that reason is not up to the demands of his position, is only personally unable to keep up. But what if there are other reasons why he does not fit into a very modern organization, such as the after-effects of peasant descent; what if he is *an earlier type*?'[40] Since these 'earlier types' were fundamental for early socialist industrialization, the communists could do nothing to stop the 'past' entering the factory gates. The categories of rule with which the state operated in the early phase of socialism represented a historical encounter between primitive accumulation and a very specific vision of the future. As my discussion about the Romanian proletarianization showed, the factory walls were porous and people's life strategies crept in, in many instances debilitating production. Although the peasant-workers were key figures of early socialist accumulation, they were also seen as 'earlier bodies [that] emerge in the Now and send a bit of prehistoric life into it',[41] penetrating the factory with their primitive practices, beliefs, allegiances and rhythms. It was in production first of all that the working class had to become the bearer of socialist ethos; and it was at the intersection between production and life that it would fail to do so.

Producing was always about placing oneself – and also the economy, the society and the state – in time. But in their confrontation with the sticky everydayness of life, the communist leaders became painfully aware of the fact that 'backwardness' was not a homogeneous realm from which they could escape. It was fluid, resistant, uneven and contagious, thus it could not simply be left behind. This is why nationalization understood as change in property relations was never enough for taking control of the factories; this is also why the rationalization of production failed to become more than a political trope during the First Five-Year Plan; this could also explain why Stakhanovism was aborted after a relatively short while, and socialist competitions became more and more an honorary enterprise.

While the revolutionary class-conscious proletarian was supposed to be the historical conclusion of the synchronous contradictions of capitalism, within the factory walls the communists battled with contradictory factors 'alien to the Now',[42] which were both subjectively nonsynchronous – 'simply torpid not wanting of the Now', and objectively nonsynchronous – 'an existing remnant of earlier times in the present'. When the (Hungarian) workers clashed with the (Romanian) students in the streets of Cluj in 1947, the right to the city was at the same time the right to be historically relevant. When workers made cruel jokes to former capitalists, clerks, artisans, kulaks and lawyers, and handed them hot tools, it was not simply an act of revenge. It was a reflection of their acute feeling that they were in the Now and the others were in the past. When peasants from the state farms or from the collective farms stopped working after eight hours and invoked their rights 'as workers', they appealed to the same Now as their industrial fellows. When the party secretaries rapidly put things in order and denied their claims because they were peasants, they were simply expressing the fact that in socialism not everybody was entitled to be in the Now. Since socialist accumulation was first of all primitive accumulation, the collectivized peasants might have seen themselves as workers (although this was rarely the case), but they could not become 'real' workers just yet.

By welcoming peasants into the factory, the communists also allowed rationalities corresponding to old relations of production to enter the gates. Moreover, as the state externalized part of labour's reproduction to subsistence economy in the countryside, these 'old forms' continued to structure people's experience and visions of the future, expecting the workers to come home to them after work or even to abandon the factory. The hailing of these proto-capitalist forms structured all the capitalist contradictions that were magnified by the socialist project in its initial phase.

In the actualization of the socialist project, accumulation as being ahead of time deeply threatened the articulation of planning as structure across practices, because at the limit each factory and each worker found themselves at a different point in time. While in the process of primitive socialist accumulation people had to work in the future, many times they actually worked in the past. Due to shortages, production stoppages and agricultural work in the countryside, people often had to catch up with past work. At the same time, they had to manufacture both the objects that belonged to the past and the ones that belonged to the future. The smooth realization of the plan required that the future was always brought into the Now, making the present virtually disappear. But when production turned out to be merely a sequence of broken tempos and rhythms, unrealized goods remained to be manufactured and the past crept into the present's economic and political requirements.

Party propaganda at the factory level made it clear that today's workload was actually the production of tomorrow, and the workers' failure to achieve the planned targets delayed a form of progress beneficial to all. In its struggle with a backward history, and in its desperate attempts to catch up, socialism placed work in the future and produced a melting present, one that was difficult to control and, at the limit, impossible to plan. The act of work connected the recent past and the near future in a present that was never valued for itself. Reduced to a mere vehicle for solving unfulfilments of the past and projects of the future, the socialist Now ended up breathing with difficulty.

Notes

Parts of this chapter appear in Alina-Sandra Cucu, 'The Impossibility of Being Planned: Slackers, Stakhanovites, and the Time of Politics in Early Socialist Romania', in *Labor in State-Socialist Europe after 1945: Contributions to a History of Work*, ed. Marsha Siefert (Budapest: CEU Press, 2019).

1. *Viața Uzinei Noastre*, 12 October 1951.
2. *Viața Uzinei Noastre*, 18 December 1951.
3. I conducted research in Cluj for eighteen months between 2011 and 2013. Apart from archival research, I collected forty life histories of labourers who were working in the city's factories at the time (most of them at János Herbák – the leather and footwear factory, at *Armătura* – a faucet factory, at the Railways Workshops, and at Tehnofrig – a manufacturer of frigorific equipment for food processing industry). I also conducted twelve interviews with former managers of the industrial units. Both types of interview included questions about the relationship between the reorganization of the labour process, socialist competitions and labour heroism.
4. There is an abundant literature focusing or explicitly touching on Stakhanovism. For the Soviet Union, see Kotkin, *Magnetic Mountain*; Siegelbaum, *Stakhanovism*. For a better understanding of how Stakhanovism was transferred to Eastern and Central Europe, see Pittaway, *From the Vanguard to the Margins*; Kenney, *Rebuilding Poland*.
5. Burawoy and Lukács, *The Radiant Past*.
6. Marx, *Grundrisse*.
7. Hanson, *Time and Revolution*, 142.
8. M. Pittaway, 'The Social Limits of State Control: Time, the Industrial Wage Relation, and Social Identity in Stalinist Hungary, 1948–53', *Journal of Historical Sociology* 12(3) (1999), 271-301.
9. Pittaway, 'The Social Limits', 96.
10. Lampland and Star, 'Reckoning with Standards', 4.
11. The 1948 Constitution, Art. 12. The Constitution was published in the Official Monitor in April 1948, just two months before the nationalization of the means of production, and opened a door for making the nationalization of the means of production legal.
12. The 1952 Constitution, Art. 15.
13. Hanson, *Time and Revolution*.
14. Pittaway, *The Workers' State*, 14.
15. Fritzsche and Hellbeck. 'The New Man', 303.
16. ANDC, Fund 13, CR PMR Cluj, 322/1952, 40.
17. *Viața Uzinei Noastre*, 1 May 1952.

18. ANDC, Fund 55, CO P.M.R. Cluj, 10/1953, 203.
19. ANDC, Fund 55, CO P.M.R. Cluj, 10/1953, 214.
20. See also Collins, *Interaction Ritual Chains*, 114.
21. ANDC, Fund 13, CR P.M.R. Cluj, 322/1952, 127.
22. Rogers, *The Old Faith*.
23. Ibid., 15.
24. ANDC, Fund 55, CO P.M.R. Cluj, 1/1951. I preserved here the sometimes strange spelling of the names used by the party organizations for the Soviet methods' inventors.
25. *Viața Uzinei Noastre*, 28 October 1951.
26. Stakhanovism cannot be understood outside a broader discussion of productivity in socialism. For an excellent account of the role of labour heroism in transformation of the wage system in early socialist Hungary, see Pittaway, 'The Social Limits'.
27. Interviews with Samuel, male, a former worker at János Herbák (1945–1990) on 13, 22 and 23 January 2013.
28. Pittaway, *The Workers' State*, 7.
29. The 1951 Decree of the Central Committee of the Romanian Workers' Party and of the Council of Ministers of the R.P.R. with regard to Stakhanovites and leaders in production and their moral and material stimulations; and Decree no. 153 with regard to income taxes, BO no. 22, 11 May 1954.
30. Mark Pittaway rightfully criticizes scholarly literature for taking for granted the enterprise as the economic unit of central planning in early socialism. Pittaway, 'The Social Limits'.
31. *Probleme economice*, no. 8, August 1957, Petru Mărculescu.
32. ANDC, Fund 13, CR P.M.R. Cluj 34/1951; ANDC, Fund 55, CO P.M.R. Cluj, 1/1951
33. ANDC, Fund 13, CR P.M.R. Cluj, 322/1952, 81.
34. Bloch and Ritter, 'Nonsynchronism'.
35. Ibid., 32.
36. Corrigan, Ramsey and Sayer, *Socialist Construction*.
37. Ibid.
38. Bloch and Ritter, 'Nonsynchronism', 22.
39. Ibid.
40. Ibid., my emphasis.
41. Ibid., 23.
42. Ibid., 31, emphasis in original.

Epilogue

REALLY EXISTING SOCIALISM AS NONSYNCHRONICITY

At first glance, the path taken by Romania at the end of the 1940s involved rapid industrialization, central planning of the economy, the nationalization of the means of production and the quick repression of alternative societal visions. With 'class struggle' as the main engine, these historical transformations were not supposed to be peaceful. They involved smashing old hierarchies in the workplace and in everyday life. For capitalists, rural landlords and the better-off categories of the peasantry, socialist construction came with raging dispossession. For industrial workers, poor peasants, women and ethnic minorities, it came with the promise of full employment, relative welfare, increased upward mobility, universal access to education and the historically unique possibility to envision one's life as a linear project with a predictable outcome.

The first postwar decade was not simply the moment of the communist takeover, but the foundation of a decisive historical advancement, projected as a way to uncage the dormant energies and forces that would have closed the modernization gap between an agrarian East European country and an advanced capitalist core. During the ten years under scrutiny, the antagonistic tendencies that socialism tried to address were actually magnified, making this moment into an extraordinarily dense time – a time when historical polyphony was still loud enough to be heard. Exploitation and existential insecurity were sometimes intensified in paroxysmal ways, while ethnic heterogeneity and the frailty of the Romanian national project only added to the lines of tension that crossed the making of a new world.

Economically backward and fragile as nation states, East and Central European postwar configurations were articulated around the simultaneous realities of exploitation and progressive societal transformation. This simultaneity was the crumbling foundation of state socialism, and it had far-reaching consequences for the way in which the project of socialist construction took up – and for a while magnified – the contradictions of capital accumulation, and for the way in which it produced its own antagonisms. The positioning of these countries on the spatial and temporal map created by the world's uneven development drove these antagonisms further, enhancing their wide-ranging implications for a large part of Europe and its people.

This book could be read as a plea for localized, in-depth and time-sensitive explorations of those realities that were so easily grouped under the label of 'socialism', and as a deconstruction of the taken-for-granted 'Soviet model' or 'Soviet blueprint', which still constitutes the starting point for most analyses of the postwar East and Central European regimes. This deconstruction did not mean ignoring what the Romanian party officials called the 'Soviet experience'. On the contrary, I considered the forced adoption of the Bolshevik path to modernization as a central explanatory dimension for the striking similarities between the initial trajectories of these countries after the Second World War, but only if taken together with the following: their historical positioning in the world economy; their emergence as nation states at the intersection of conflicting imperial policies; the longer involvement with the tradition of West European industrialism; and with the myriad of ways in which local relations of production were embedded in the sticky, never fully controllable everydayness of the postwar years. Only in this way can the 1930s revolutionary debates on the Soviet industrialization become a fecund line of thinking about East European state socialism as being simultaneously a very particular historical configuration and one attempt among others to transcend a broader history of exploitation and injustice.

Hence, my exploration started from problematizing the Bolshevik blueprint itself.[1] The position I adopted here was that the 'Soviet model' came into being as an abstraction of a concrete historical experience, which characterized not only the Soviet Union of the 1930s but also interwar Eastern and Central Europe: the agrarian and unmechanized character of the economy, low capital investment, peasant poverty, weak to non-existent infrastructure, the lack of an adequately trained bureaucracy, overwhelming illiteracy, widespread illness and malnutrition, and fragile multi-ethnic national constructions. What stood behind the similarities between the narratives about the communist takeover in Eastern and Central Europe was not simply the imposition of a Stalinist model of development but the emulation of a historical experience set against akin conditions and producing similar contradictions. It was not a propaganda artifice that the Romanian communists rarely referred to the Soviet 'model' but often to the Soviet 'experience'.

Seen from this angle, the post-1945 societal transformations appear as just one moment in a series of modernizing plans that juggled with the thorny entanglement between national independence and economic backwardness, and with the historical possibility to bring the future into the present. The socialist state was going to deal with the same issues as its predecessors: an ethnicized class structure and a lack of proletarians as the foundation for its productive and political reasoning. Its solutions were different, not because they placed top-down industrialization and central planning at their centre, but because they made the working class the main subject/object of state politics. Thus, the socialist state was going to assume and expand both a modernizing ethos and a paternalist role, and to firmly establish the factories as its productive and redistributive arms.

While the whole world can be seen as a rich polyphonic unfolding of multi-temporal and multi-spatial forces and processes, the social fabric of backward countries is especially dominated by what Ernst Bloch called 'nonsynchronicity'. They are marked by hard-to-resolve 'polyphonous dialectics', which are at the same time synchronous – the fundamental capitalist contradictions that need to be transcended by revolution. They belong to different times and spaces – like the power of the archaic to trail the rural into a dream of urban modernity, the peasants into the proletariat, and the petty bourgeois craftsmen and shopkeepers into the state economy. Thus, the historical struggle of the 1950s was not simply between two modes of production. It became a critical battle to connect the master aim of superseding capitalism with the concrete conditions in which capitalism – with its rationalizing and productive obsessions – still needed to be produced. In the Romanian factories, working according to the plan became the predilect way to experience and embody this battle.

The contradictory mixture of accumulation mechanisms, pains of 'catching-up' and emancipatory prospects that were articulated in the East Central European postwar regimes met a vision of industrial modernization centred around the most vivid expression of their lived nonsynchronicity – the reproduction and expansion of labour. This was a story of uneven and postponed proletarianization, rooted in the non-socialist exterior that Preobrazhensky made us aware of. If capitalism can (and must) produce non-linear and reversible class trajectories, this was also true for state socialism in Eastern and Central Europe, a space that offers yet another possibility to implode the classical narrative of industrialization.

In the standard scenario of Soviet-style proletarianization, the collectivization of land in the countryside would have ensured the timely release of the workforce for the flourishing socialist industry. This expansion of labour was going to condense social processes, compress time and burn historical stages. It was going to completely redefine the worker/ peasant and the worker/craftsman nexuses. On the ground, making proletarians was going to entail processes of social mobility and personal stories of becoming or falling apart, as well as radical ruptures in attitudes towards work, family, friendship, politics and money.[2] Proletarianization was going to proceed through the transformation of some categories and the exclusion of others, producing winners and losers of history and reshaping people's biographies for generations to come. A new urban fabric was going to be weaved around the factories, bringing together people and materialities, and constituting networks of houses, neighbourhoods, sport teams, cultural programmes, health facilities, childcare, education and leisure. Because of the increasing pressure of collectivization, life with all its possibilities was going to slowly move into the cities, which were going to become the cradle of a new working class, the bearer of a progressive *Weltanschauung*. The past as represented by the rural would never have crawled into the factories or into the new neighbourhoods.

In this sense, the collectivization process was going to make people 'free' to sell their work by leaving them with almost no means of subsistence in the countryside. However, as the convoluted global history of industrialization shows, a field of battle emerged at the intersection between production and life in the twentieth century. Pressures have been exercised and struggles have been fought around the inherent tensions between the tendency of commodity production to make the 'worker-behind-the-work' completely invisible, and the impossibility of decoupling labour power from the complex field of workers' reproduction. Historically, notions of 'welfare', 'solidarity' and 'social responsibility' have never been separated from working hours, wages or pensions. From this perspective, a rather thin analytical line separated Bismarckian social security ideas or their post-Second World War welfare state variations from state socialism's emancipatory dream.

Primitive socialist accumulation appeared as a violent abstraction of the spatially and temporally located process on which Marx built his account of the emergence of capitalism as a mode of production. The classical (and also the most atypical) case analysed by Marx is well known. Primitive accumulation was the zero point for the formation of capital and for turning an important part of the population into wage-labourers. The dispossessed and pauperized rural population was partly absorbed into the new structure of employment in the countryside, and partly attracted by the flourishing manufacturing in urban centres. While for Marx the fracture between the worker and his/her means of production and subsistence constituted the precondition for capitalist accumulation, a line of thinking that started with Rosa Luxemburg and Hannah Arendt brilliantly argued that violent dispossession was not simply the original sin of capitalism.[3] The realization of surplus value always needs a generic 'third person', who stands outside the relationship between workers and capitalists as immediate agents of capitalist production, simply because '[c]apitalism needs non-capitalist social strata as a market for its surplus value, as a source of supply for its means of production and as a reservoir of labour power for its wage system'.[4]

It was in this form that capitalism violently travelled in colonial contexts, where it deeply transformed local notions and relations of 'property' by circumventing them, (re)producing them, using them for its own purposes or simply deleting them from the historical scene. At the intersection of these relations, the control, exploitation, reproduction and expansion of labour took various and complex forms that combined wage labour with slavery, serfdom, debt bondage, petty-commodity production, or reciprocity. Thus, the existence of a 'non-capitalist exterior' has always been a critical condition for capitalism, and until these days, the emperor has stayed naked: what David Harvey recoined as 'accumulation by dispossession' remains central to the reproduction of capital, hidden under the shallow veil of 'legality' and 'democracy'.[5]

Thus, any exploration of the processes through which labour is supposed to become something objective and independent from people's bodies requires at the same time an effort to reveal the limits of these processes. Any discussion about 'proletarianization' needs to be decentred from its original context of Marx's England by rescuing it both from the Anglo-Saxon language of rights and from the translation of a particular industrialization narrative into a universal model. The debate needs to be rescaled in order to avoid methodological nationalism and the assumption that the making of work into labour is a process that ever develops nationally. And lastly, it is necessary to move on from a universalistic and unidirectional grand narrative that frames proletarianization as a linear process. As history shows, this was basically never the case for the capitalist world. From the Zambian copperbelt,[6] to the Venezuelan Andes' coffee and petroleum,[7] and to contemporary Mexico's stonemasonry, there are endless examples of how uneven and combined development produced sometimes striking entanglements between various forms of labour, in which complete dispossession and full reliance on wage labour were never achieved.[8] Probably the most dramatic example is contemporary China, with its 'scattered sand' workforce of 200 million people migrating for work every year from the rural interior to the urban factories, mines and construction yards.[9] Both capitalism and state socialism as its 'eccentricity'[10] had rather complex and fragmented trajectories that produced localized pockets of class formation around processes of depeasantization and peasantization; and of proletarianization and deproletarianization, or reproletarianization.[11] They were essentially linked to mechanisms of accumulation, dispossession and disenfranchisement. Managing the temporalities of these processes has always been crucial for capital and labour alike.

Notes

1. For a different discussion of the tensions between Soviet ideology, path-dependent local realities and conflicting values in the materialization of the socialist project in Romania, see Mărginean, *Ferestre spre furnalul roșu*.
2. On the Soviet ideal of proletarianization, see Siegelbaum and Suny, *Making Workers Soviet*. On personal histories of mobility, see Bertaux, Thompson and Rotkirch, *On Living Through Soviet Russia*.
3. Marx, *Capital*; Luxemburg, *Accumulation of Capital*; Arendt, *Origins of Totalitarianism*.
4. Luxemburg, *Origins of Totalitarianism*, 348–49.
5. Harvey, *New Imperialism*.
6. Ferguson, *Expectations of Modernity*.
7. Roseberry, *Anthropologies and Histories*.
8. Munslow and Finch, *Proletarianisation in the Third World*; Cooper, *Decolonization and African Society*; Cooper et al., *Confronting Historical Paradigms*.
9. Pai, *Scattered Sand*.
10. Lampland, *The Object of Labor*.
11. Brass, 'Unfree Labour as Primitive Accumulation?'; Brass and Bernstein, 'Introduction: Proletarianisation and Deproletarianisation'.

BIBLIOGRAPHY

Archival Sources
The Romanian National Archives Cluj, The Romanian Workers' Party City Committee (1944–1962).
The Romanian National Archives Cluj, The Romanian Workers' Party County Committee (1944–1970).
The Romanian National Archives Cluj, The Romanian Workers' Party Regional Committee (1944–1955).
The Romanian National Archives Cluj, The County Police Inspectorate (1944–1955).
The Romanian National Archives Cluj, Clujana.
The Romanian National Archives, The Central Committee of the Romanian Communist Party, The Economic Section (1950–1965).
The Romanian National Archives, State Planning Committee (1948–1951).
Open Society Archives Budapest, Romanian Unit.
The Romanian National Archives, Ministry of Labour.

Newspapers and Journals
Monitorul oficial [The official monitor].
Lupta de clasă [Class struggle].
Probleme economice [Economic problems].
Viața uzinei noastre [The life of our factory].
Scânteia [The spark].
Făclia [The torch].
Liberalul [The liberal].

Books and Articles
Abrams, P. 'Notes on the Difficulty of Studying the State', in A. Sharma and A. Gupta, *The Anthropology of the State: A Reader* (Malden, MA: Blackwell Publishing, [1977] 2006), 112–30.
Akgöz, G. 'The German Way to Scientific Management: German Industrial Experts on the Turkish Shop Floor in the 1930s'. Conference paper, IGK Work and Human Lifecycle in Global History, Ninth Annual Conference, 4–5 July 2018.
Allinson, J.C., and A. Anievas. 'The Uses and Misuses of Uneven and Combined Development An Anatomy of a Concept', *Cambridge Review of International Affairs* 22(1) (2009), 47–67.
Anievas, A., and K. Matin (eds). *Historical Sociology and World History: Uneven and Combined Development over the Longue Dureé*. Lanham, MD: Rowman & Littlefield, 2016.
Arendt, H. *The Origins of Totalitarianism*. New York: Harcourt Brace Jovanovich, (1951) 1975.
Asad, T. 'Ethnographic Representation, Statistics, and Modern Power'. *Social Research* 61(1) (1994).
Bakunin, M. 'The International and Karl Marx', in Sam Dolgoff (ed.), *Bakunin on Anarchy:*

Selected Works of the Founder of World Anarchism. London: Allen & Unwin, [1872] 1973), 286–320.
Balas, E. *Will to Freedom: A Perilous Journey through Fascism and Communism*. Syracuse, NY: Syracuse University Press, 2000.
Baronian, L. *Marx and Living Labour*. London: Routledge, 2013.
Bedeian, A.C., and C.R. Phillips. 'Scientific Management and Stakhanovism in the Soviet Union: A Historical Perspective'. *International Journal of Social Economics* 17(10) (1990), 28–35.
Beissinger, M. *Scientific Management, Socialist Discipline, and Soviet Power*. London: Tauris, 1988.
Bertaux, D., P. Thompson and A. Rotkirch (eds). *On Living through Soviet Russia*. New York: Routledge, 2004.
Bindea, T.V. 'Conditiunile de munca si de traiu ale muncitorilor din Cluj' [Work and living conditions of the workers in Cluj], *Buletinul Camerei de Munca Cluj*, anul I, (1939), 7–9.
Binns, P. 'State Capitalism'. *Education for Socialists* 1 (1986).
Bloch, E., and M. Ritter. 'Nonsynchronism and the Obligation to Its Dialectics'. *New German Critique* 11 (1977), 22–38.
Boc, C.I. *Întreprinderea și contabilul față de legea stabilizării: Conferință ținută în ziua de 4 octombrie 1947* [The enterprise and the accountant facing the law of stabilization: Conference held on 4 October 1947]. București: Tipografia Urania, 1947.
Bockman, J. *Markets in the Name of Socialism: The Left-Wing Origins of Neoliberalism*. Stanford, CA: Stanford University Press, 2011.
Bockman, J., and G. Eyal. 'Eastern Europe as a Laboratory for Economic Knowledge: The Transnational Roots of Neoliberalism'. *American Journal of Sociology* 108(2) (2002), 310–52.
Bodnar, J. *Fin de Millénaire Budapest: Metamorphoses of Urban Life*. Minneapolis: University of Minnesota Press, 2000.
Bottoni, S. 'A sztálini "Kis Magyarország" megalakítása, 1952' [The creation of Stalin's 'Little Hungary', 1952]. *REGIO* 3 (2003), 89–125.
Brass, T. 'Unfree Labour as Primitive Accumulation?'. *Capital & Class* 35(1) (2011), 23–38.
Brass, T., and H. Bernstein. 'Introduction: Proletarianisation and Deproletarianisation on the Colonial Plantation', in E. Valentine Daniel, H. Bernstein and T. Brass, *Plantations, Proletarians, and Peasants in Colonial Asia* (London: Frank Cass, 1992), 1–67.
Braverman, H. *Labour and Monopoly Capital: The Degradation of Work in the Twentieth Century*. New York: Monthly Review Press, [1975] 1998.
Brubaker, R., et al. *Nationalist Politics and Everyday Ethnicity in a Transylvanian Town*. Princeton, NJ: Princeton University Press, 2006.
Bucur, M., et al. 'Six Historians in Search of *Alltagsgeschichte*'. *Aspasia* 3 (2009), 189–212.
Burawoy, M. *The Politics of Production: Factory Regimes under Capitalism and Socialism*. London: Verso, 1985.
———. *The Extended Case Method: Four Countries, Four Decades, Four Great Transformations, and One Theoretical Tradition*. Berkeley: University of California Press, 1998.
Burawoy, M., and J. Lukács. *The Radiant Past: Ideology and Reality in Hungary's Road to Capitalism*. Chicago: University of Chicago Press, 1992.
Burtan, F. 'Principalele transformări economico-sociale în perioada 1944–1947' [The main economic and social transformations in the 1944–1947 period], in I.V. Totu (ed.), *Progresul Economic în România 1877–1977* [The Romanian economic progress in Romania, 1877–1977]. Bucharest: Editura Politică, 1977), 366–72.
Carmona, S., M. Ezzamel and F. Gutierrez. 'Control and Cost Accounting Practices in the Spanish Royal Tobacco Factory'. *Accounting, Organizations and Society* 22(5) (1997), 411–46.
Case, H. *Between States: The Transylvanian Question and the European Idea during World War II*. Stanford, CA: Stanford University Press, 2009.

Cioroianu, A. *Pe umerii lui Marx: O introducere în istoria comunismului românesc* [On Marx's shoulders: An introduction in the history of Romanian Communism]. Bucharest: Curtea Veche, 2007.

Cîrjan, M.D. 'Reimagining the State after the Crisis: Psychotechnics and the Evaluation of Labour in Post-Depression Romania'. Conference paper, Europe and the World Workshop, SciencesPo, Reims (2014).

Clarke, S. 'What in the Ford's Name is Fordism?'. British Sociological Association Conference, University of Surrey (1990).

———. 'The Contradictions of "State Socialism"', in S. Clarke et al. (eds), *What About the Workers? Workers and the Transition to Capitalism in Russia* (London: Verso, 1993), 5–29.

Cliff, T. *State Capitalism in Russia*. London: Pluto Press, (1955) 1974.

Cohen, Y. 'Matter Matters to Authority: Some Aspects of Soviet Industrial Management in the 1930s from a Multi-Sited Perspective'. *Business and Economic History On-Line* 2 (2004).

———. *Le siècle des chefs: Une histoire transnationale du commandement et de l'autorité (1891–1940)*. Paris: Éditions Amsterdam, 2013.

Collins, R. *Interaction Ritual Chains*. Princeton, NJ: Princeton University Press, 2004.

Comaroff, J., and J.L. Comaroff. 'Figuring Crime: Quantifacts and the Production of the Un/real'. *Public Culture* 18(1) (2006), 209–46.

Cooper, F. *Decolonization and African Society: The Labor Question in French and British Africa*. Cambridge: Cambridge University Press, 1996.

Cooper, F., et al. *Confronting Historical Paradigms: Peasants, Labor, and the Capitalist World System in Africa and Latin America*. Madison: University of Wisconsin Press, 1993.

Corrigan, P., H. Ramsey and D. Sayer. *Socialist Construction and Marxist Theory: Bolshevism and Its Critique*. New York: Monthly Review Press, 1978.

Corrigan, P., and D. Sayer. *The Great Arch: English State Formation as Cultural Revolution*. Oxford: Blackwell, 1985.

Creed, G. *Domesticating Revolution: From Socialist Reform to Ambivalent Transition in a Bulgarian Village*. University Park, PA: Penn State University Press, 1998.

Cucu, A. 'Producing Knowledge in Productive Spaces: Ethnography and Planning in Early Socialist Romania'. *Economy and Society* 43(2) (2014), 211–32.

———. 'Why Hegemony Was Not Born in the Factory: Twentieth-Century Sciences of Labour from a Gramscian Angle', in M. Badino and P.D. Omodeo, *Cultural Hegemony in a Scientific World: Gramscian Concepts for the History of Science*, Vol. 1 (Leiden: Brill, Historical Materialism series, 2019).

Daele, W. van den. 'Traditional Knowledge in Modern Society', in N. Stehr (ed.), *The Governance of Knowledge* (New Brunswick, NJ: Transaction Publishers, 2004), 27–39.

Day, R. 'On "Primitive" and Other Forms of Socialist Accumulation', *Labour/Le Travailleur* 10 (1982), 165–74.

Djilas, M. *The New Class: An Analysis of the Communist System*. London: Thames and Hudson, 1957.

Dunn, B., and H. Radice (eds). *100 Years of Permanent Revolution: Results and Prospects*. London: Pluto Press, 2006.

Dunn, E. *Privatizing Poland: Baby Food, Big Business, and the Remaking of Labor*. Ithaca, NY: Cornell University Press, 2004.

Durkheim, E. *The Division of Labor in Society*. Houndmills: Macmillan, (1893) 1984.

Eeckhout, P. van den (ed.). *Supervision and Authority in Industry: Western European Experiences, 1830–1939*. New York: Berghahn Books, 2009.

Eley, G. 'Labor History, Social History, "Alltagsgeschichte": Experience, Culture, and the Politics of the Everyday – A New Direction for German Social History?'. *Journal of Modern History* 61(2) (1989), 297–343.

Ellman, M. 'Did the Agricultural Surplus Provide the Resources for the Increase in Investment in the USSR during the First Five-Year Plan?'. *The Economic Journal* 85(340) (1975), 844–63

———. *Socialist Planning*. Cambridge: Cambridge University Press, 1989.
Erlich, A. 'Preobrazhensky and the Economics of Soviet Industrialization'. *Quaterly Journal of Economics* 64(1) (1950), 57–88.
Faje, F. 'Playing to Win, Learning to Lose: Sport, Nation and State in Interwar Romania'. PhD dissertation. Budapest: Central European University, 2014.
Ferguson, J. *Expectations of Modernity: Myths and Meanings of Urban Life on the Zambian Copperbelt*. Berkeley: University of California Press, 1999.
Filtzer, D. *Soviet Workers and Stalinist Industrialization: The Formation of Modern Soviet Production Relations, 1928–1941*. New York: M.E. Sharpe, 1986.
———. 'Labor Discipline, the Use of Work Time, and the Decline of the Soviet System, 1928–1991'. *International Labor and Working-Class History* 50 (1996), 9–28.
Fitzpatrick, S. *Everyday Stalinism: Ordinary Life in Extraordinary Times: Soviet Russia in the 1930s*. Oxford: Oxford University Press, 1999.
Friedmann, G. 'Esquisse d'une psycho-sociologie du travail à la chaîne'. *Journal de Psychologie normale et pathologique* 41 (1948).
Fritzsche, P., and J. Hellbeck. 'The New Man in Stalinist Russia and Nazi Germany', in Michael Geyer and Sheila Fitzpatrick (eds), *Beyond Totalitarianism: Stalinism and Nazism Compared* (Cambridge: Cambridge University Press, 2008), 302–44.
Frunză, V.I. *Istoria stalinismului în România*. Bucharest: Humanitas, 1990.
Fulbrook, M. *Power and Society in the GDR, 1961–1979: The 'Normalisation of Rule'?* New York: Berghahn Books, 2009.
Geertz, C. *Works and Lives: The Anthropologist As Author*. Stanford, CA: Stanford University Press, 1988.
Gibson-Graham, J.K., et al. (eds), *Re/presenting Class: Essays in Postmodern Marxism*. Durham, NC: Duke University Press, 2001.
Glassman, J. 'Primitive Accumulation, Accumulation by Dispossession, Accumulation by "Extra-Economic" Means'. *Progress in Human Geography* 30(5) (2006), 608–25.
Glonț, A. 'Nihil Sine Carbo: Politics, Labor, and the Coal Industry in the Towns of the Jiu Valley, 1850–1999'. PhD dissertation. University of Illinois at Urbana-Champaign, 2015.
Goldman, W. *Women at the Gates: Gender and Industry in Stalin's Russia*. Cambridge: Cambridge University Press, 2002.
Gordeeva, Y., D. Drancă and F. Orăștean. 'Cluj-Napoca 1939–1960: Diversity of Remembrances'. Geschichtswerkstatt Europa, 2012.
Goswami, M. *Producing India: From Colonial Economy to National Space*. Chicago: University of Chicago Press, 2004.
Grama, A. 'Nationalization, Early Planning and the Monetarized Everyday in Postwar Romania (1947–1950)'. Unpublished manuscript.
———. 'Laboring Along: Industrial Workers in Postwar Romania, 1944–1954'. PhD dissertation. Budapest: Central European University, 2018.
Guillén, M.F. *Models of Management: Work, Authority, and Organization in a Comparative Perspective*. Chicago: Chicago University Press, 1994.
Gurley, J.G. 'Excess Liquidity and European Monetary Reforms, 1944–1952'. *The American Economic Review* 43(1) (1953), 76–100.
Hanson, S.E. *Time and Revolution: Marxism and the Design of Soviet Institutions*. University of North Carolina Press, 1998.
Haraszti, M. *A Worker in a Worker's State: Piece-Rates in Hungary*. Harmondsworth: Penguin Books, 1977.
Harloe, M., G. Andrusz and I. Szelenyi (eds). *Cities After Socialism: Urban and Regional Change and Conflict in Post-Socialist Societies*. Oxford: Blackwell, 1996.
Harvey, D. *The New Imperialism*. Oxford: Oxford University Press, 2003.
———. *Spaces of Global Capitalism: A Theory of Uneven Geographical Development*. London: Verso, 2006.

Hayek, F.A. 'The Use of Knowledge in Society'. *The American Economic Review* 35(4) (1945), 519–30.
Hirsch, F. *Empire of Nations: Ethnographic Knowledge and the Making of the Soviet Union*. Ithaca, NY: Cornell University Press, 2005.
Howard, M.C., and J.E. King. 'State Capitalism in the Soviet Union'. *History of Economics Review* (2001), 110–26.
Ionescu, G. *Communism in Romania, 1944–1962* (London: Oxford University Press, 1964).
Iordachi, C., and D. Dobrincu (eds). *Transforming Peasants, Property and Power: The Collectivization of Agriculture in Romania, 1949–1962*. Budapest: Central European University Press, 2009.
Jowitt, K. *Social Change in Romania, 1860–1940: A Debate on Development in a European Nation* (Berkeley: University of California Press, 1971).
Kalb, D. 'Frameworks of Culture and Class in Historical Research'. *Theory and Society* 22 (1993), 513–37.
———. *Expanding Class: Power and Everyday Politics in Industrial Communities, The Netherlands, 1850–1950*. Durham: Duke University Press, 1997.
———. '"Bare Legs Like Ice": Recasting Class for Local/Global Inquiry', in D. Kalb and H. Tak (eds), *Critical Junctions: Anthropology and History beyond the Cultural Turn* (New York: Berghahn Books, 2005), 109–36.
Kecskes, I., and Kerekes O. 'O metodă' de a descoperi rezervele interne ale timpului de lucru în unitățile industriale' [A method of discovery for the inner reserves of the working-time in the industrial units], *Probleme economice*, March 1955.
Kenney, P. *Rebuilding Poland: Workers and Communists, 1945–1950*. Ithaca, NY: Cornell University Press, 1997.
Konrád, G., and I. Szelenyi. 'Social Conflicts of Underurbanization', in M. Harloe (ed.), *Captive Cities: Studies in the Political Economy of Cities and Regions* (London: John Wiley & Sons, 1977), 157–74.
———. *The Intellectuals on the Road to Class Power*. Brighton: Harvester Press, 1979.
Kornai, J. *Economics of Shortage*. Amsterdam: North Holland, 1979.
———. 'Resource-Constrained versus Demand–Constrained Systems'. *Econometrica: Journal of the Econometric Society* 7(1) (1979), 801–19.
———. 'The Soft Budget Constraint'. *Kyklos* 39(1) (1986), 3–30.
———. *The Socialist System: The Political Economy of Communism*. Oxford: Oxford University Press, (1992) 2007.
———. 'Socialism and the Market: Conceptual Clarification', in J. Kornai and Y. Qian (eds), *Market and Socialism: In the Light of the Experiences of China and Vietnam* (London: Palgrave Macmillan, 2009).
Kornai, J., and T. Liptak. 'Two-Level Planning'. *Econometrica* 33(1) (1965).
Kotkin, S. *Magnetic Mountain: Stalinism as a Civilization*. Berkeley: University of California Press, 1997.
Lampland, M. *The Object of Labor: Commodification in Socialist Hungary*. Chicago: University of Chicago Press, 1995.
———. *The Value of Labor: The Science of Commodification in Hungary, 1920–1956*. Chicago: University of Chicago Press, 2016.
Lampland, M., and L. Star. 'Reckoning with Standards', in M. Lampland and L. Star (eds), *How Quantifying, Classifying, and Formalizing Practices Shape Everyday Life* (Ithaca, NY: Cornell University Press, 2009), 3–24.
Lascu, A. *Minimum de existență, salarizare, norme de salarizare* [Basic income, salary, salary norms] Bucharest: Atelierele Grafice Socec, 1947.
Lebow, K. *Unfinished Utopia: Nowa Huta, Stalinism, and Polish Society, 1949–56*. Ithaca, NY: Cornell University Press, 2013.
Levy, R. *Ana Pauker: The Rise and Fall of a Jewish Communist*. Berkeley: University of California Press, 2001.

Lewin, M. *The Soviet Century*. London: Verso, 2005.
Linden, M. van der. 'Socialisme ou Barbarie: A French Revolutionary Group (1949–65). In memory of Cornelius Castoriadis, 11 March 1922 – 26 December 1997'. *Left History* 5(1) (1997).
Lüdtke, A. 'Introduction: What Is the History of Everyday Life and Who Are Its Practitioners?', in A. Lüdtke (ed.), *The History of Everyday Life: Reconstructing Historical Experiences and Ways of Life* (Princeton, NJ: Princeton University Press, 1995), 3–40.
Lüdtke, A., and W. Templer. 'Polymorphous Synchrony: German Industrial Workers and the Politics of Everyday Life'. *International Review of Social History* 38 (1993), 39–84.
Lux, G. 'Industrial Development, Public Policy and Spatial Differentiation in Central Europe: Continuities and Change'. *Discussion papers* 62 (2008). Centre for Regional Studies of Hungarian Academy of Sciences.
Luxemburg, R. *The Accumulation of Capital*. London: Routledge, (1913) 2003.
MacKenzie, D., F. Muniesa and L. Siu. *Do Economists Make Markets? On the Performativity of Economics*. Princeton, NJ: Princeton University Press, 2008.
Madgearu, V. *Agrarianism, Capitalism, and Imperialism*. Bucharest: Economistul, 1936.
Maier, C.S. 'The Postwar Social Contract'. *International Labour and Working-Class History* 50 (1996), 148–56.
Mandel, E. 'The Theory of State Capitalism'. *Fourth International* 12(5) (1951): 145–56.
Mărginean, M. *Ferestre spre furnalul roșu: Urbanism și cotidian în Hunedoara și Călan (1945–1968)* [Windows to the red furnace: Urbanism and everydayness in Hunedoara and Călan]. Iași: Polirom, 2015.
Marx, K. *Capital: Critique of Political Economy*, Vol. 1. London: Penguin Books, (1867) 1992.
———. *Grundrisse: Foundations of the Critique of Political Economy*. London: Penguin Books, (1939) 1993.
Meehan, K., and K. Strauss. *Precarious Worlds: Contested Geographies of Social Reproduction*. Athens, GA: University of Georgia Press, 2015.
Millar, J.R. 'Soviet Rapid Development and the Agricultural Surplus Hypothesis'. *Soviet Studies* 22(1) (1970), 77–93.
———. 'Mass Collectivization and the Contribution of Soviet Agriculture to the First Five-Year Plan: A Review Article'. *Slavic Review* 33(4) (1974), 750–66.
———. 'A Note on Primitive Accumulation in Marx and Preobrazhensky'. *Soviet Studies* 30(3) (1978), 384–93.
Montias, J.M. *Economic Development in Communist Romania*. Cambridge: MIT Press, 1967.
Munslow, B., and M.H.J. Finch. *Proletarianisation in the Third World: Studies in the Creation of a Labour Force under Dependent Capitalism*. London: Croom Helm, 1984.
Murgescu, B. *România și Europa: Acumularea decalajelor economice (1500–2010)* [Romania and Europe: The accumulation of economic disparities]. Iași: Polirom, 2010.
Neuburger, M., and P. Bren (eds). *Communism Unwrapped: Consumption in Cold War Eastern Europe*. Oxford: Oxford University Press, 2012.
Nistor, I.S. 'Constituirea si activitatea Comisariatului pentru administrarea Transilvaniei eliberate (octombrie 1944 – martie 1945)' [The constitution and activity of the commissariat for Free Transylvania]. *Anuarul Institutului de istorie si arheologie Cluj-Napoca* XXVI (1984), 491–98.
Nove, A. *An Economic History of the USSR*. London: Penguin Books, (1969) 1989.
Ong, A. *Spirits of Resistance and Capitalist Discipline: Factory Women in Malaysia*. Albany: State University of New York Press, 1987.
Ost, D. *Solidarity and the Politics of Anti-Politics: Opposition and Reform in Poland since 1968*. Philadelphia: Temple University Press, 1991.
Pai, H.-H. *Scattered Sand: The Story of China's Rural Migrants*. London: Verso Books, 2013.
Painter, J. 'Prosaic Geographies of Stateness'. *Political Geography* 25(7) (2006), 752–74.
Pearce, F. *The Radical Durkheim*. Toronto: Canadian Scholars' Press, 2001.

Perrot, M. 'The Three Ages of Industrial Discipline in Nineteenth-Century France', in J. Merriman, *Consciousness and Class Experience in Nineteenth-Century Europe* (New York: Holmes & Meier, 1979).

Petrovici, N. 'Neoliberal Proletarization along the Urban–Rural Divide in Postsocialist Romania'. *Studia Universitatis Babes-Bolyai Sociologia* 58(LVIII) (2013), 23–54.

———. *Zona urbană: O economie politică a socialismului românesc* [The urban zone: A political economy of the Romanian socialism]. Cluj: Tact, 2018.

Pittaway, M., 'The Social Limits of State Control: Time, the Industrial Wage Relation, and Social Identity in Stalinist Hungary, 1948–53'. *Journal of Historical Sociology* 12(3) (1999), 271–301.

———. *The Workers' State: Industrial Labor and the Making of Socialist Hungary, 1944–1958*. Pittsburgh: University of Pittsburgh Press, 2012.

———. *From the Vanguard to the Margins: Workers in Hungary, 1939 to the Present*. Selected essays by Mark Pittaway, ed. by Adam Fabry. Leiden: Brill, 2014.

Pittaway, M., and H.F. Dahl. 'Legitimacy and the Making of the Post-War Order', in M. Conway and P. Romijn (eds), *The War for Legitimacy in Politics and Culture 1936–1946* (Oxford: Berg, 2008), 177–209.

Pobłocki, K. 'The Cunning of Class: Urbanization of Inequality in Post-War Poland'. Unpublished PhD dissertation. Budapest: Central European University, 2010.

Poenaru, F. 'Methodological State Apparatuses'. Position paper for the Methodological Workshop of the Young Researchers, Sociology Department, Babeş-Bolyai University, Cluj-Napoca (2010).

Postone, M. 'Necessity, Labor, and Time: A Reinterpretation of the Marxian Critique of Capitalism'. *Social Research* 45(4) (1978), 739–88.

———. *Time, Labor and Social Domination: A Reinterpretation of Marx's Critical Theory*. New York: Cambridge University Press, (1993) 2003.

Preobrazhensky, Y. *The New Economics*. Oxford: Clarendon Press, (1926) 1965.

Rabinbach, A. *The Human Motor: Energy, Fatigue, and the Origins of Modernity*. Berkeley: University of California Press, 1992.

Reid, D. 'Industrial Paternalism: Discourse and Practice in Nineteenth-Century French Mining and Metallurgy'. *Comparative Studies in Society and History* 27(4) (1985), 579–607.

Rogers, D. *The Old Faith and the Russian Land: A Historical Ethnography of Ethics in the Urals*. Ithaca, NY: Cornell University Press, 2009.

Ronnås, P. *Urbanization in Romania: A Geography of Social and Economic Change since Independence*. Economic Research Institute, Stockholm School of Economics, 1984.

Rose, N. 'Governing by Numbers: Figuring Out Democracy'. *Accounting Organizations and Society* 16(7) (1991), 673–92.

Rose, N., and P. Miller. 'Political Power beyond the State: Problematics of Government'. *The British Journal of Sociology* 43(2) (1992), 173–205.

Roseberry, W. *Anthropologies and Histories: Essays in Culture, History, and Political Economy*. London: Rutgers University Press, 1991.

Rostás, Z. *O Istorie Orală a Şcolii Sociologice de la Bucureşti* [An oral history of Bucharest Sociological School]. Bucharest: Paideia, 2001.

Sampson, S. *National Integration through Socialist Planning: An Anthropological Study of a Romanian New Town*. New York: Columbia University Press, 1984.

Scott, J. *Seeing Like a State: How Certain Schemes to Improve the Human Condition Have Failed*. New Haven, CT: Yale University Press, 1999.

Şerban, M. 'Surviving Property: The Making and Unmaking of Hegemony in Law (Romania. 1945–1965)'. Unpublished PhD dissertation, New York University, 2010.

Sider, G. *Culture and Class in Anthropology and History*. Cambridge: Cambridge University Press, 1986.

Siegelbaum, L.H. *Stakhanovism and the Politics of Productivity in the USSR, 1935–1941.* Cambridge: Cambridge University Press, 1990.

Siegelbaum, L.H., and R.G. Suny (eds). *Making Workers Soviet: Power, Class, and Identity.* Ithaca, NY: Cornell University Press, 1994.

Sochor, Z. 'Soviet Taylorism Revisited'. *Soviet Studies* 33(2) (1981), 246–64.

Stalin, J.V. 'New Conditions – New Tasks in Economic Construction', in J.V. Stalin, *Problems of Leninism* (Peking: Foreign Languages Press, 1976).

Steinberg, M. '"The Great End of All Government ...": Working People's Construction of Citizenship Claims in Early Nineteenth-Century England and the Matter of Class', in C. Tilly (ed.), *Citizenship, Identity, and Social History* (Cambridge: Press Syndicate of the University of Cambridge, 1996), 19–50.

Sweezy, P.M. *Post-Revolutionary Society.* New York: Monthly Review Press, 1980.

Szelenyi, I. 'East European Socialist Cities: How Different Are They?', in G. Guldin and A. Southall (eds), *Urban Anthropology in China* (Leiden, Netherlands: E.J. Brill, 1993), 41–64.

Țărău, V. 'Campania electorală și rezultatul real al alegerilor din 19 noiembrie 1946 în județele Cluj, Someș și Turda' [The electoral campaign and the real result of the elections of November 1946 in Cluj, Someș and Turda counties], in S. Mitu and F. Gogâltan (eds), *Studii de istorie a Transilvaniei* [Studies of Transylvanian History] (Cluj: Presa Universitară, 1994).

Thelen, T. 'Shortage, Fuzzy Property and Other Dead Ends in the Anthropological Analysis of (Post)socialism'. *Critique of Anthropology* 31(1) (2011), 43–61.

Thomas, V. 'Les travailleurs roumains après cinq ans de République populaire', *La Revue Syndical Suisse* (1953).

Thompson, E.P. 'Time, Work-Discipline, and Industrial Capitalism'. *Past and Present* 38 (1967), 56–97.

Trotsky, L. *The History of the Russian Revolution.* Chicago: Haymarket Books, (1930) 2008.

Turnock, D. *An Economic Geography of Romania.* Boulder, CO: Westview, 1974.

———. *The Romanian Economy in the Twentieth Century.* London: Croom Helm, 1986.

Vasile, C. *Politicile culturale comuniste în timpul regimului Gheorghiu-Dej* [Communist cultural politics during Gheorghiu-Dej regime]. Bucharest: Humanitas, 2013.

Verdery, K. *National Ideology under Socialism: Identity and Cultural Politics in Ceaușescu's Romania.* Berkeley: University of California Press, 1991.

———. *What Was Socialism, and What Comes Next?* Princeton, NJ: Princeton University Press, 1996.

Verdery, K., and G. Kligman. *Peasants under Siege: The Collectivization of Romanian Agriculture, 1949–1962.* Princeton, NJ: Princeton University Press, 2011.

Warde, A. 'Industrial Restructuring, Local Politics and the Reproduction of Labour Power: Some Theoretical Considerations'. *Society and Space* 6 (1988), 75–95.

Weber, E. *Peasants into Frenchmen: The Modernization of Rural France, 1870–1914.* Stanford, CA: Stanford University Press, [1976] 1992.

Wise, N.M. 'Work and Waste: Political Economy and Natural Philosophy in Nineteenth-Century Britain (II)'. *History of Science* 27(4) (1989), 392–449.

Yurchak, A. *Everything Was Forever, Until It Was No More: The Last Soviet Generation.* Princeton, NJ: Princeton University Press, 2005.

Zerubavel, E. *Hidden Rhythms: Schedules and Calendars in Social Life.* Berkeley: University of California Press, 1985.

Index

Abrams, Philip, 33n52, 33n53, 34n63, 153
agriculture, 4, 8, 9, 11–12, 24, 44, 78, 94, 109, 113, 117, 118, 120, 133, 136, 142n6, 179, 201
Armătura, xi, 31–32, 90, 93, 97, 98, 104, 105, 144n49, 166, 170, 192, 226n3
austerity, 10, 79

backwardness, 3–4, 6, 9, 13, 23, 110, 147, 169, 208, 210, 212, 221–224, 230
Bakunin, Mikhail Alexandrovich, 32n14
Bloch, Ernst, ix, 32n8, 222, 224, 227nn34–35, 230
Burawoy, Michael, 6, 32n13, 33n37, 34n65, 34n72, 108n67, 207, 226n5

capitalism, vii, viii, 8, 9, 12, 19, 34n55, 34n59, 42, 84, 182, 193, 201, 223, 224, 230, 231, 232
CASBI, 41, 44, 63
Case, Holly, 29, 32n4, 34n67
class, viii–ix, x, 2, 3, 4, 5, 6, 8, 9, 12, 13–17, 22, 24–26, 28, 29, 40, 42, 58, 59, 65, 75, 79, 105, 109, 112, 113, 114, 117, 134, 141, 160, 164, 205, 206, 209, 216, 221, 223, 224, 229, 230, 231
    and ethnicity, 56
    formation, 232
    relations, 76, 116
    struggle, 55, 211
Class Struggle (journal), 1, 161
Cliff, Tony, 32n16, 33n24
Cluj, 2, 24–34, 37–42, 49–50, 56–57, 60–63, 67, 78, 79, 81, 82, 86, 90, 102, 110, 111, 112, 121–122, 124–128, 135, 136, 139, 140, 157, 158, 160, 179, 192, 217, 221, 225
collectivization of land, ix, 3, 4, 9, 10–12, 14, 33n24, 60, 66, 110, 111, 115–120, 122, 133, 154, 175n12, 179, 208, 231

commuting, ix, 31, 121, 128–134, 143n33
conveyor belt, 152, 180

Dej, Gheorghe Gheorghiu, 117, 119
Dermata, 26, 27, 29, 51, 53–55, 58, 59, 61, 62, 65, 66, 68, 77, 78, 136
director's fund, 130, 218

Economats, 45, 47, 52, 53, 59, 77, 78, 132
elections, 43, 44, 52, 56, 59, 87
everyday life, 1, 2, 3, 4, 15, 17, 18, 31, 42, 49, 60, 72, 76, 82, 98, 110, 114, 127, 134, 153, 156, 163, 175, 188, 208, 209, 211, 224, 228, 229
expanded reproduction, 3

factory
    administration councils, 61
    committees, 48, 51, 52, 55, 77, 78, 87, 97, 155, 178, 187, 199
    disciplinary committees, 102
    discipline (*see* labour discipline)
    management, 21, 31, 50, 63–65, 68–70, 75, 81, 88, 89, 90, 91, 92, 93, 96, 97, 100, 104, 105, 129, 130, 140, 149, 159, 160, 161, 162, 165, 166, 182, 184, 186, 188, 189, 191, 197, 198, 199, 200, 215, 217, 218, 219, 221
    as object of knowledge, 151, 170, 172–175
familialism, 63, 70, 95, 100, 105, 130, 186, 188, 189
the Final Solution, 28
financial reforms, 155
    1947, 44–45, 73n13, 78–80, 106n7
    1952, 118–119, 100, 143n25
Fordism, 76, 111, 169, 178, 179, 180
Friedmann, Georges, 180, 202n7

Gastev, Aleksei, 166
Geertz, Clifford, 174
gender, x, 2, 5, 12, 49, 97, 133–138, 141, 212
General Confederation of Labour, 156
Gibson-Graham, 175
Greater Romania, 25, 37–38

Hanson, Stephen, 211
Hayek, Friedrich August von, 173–174
Herbák, János,
  factory, 31–32, 41, 66, 88–96, 98–100, 124, 126, 127, 129, 135, 138, 162, 171, 178, 182–183, 184–185, 187–189, 190–192, 195–200, 204, 212, 216, 219
  communist fighter, 26
'The History of the Russian Revolution'. *See* Trotsky, Leon
hoarding, 6, 21, 22, 87, 118, 119, 185, 186, 219
Hungarians in Cluj, 30–31, 46, 49, 51, 59, 126–127, 172, 196
Hungarianization of the economic life, 28
Hungary, 2, 5, 14, 16, 28, 29, 38, 40, 57, 62, 86, 88, 96, 115, 179

indiscipline. *See* labour discipline
Industria Sârmei, 90
Industrial Offices, 45–46, 107n28, 128
industrial paternalism, 53
industrialism, 3, 77, 201, 229
industrialization waves, 10, 24, 30, 115, 116, 124, 207
industry
  heavy industry, 4, 10, 44, 47, 82, 85, 89, 90, 96, 117, 163, 179, 186, 208
  light industry, 82, 96, 117
inflation, 3, 44, 45, 46, 59, 76, 77, 79, 80, 106n10, 118, 119
The Institute for Planning and Economic Administration, 159, 161
internal migration, 11, 24, 115, 121, 128, 129
the interwar period, 2, 3, 5, 9, 24, 25, 27, 38, 43, 49, 50, 53, 55, 57, 77, 81, 89, 113, 116, 135, 136, 137, 151, 157, 159, 163, 165, 193, 229
investment, 2, 4, 7, 8, 10, 19, 21, 22, 69, 83, 96, 110, 114–115, 120, 122, 130, 150, 155, 179, 208, 229

Jowitt, Kenneth, 46

knowledge, 2, 14, 17, 20, 48, 64, 79, 96, 180, 210
  embodied and embedded knowledge, 165
  ethnographic knowledge, 31, 149, 150–153, 169–175
  knowledge production in the planning process, 148–154
  legibility, 148, 149, 150–153, 154–162
  managerial knowledge, 163–169
  mētis, 156
  practical knowledge, 2, 10, 22, 168
Kolozsvár. *See* Cluj
Kornai, János, vii, 21, 34n56, 179, 180, 202n25

labour
  cheap, x, 2, 3, 9, 109–140, 148, 179, 181, 211
  commodification of, 5, 77, 83, 164, 220
  control of, 2, 18, 22, 30, 42, 51, 55, 60, 63, 65, 71, 75, 86, 88, 98, 101, 105, 139, 141, 148, 165, 169, 180, 181, 184–185, 212, 215, 221
  discipline, 5, 10, 16, 17, 22, 90, 91, 92, 94, 96, 98, 101, 103, 129, 131, 139, 164, 165, 168, 171, 179, 181, 182, 184, 189, 194, 195, 201, 204, 205, 208, 209, 214, 221
  expansion of, 2, 4, 12, 18, 232
  female labour, x, 48, 50, 90, 96–98, 103, 104, 133–138, 196, 21
  flexibility of, 2, 3, 5, 110–112, 115–116, 120, 129, 141, 148, 179
  fluctuations, 9, 89, 97, 132, 189
  forced, 99, 102, 111, 125
  heroism, 204–210, 214, 222
  labour power, 2, 5, 22, 83, 84, 85, 86, 104, 148, 209, 219, 222, 231, 232
  living labour, 2–6, 22, 83, 148, 222
  markets, 76, 83, 86, 89, 98
  mobilization of, 2, 9, 10, 57, 150, 168, 169, 174, 185, 207
  multivocal nature of, 2, 24, 148
  planned resource, 18–24
  reproduction of, x, 2, 3, 4, 12, 13, 27, 51, 55, 66, 76, 83, 85, 105, 111, 112, 133, 135, 147, 222, 225, 231, 232
  shortage of, 9, 21, 31, 70, 86, 87, 98, 104, 110, 120, 133, 135, 179, 186, 198, 218

skilled/unskilled, 13, 24, 25, 26, 27, 29, 30, 31, 81, 82, 89, 90, 92, 95, 96, 98, 122, 123, 126, 128, 131, 132, 135, 136, 137, 140, 141, 156, 165, 166, 186, 193, 199, 215, 216, 218, 220, 224
  turnover of, x, 31, 91, 94, 97, 131, 139
  unrest of, 3, 52, 120
Lampland, Martha, 5, 83, 133, 147
law of value, 19–20
living conditions, 57, 58, 81, 123, 130, 157
living standards, 15, 81, 119, 156, 157, 179
Luca, Vasile, 11, 56, 117, 119

Mandel, Ernest, 7
Marx, Karl, ix, 8, 11, 83–84, 180, 209, 223, 231, 232

nation building, 25, 151
National Democratic Bloc, 43, 56, 57, 59
nationalization of the means of production, 3, 4, 10, 12, 19, 31, 42, 43, 52, 55, 60–74, 77, 78, 79, 87, 101, 111–112, 115, 116, 130, 154–156, 159–162, 198, 208, 210, 224
newcomer. See *vinituri*
nonsynchronicity, ix, 5, 23, 219, 222–226, 230
nostrification, 27

Pauker, Ana, 11, 117, 119
Pătrășcanu, Lucrețiu, 51
peasant-workers, 13, 40, 110, 130, 196, 218, 221, 224
peasantry, viii, ix, 3, 6, 8, 9, 11, 13, 14, 23, 29, 30, 37, 45, 57, 64, 66, 71, 78, 79, 80, 91, 92, 111, 112, 116, 117–121, 123, 126, 128, 130, 134, 141, 157, 179, 201, 205, 206, 216, 222, 225, 228, 229, 230
piece-rate, 65, 80, 82, 89, 91, 92, 95, 105, 139, 147, 163, 165, 179, 186, 194, 219, 220
piecework. See piece-rate
Pittaway, Mark, 16, 71, 179, 180, 209
planned heroism, 5, 10, 208, 211, 218, 222. See also Hanson, Stephen
planning, vii, 3, 4, 5, 7, 17–24, 31, 75, 101, 112, 130, 135, 148–149, 150, 151, 152, 153, 154, 157, 158–159, 173, 174, 175, 179, 180, 181, 183, 191, 192, 197, 208, 209, 211, 219, 223, 224, 225

political parties, other than the Romanian Workers' Party, 43
  National Peasants' Party, 49, 56, 57
political subjectivity, 2, 4, 18, 22, 23, 55, 30, 102, 168, 169, 205, 206, 222, 230
productivity, x, 2, 3, 5, 8, 10, 15, 22, 24, 66, 76, 80, 83, 86, 87, 90, 94, 98, 148, 150, 169, 147, 149, 152, 155, 161, 163, 164, 175, 178, 181, 188, 193, 207, 208, 209, 211, 212, 215, 216, 222, 227n26
  hidden/inner reserves of productivity, x, 3, 10, 15, 149–150, 152, 154, 185, 167, 169, 209
politics of calculation, 23, 83, 160
politics of productivity, 2, 5, 22, 148, 207, 208
Postone, Moishe, 7
postwar reconstruction years, 3, 43–60, 154
Preobrazhensky, Yevgeni, ix, 9, 12, 22, 76, 111, 112, 149, 208, 230
primitive socialist accumulation, x, 2–12, 43, 60, 66, 67, 76, 109, 112, 114, 115, 119, 122, 201, 208, 224, 225, 230, 231
price scissors, 8, 11, 12, 33n22, 80, 111, 118, 208
professional schools, 27, 67, 124, 138–139, 199
proletarian, 13, 17, 23, 24, 110, 111, 116, 141
  non-proletarians, 223
  semi-proletarians, 31, 92, 132, 212, 221
proletarian ethics and proletarian morals, 103, 214
proletarianization, 12, 84, 110, 115, 122, 221, 224, 230–233

The Railways Workshops, 25, 26, 27, 41, 50, 52, 58, 59, 61, 64, 89, 92, 97, 98, 100, 124, 27, 128, 212, 213
rationalization of production, 3, 5, 10, 164, 147–149, 163–169, 198, 211, 220, 224
really existing socialism, vii, viii, x, 3, 6, 7, 20
the Red Army, 37–41, 42, 43, 53, 61, 87, 160, 187
the right to the city, 30, 42, 43–51, 56, 58, 225
The Romanian Workers' Party, 1, 11, 31, 42–47, 55–57, 60, 61, 76, 86, 93, 99, 101, 117, 118, 124, 127, 128, 139, 158, 160, 169, 170, 219, 221

scientific management. *See* Taylorism
Scott, James, 150–153
The Second World War, 2, 3, 5, 6, 9, 10, 11, 24, 25, 27, 28, 38, 43, 50, 76, 77, 79, 119, 136, 223, 229, 231
The Second Vienna Arbitration, 28, 29, 38
shop floor, 2, 5, 9, 10, 14–23, 43, 50, 51, 52, 55, 60, 61, 66, 72, 76, 89, 92, 99–101, 104, 105, 109, 112, 122, 129, 137, 139, 147–151, 154, 162, 163–168, 170, 175, 179–182, 184, 188, 189, 191, 194, 198, 201, 208, 209, 211–222
shortage economy, 21–22, 34n54, 44, 91, 92, 93, 118, 182, 225
slacking, 23, 104, 206, 207, 208, 211–214, 216, 220, 221, 223, 226
socialist calculation debate, 173
Soviet methods of organizing production, 165, 207, 214–215
The Soviet Union, 6, 7, 8, 10, 44, 46, 52, 109, 164, 165, 171, 204, 207, 208, 229
Stakhanovite movement, x, 10, 13, 105, 130, 165, 166, 206–209, 210–222, 223, 224
Stalin, Joseph Vissarionovich, 1, 9, 11, 120, 147, 159, 208
state
  fragility of, 9, 16, 17, 56, 182
  legitimacy of, 4, 16–17, 47, 71, 76
  manager state, 16–17, 23, 76, 141, 152, 153, 163–168, 169, 188, 206, 219
  'state-system' and 'state-idea', 21, 153 (*see also* Abrams, Philip)
  workers' state, 4, 7, 16, 29, 69, 102, 130, 152, 153, 169, 188
state capitalism, 7, 32nn14–16, 33n24
State Planning Commission, 158
stealing, 31, 40, 75, 76, 98–106
surplus extraction, 3, 4, 6, 9, 13, 19, 22, 149
Sweezy, Paul, 7

Taylorism, 2, 3, 5, 9, 22, 76, 80, 82, 148, 149, 152, 153, 163–169, 173, 193, 208, 211, 214, 215

Tehnofrig, 70, 92, 102, 105, 126, 217, 223, 226
time
  compression, 23, 210, 211, 218
  rhythms, x, 4, 12, 13, 95, 114, 115, 179, 182, 183, 185, 196, 220, 225
  time of production and time of politics, 23, 24, 53, 148, 208, 209
The Tobacco Factory, 27, 50, 136–137
Trotsky, Leon, ix. *See also* uneven and combined development

unemployment, 81, 86, 87, 136
uneven and combined development, ix, 34n59, 232
unions, 26, 27, 47, 42, 48–57, 59, 61, 77, 78, 81, 85, 88, 104, 154, 155, 162, 164, 165, 168, 174, 187, 189, 194, 198, 199, 212
university, 38, 49, 57, 59, 125, 166, 173
under-urbanization, 110

Verdery, Katherine, vii
Victoria Cooperative, 64, 98
vinituri, 29, 97, 98, 110, 112, 122–128, 141, 194

wages, 3, 4, 10, 12, 13, 19, 44–45, 47–48, 52–53, 59, 61, 65, 66, 70, 75–85, 87, 88, 89, 92, 93, 94, 96, 97, 111, 118–121, 130, 131, 135, 137, 155, 156, 158, 166, 168, 179, 186, 188, 193, 207, 209, 211, 215, 219–222, 231
work norms, 77, 80, 82, 83, 92, 93, 94, 95, 97, 131, 137, 149, 162, 164, 166, 167, 171, 207, 209, 211, 215, 216, 217, 219, 220
working-class
  alliance with peasantry, 119, 121
  families, 26, 78, 121, 123, 126, 135, 136, 156, 157
  identity, 180
  imagined working-class, 212
  neighbourhoods, 25, 27, 30, 41, 59, 123, 136, 137
  solidarity, 213

www.ingramcontent.com/pod-product-compliance
Lightning Source LLC
Chambersburg PA
CBHW071154070526
44584CB00019B/2785